THE STUDENT COUNCIL

The quality of the materials used in the manufacture of this book is governed by continued postwar shortages.

Books by

HARRY C. McKOWN

THE TREND OF COLLEGE ENTRANCE REQUIREMENTS, 1913–1922

EXTRACURRICULAR ACTIVITIES

SCHOOL CLUBS

ASSEMBLY AND AUDITORIUM ACTIVITIES

COMMENCEMENT ACTIVITIES

HOME ROOM GUIDANCE

HOW TO PASS A WRITTEN EXAMINATION

THE STUDENT COUNCIL

CHARACTER EDUCATION

ACTIVITIES IN THE ELEMENTARY SCHOOL

FOOLS AND FOOLISHNESS

With ALVIN B. ROBERTS

AUDIO-VISUAL AIDS TO INSTRUCTION

With MARION LEBRON

A BOY GROWS UP

HARRY C. McKOWN

THE STUDENT COUNCIL

McGRAW-HILL BOOK COMPANY, INC.
New York . . . . London

THE STUDENT COUNCIL

PRINTED IN THE UNITED STATES OF AMERICA

IV

COMPOSITION BY THE MAPLE PRESS COMPANY, YORK, PA.
PRINTED AND BOUND BY COMAC PRESS, INC., BROOKLYN, N. Y.

TO THE GRAND OLD MAN

OF THE PARTICIPATION MOVEMENT

Richard Welling

Preface

ALTHOUGH the basic ideas and principles of democratic government are centuries old, our American application is of comparatively recent origin and, despite the beliefs of the average man, our form of government is still on trial. At the present time it faces two kinds of enemies—external and internal, and the latter are as vicious and destructive as the former and much more difficult to fight because they are insidious. One type of these internal enemies is well known and widely recognized, gangsterism—political, industrial, commercial, and moral. A less well known and less widely recognized group is composed of such elements as fear, doubt, prejudice, smugness, cynicism, indifference to personal social responsibility, lack of civic consciousness, and a childish faith in human "saviors." A government which is "of the people, by the politicians, and for the pressure groups" is a diseased government. Armies and navies can crush external foes, but they cannot vanquish internal enemies. These must be conquered by education.

The fundamental assumptions of democracy are that men are competent to govern themselves and that their efforts will result in an organization "of the people, by the people, and for the people." Such an organization necessitates appropriate social and political ideals, understandings, and habits, and a willingness to live, as well as die, for the common good. These elements are not in the original nature of man. They must be developed, and, as will be shown later, this development comes most easily and surely through practice in a setting that resembles that of ultimate citizenship. Student participation in school government represents such a setting.

Preface

During the past two or three decades, student participation has spread so rapidly that it can no longer be considered as an innovation or an experiment. As pointed out in Chap. I, it is now to be found in practically all junior high schools, junior colleges, and colleges, in at least two-thirds of all senior high schools, and to a lesser extent in elementary schools. True, participation in these schools varies in purpose, form, and function all the way from hypocritical window dressing to plans in which the students assume real and vital responsibilities. But, at least, the plan has been accepted and is now well established.

The purpose of this book is to define the ideals and the place of student participation, to establish justifiable principles, and to provide definite suggestions for its organization, administration, procedures, and activities. In order to make the book immediately useful, theory has been kept to a minimum. In the establishment of basic ideals and principles, commonly accepted and used practices have been critically examined, and some of them have been thoroughly condemned, not on the basis of the author's personal opinion, but on the basis of logic and reflected school experience. Only through such critical examination can desirable improvement be made.

With few exceptions, identified practices of individual schools and councils have not been included because such inclusion is always excessively duplicative, detracts from the idea being presented, and tends to justify an item largely on the basis of its source. The practices of consciously or unconsciously accepting a procedure because it originated in a large well-known school, or refusing to accept it because it came from a small unknown school are all too common in our American system of education.

"School council" is a more accurate and desirable designation than "student council," especially in settings in which teachers are elected to represent the faculty. However, because the emphasis is upon student participation and also because the expression is so well known and widely accepted, "student council" will be used throughout the book.

Although it might appear at first glance that this book will be useful only in the upper grades and the junior and senior high schools, this is not the case. Because these settings, basically, are about the same as those found in the middle and lower grades, junior college, college, university, and professional and technical schools, as well as in youth groups, community centers, and similar organizations, the material suggested should be found valuable by those interested in these institutions and situations.

Every chapter of this book has been read by from three to five critics, and all these, with one exception, have had or are having direct firsthand experience with the student council plan. These critics are: Dr. Fred B. Dixon, Superintendent of Schools, East Lansing, Mich.; Adah H. Pratt, Council Sponsor, Elgin High School, Elgin, Ill.; Prof. Clifford E. Erickson, Northwestern University; Supt. Elden D. Finley, Community High School, Delavan, Illinois; Harold E. Gibson, Director of Admissions, MacMurray College, Jacksonville, Ill.; C. C. Harvey, Nyssa, Ore.; Prof. Edgar G. Johnston, University of Michigan; Prof. E. C. Kelley, Wayne University; Alice G. Langford, Secretary-treasurer, National Association of Student Councils, Fall River, Mass.; Frank Meyer, Council Sponsor, Junior High School, Grand Haven, Mich.; Allegra Nesbit, Guidance Director, Lew Wallace High School, Gary, Ind.; Sophia Pollack, Secretary-treasurer, National Self Government Committee, Inc., New York; Arthur Shirey, Council Sponsor, Senior High School, Anderson, Ind.; Adeline M. Smith, formerly of Bloom Township High School, Chicago Heights, Ill., and Acting President, National Association of Sponsors of Student Participation in School Administration, St. Petersburg,

Fla.; Prof. Paul W. Terry, University of Alabama; Gertrude Thuemler, Dean, Arsenal Technical Schools, Indianapolis; C. R. Van Nice, Managing Editor, *School Activities* Magazine, Topeka, Kans.; and Richard Welling, Chairman, National Self Government Committee, Inc., New York. To these, and to the many unidentified helpers who have contributed to this book, and to the publishers for permission to quote from copyrighted material, the author expresses his sincere gratitude.

HARRY C. McKOWN.

GILSON, KNOX COUNTY, ILL.,
October, 1944.

Contents

Contents

THE STUDENT COUNCIL

Chapter I

The Origin and Development of Participation in School Control

ALTHOUGH the expression "student council" is of recent origin, the basic idea is centuries old. Naturally, the records of the development of this idea are scattered and incomplete, and consequently a closely connected story cannot be told. However, a brief discussion of some of the early examples will prove that the idea has been struggling for recognition from ancient times and will also lay a foundation upon which a description of the modern movement may be based. For our purposes here, that is all that is necessary.

The Origin and Development of Participation in Lower Schools.[1]—Perhaps the conception of participation in school administration did not originate with Plato, since there are references to the "Irenes," or pupil companies under the direction of the older boys, in accounts of Spartan boarding schools, but at least our first definite descriptions date from this brilliant Athenian educator. Plato, Socrates's greatest disciple, was a wealthy citizen who, because of his interest in philosophy, forsook a political career. In 386 B.C., he gathered a group of young philosophers around him and established his

[1] The expression "lower schools" refers to all types of institutions below the college and university. It should not be interpreted in its modern meaning.

"Academy," a unique institution in which the teachers and students together owned and operated the school's property, chapel, library, lecture and discussion rooms, and living quarters. In it the scholarchs, or student leaders, were elected every 10 days on secret ballots by the students themselves. This school soon became the pattern for many other institutions established throughout Greece by Plato's disciples and others. It is interesting to note that the Academy existed for more than 900 years. In A.D. 529, the Emperor Justinian, because of his zeal for Christian orthodoxy, abolished all Athenian schools—and appropriated their properties.

Aristotle entered the Academy at the age of seventeen and studied and taught there until Plato's death 20 years later. Then he organized a similar institution, which he called the "Lyceum." In this he further developed and incorporated the idea of student participation, adding such offices as that of master of sacrifices and that of overseer of good order, to which the students elected their fellows. The main purpose of student participation in both the Academy and the Lyceum was educational; it was not, as it was in some of the later schools, for economy of administration. Aristotle, like his teacher, developed and supported in his writings the theory of education for cooperative living.

Following these beginnings in the development of the student participation idea came a long period that saw the decline of the Grecian state, the development of the Roman Empire, the rise of Christianity, and the barbarian invasions, a period of numerous, varied, and conflicting educational ideals and institutions, but a period in which the philosophy of the student council was apparently nonexistent.

However, with the Revival of Learning this idea again began to emerge. Vittorino da Feltra, "the first modern schoolmaster," who had taught privately at Padua and Venice and later at the University of Venice, in 1428 at the request of the Prince of Mantua established a court school. Da Feltra's educational philosophy and psychology were really quite modern. He believed in making education attractive and developed a curriculum for his "Pleasant House," as he called it, that was based upon natural interests and abilities, and built around active and constructive projects which, he held, would furnish an immediate introduction to a useful and happy life. To achieve this ideal of an education that would prepare for leadership in secular and religious affairs, da Feltra incorporated several radical features into the school's curriculum and organization. Among other things, in addition to a curriculum of the seven liberal arts, he stressed health and developed a program of physical activities and competitive sports. Naturally, such a program required student organizers, leaders, and officials. Later this student participation spread into other areas of student life and activity and finally grew into a rather modern form of "self-government." Incidentally, da Feltra was probably the first promoter of interscholastic athletics. His program of intrascholastic athletics was copied by other schools, and the natural result was a program of athletics and sports between these schools. Here again, the students assumed most of the responsibility for these events.

In 1531 at Goldberg, Germany, Valentino Trotzendorf organized a plan of participation that was built around a senate of twelve elected representatives, a larger council, and the necessary administrative and recording officers. Very formal and dignified court trials were held for students who were unmannerly at the table, tardy, unnecessarily absent, lazy, etc. Incidentally, Trotzendorf was a forerunner of Lancaster and Bell in that he assigned the older and more competent students to help teach the younger. As a result, graduates of his school were in great demand as teachers. In England, about 1700, Thomas Hill organized his school so that the students could participate in its administration. By the time of the American Revolution both Eton and Rugby had well-established plans. Undoubtedly there were similar organizations in various stages of development in other European schools.

A little more than a century ago three great educators, Rousseau, Froebel, and Pestalozzi, added impetus to the development of the student-council idea. In Book IV of "Emile," Rousseau discusses the proper education of the boy from fifteen to twenty, an education which, unlike that of the first three periods, one to five, five to twelve, and twelve to fifteen, designed largely for the purpose of discovering, understanding, and developing himself as an individual, is organized to train him through actual social settings and relationships for a life with others. In this setting the boy learns to follow, to lead, and to cooperate. In his new institution, the kindergarten, Froebel stressed the importance of social relationships and responsibilities by building his classroom into a miniature democracy, while Pestalozzi introduced a system of participation into his Institute at Bergdorf.

Another type of student participation was that to be found in the monitorial schools. In 1797, Rev. Andrew Bell published a report of his work in using mutual or monitorial instruction in a school in India, and shortly thereafter Joseph Lancaster, working independently, incorporated such a plan into his school because he needed assistance and was too poor to employ it. The plan was simple; a monitor, one of the older pupils, was assigned as an assistant teacher to a group of ten or twelve younger pupils. As ultimately developed, the plan was a bit more complex, utilizing both conduct and teaching monitors. These monitors handled nearly all the detail work of the school, assigning pupils to classes, checking absences and the reasons therefor, examining and promoting the pupils, ruling the writing paper, assuming charge of slates, books, and other equipment, etc. In addition, a monitor-general acted as a sort of supervisor of all the other monitors. Obviously, the reason for this plan was purely economic; a very large school could be handled by one paid teacher and several unpaid monitors. The plan was widely copied in England and on the continent and even in America, as will be shown later. Although differing in purpose and organization from the participation plans discussed previously, undoubtedly this system did contribute much to the general development of the student-council idea.

Turning now to America[1] we find in *The Students' Gazette* of the William Penn Charter School, July 23, 1777 (No. 7, pp. 1–2) an interesting account of how the boys "actuated by a noble principle and desirous to prevent the ill effects of internal broils, have established a constitution founded on their own authority." In this plan an "assembly" was chosen every month and was "empowered to make such laws as they shall think necessary or useful." Judges and other necessary officers were elected by the students. All offenders were tried publicly. Apparently the plan was successful judging by the statement, "Since this valuable institution has been adopted the absurd practices of fighting and calling names have visibly declined among the boys who now carry themselves toward one another with a delightful and polite behavior." Concerning the future value of such experiences the writer of this article states, "This will certainly be of great advantage to them hereafter, for when they are arrived at manhood and entered upon the busy scenes of life they will be useful mem-

[1] It is interesting to note that this plan is little mentioned in standard histories of American education. For instance, E. W. Knight's "Education in the United States" covers it with one sentence, while E. P. Cubberley's "Public Education in the United States" does not even mention it. Probably the first book on this topic published in America was Frederick S. Jewell's "School Government, a Practical Treatise," A. S. Barnes & Co., New York, 1866.

bers of society and qualified to serve their country in distinguished posts of honor and profit."

The influence of the monitorial schools in England was suggested in a previous paragraph. It is now pertinent to show how in America, where the plan was less hampered by tradition, conservatism, and religious limitations, its influence on educational thought and practice was still more pronounced. It will be recalled that this system of mutual instruction was proposed at about the same time by two men, Rev. Andrew Bell and Joseph Lancaster. However, because Bell was a clergyman of the Church of England and after the Revolution America wanted none of his doctrines, the plan in America became known as the "Lancastrian system." This was also due to the fact that Lancaster came to America in 1818 and spent most of the remaining 20 years of his life here organizing and promoting these schools.

The first Lancastrian school was opened in New York City in 1805, and the system was incorporated into the New York High School in 1825. Within a very few years the system had spread all through New England, as far south as Georgia, and as far west as Cincinnati, Louisville, and Detroit. Maryland instituted a state system of monitorial schools as did also Mexico for the state of Texas. This rapid development not only paved the way for the organization of a public education system but, more important for our purpose here, it paved the way for the development of student participation by demonstrating that, when properly selected, trained, and supervised, students can actually handle many of the school's affairs. Although the monitorial system (1) was designed in order to provide an inexpensive schooling, and (2) was obsolete by 1840 as a result of an awakened sense of the state's responsibility for its schools, it did have considerable influence on the development of the student-participation idea.

In addition to its appearance in New England schools as indicated above, student participation was introduced into the New York High School in 1825; into the Temple School, Boston, by Bronson Alcott in 1834; into her Hartford, Conn., private school for girls by Catherine Beecher in 1830; into the Hartford public school in 1852; and into the Mattakeesett School, Duxbury, Mass., about 1840.[1] These plans varied considerably in purpose and organization. The New York plan was an extension of the monitorial system; that at Boston included a provision in which the students elected a superintendent of activities; the first Hartford and the Mattakeesett plans rather closely resembled modern council organization even to a definite provision for the headmaster's veto: while the second Hartford plan was built around a student court and emphasized this phase of activity. In the 1860's John MacMullen developed a plan of participation in his New York City school, and Theodore Roosevelt and George Haven Putnam were elected to head the organization.

Dr. Bernard Cronson initiated "self-government" in the form of a "school city" in the New York schools in 1893 and made a rather startling success of it in School 69, and subsequently through his addresses, articles, and book[2] was directly responsible for the organization of many similar councils in American schools. Incidentally, Dr. Cronson, a close student of failures as well as successes, put most of the blame of the former onto the fact that the councils were planned, organized, and "run" by enthusiastic principals and teachers and were not the logical outgrowth of felt needs in the schools. His criticism still holds today.

Wilson L. Gill, another New Yorker, organized the Patriotic League of America in 1891, an elaborate scheme of

[1] The students of this school occasionally even voted a shorter school day or a day's vacation. However, they more frequently voted themselves additional evening periods of instruction. Several pages of the minutes of this organization will be found in E. C. Kelley's unpublished doctoral dissertation, "An Evaluation of Student Participation in Government in American Secondary Schools," pp. 16–23, Northwestern University, 1941.

[2] "Pupil Self-government," The Macmillan Company, New York, 1907.

self-government designed to teach citizenship. He later simplified it and introduced it as the "School City" into the Norfolk Street Vacation School in 1897. Later General Leonard Wood became interested in this plan, and as a result Mr. Gill went to Cuba to develop similar organizations there. In 1930 William McAndrew, formerly superintendent of schools in Chicago, stated that for 40 years he had had pupil participation in every school in which he worked. And, he added, "It worked." Throughout his life, McAndrew was continuously "pegging away at the practice," as he expressed it, by means of addresses, editorials, articles, forewords, activities, personal contacts, and other media.

In 1894 came William R. George's epoch-making experiment in self-government, the George Junior Republic at Freeville, N.Y. This was a sort of self-governing community patterned after the federal government. Originally designed as a summer vacation device for a group of underprivileged young folks, this Republic finally developed into an all-year plan.[1] In a later extension (1916), Mr. George designed a plan to fill the gap between leaving-school and voting ages, sixteen to twenty-one, the "Junior City" of Ithaca, N.Y. This Junior City was organized like Ithaca, with a mayor, council, and other municipal officials. These young people attended the meetings of the city council and in other ways kept in close touch with the municipal authorities and their activities. Similar junior cities were later organized in other parts of the country.

In 1919, McClure reported a "brief summary of the rise and fall of public attention with regard to pupil self-government" as shown by the number of articles appearing in pro-

[1] George, W. R., "Junior Republic," D. Appleton-Century Company, Inc., New York, 1910. A shorter account will be found in A. O. Bowden and I. C. Clark, "Tomorrow's Americans," pp. 88–89, G. P. Putnam's Sons, New York, 1930.

fessional journals from 1900–1918. These articles were as follows: 2 in 1900–1904; 7 in 1905–1909; 27 in 1910–1914; 11 in 1915–1918. The author knows of no similar study since 1918. However, in order to obtain somewhat comparable figures for the last decade, he listed, by years, the number of articles quoted and referred to in this book. The totals were 92 in 1934–1938 and 126 in 1939–1943. The peak year was 1942 with 32 articles. These figures do not include all the articles published during these years, because quite a number of those read were not used in the lists of references. Hence, the above figures for 1934–1943 represent a minimum rather than a maximum record. The complete record would probably include from one-fourth to one-third more than were used. Referring again to the first study, two of McClure's conclusions were: (1) "The extended discussion accorded the plan indicates that it contains a certain element of success"; (2) "The recent slackening of public attention suggests the presence of some characteristic weakness so persistent as to register a large percentage of failures."[1] In any case, the increase in number of articles in the last over the earlier period is significant.

Development of Participation in Higher Institutions of Learning.—For centuries participation plans have also been found in the universities. In an early day a university was merely an unorganized group of teachers around each of whom gathered interested students. Later definite authorization and organization became necessary, and buildings and accommodations were needed. These were supplied or promoted by the state, municipality, or church. Students came from all parts of the known world in response to the efforts of the sponsoring institutions in competing for famous teachers and large enrollments. By about 1200, university teachers and students became so numerous that they began to organize themselves

[1] McClure, W.: Morale by Rote, *School Review*, 27: 458–464, June, 1939.

into associations or guilds for protection against oppression of all kinds. The term *universitas*, from which our word "university" comes, was a Roman legal term corresponding to our modern word "corporation." As a result of this organization, the members of these guilds won practical respect in the form of special privileges and immunities such as, for example, exemptions from taxes and civil and military service, freedom from trial by civil courts, and the *cessatio*, the right to strike, in case of grievance, against either church or civil authorities.

By the very nature of the case, these privileges and immunities had to be conferred upon definite bodies, and a more exact organization became necessary. Students came from afar, and, because territorial lines were very indefinite, the most natural bases for the university's divisions were language and kinship. Hence the divisions took the form of "nations," each being duly chartered by the university's sponsor. Each of these nations elected, usually annually, a councilor or procurator, and these representatives, together with the heads or deans of the various schools elected by the teachers of these schools, named a rector of the university. This rector, generally elected annually, often was a student. The real governing authority of the university was, of course, the nations. In addition to electing the head of the university, and often the teachers, and even sometimes the town in which the university existed, the representatives decided upon policies, housing, routines, schedules, fees, and similar university matters, and handled all cases of discipline irrespective of whether the misdemeanor was against the "gown" or the "town." Here, indeed, in the fourteenth century, was a very powerful student council, and it was hardly "extracurricular" in any sense of the term.

Two early English colleges have left written records of the organization and activities of student participation plans. Winchester College in 1382 had a prefect system in which the older boys supervised the younger. This plan may have originated earlier than 1382, but at least it was used by this time. In Westminster by 1630 there was a system by which student officers or monitors with various types of specialized duties exercised considerable control over both the curricular and the extracurricular activities of the students. The chief monitor or *monitor monitorum* supervised the work of these monitors.

Probably the first example of student participation in American colleges was at William and Mary, Williamsburg, Va., in 1779, after the college had been in existence for more than three-quarters of a century. The political break with England and the emergence of the democratic ideal were undoubtedly responsible for this development. The students elected representatives to a central body and this handled lesser details of "general improvement," routine discipline. The plan was very simple, but it was a beginning. Probably it had some influence on its famous alumnus, Thomas Jefferson, who later organized the University of Virginia after an earlier movement to make a state university out of William and Mary College had failed.

In a way, the University of Virginia had its beginning when in 1803 the legislature passed an act incorporating the "trustees of Albemarle College," but it was not until 1819 that the university, under the leadership of Jefferson, a great champion of education, opened at Charlottesville. From its very beginning the University of Virginia was undoubtedly the most liberal institution of higher education in the whole world. It had an elective curriculum, freedom from religious tests and practices, equality of professors, rotating election of department chairmen, and other unorthodox policies and procedures. Little wonder that self-government was included, a system that went far beyond that of William and Mary College. This plan included an honor system for all examinations and control of nearly all student activities. It also handled ordinary cases of discipline.

In 1833, Oberlin College, named after a famous Alsatian churchman and philanthropist, was founded by John J. Shipherd and Philo P. Stewart at Oberlin, Ohio. This college was revolutionary because it admitted students of all races. It also provided for student cooperation in its management. Its critics laughed it to scorn and prophesied an early demise. However, these critics were wrong; Oberlin not only flourished from the start but became the pattern followed by many subsequently organized private and public institutions, notably the University of Michigan, established in 1837.

Frances E. Willard, best known for her work as secretary of the National Woman's Christian Temperance Union, and later as president of the World's Woman's Christian Temperance Union, was a very practical-minded and energetic advocate of the student-council idea. After graduating from the Northwestern Female College at Evanston, Ill., in 1859, she taught for a number of years and in 1871 became president and professor of aesthetics at her alma mater, by then called the Evanston College for Ladies. Student participation was an important phase of her program, something quite unusual in a women's college. In 1873 her college was incorporated into Northwestern University and she resigned her position, largely because her ideas of democratic education conflicted with those of the president and trustees. However, she always retained her interest in the subject and in later years never failed to express her views at every opportunity and to voice her satisfaction at reports of successful student participation. To her sturdy pioneering can be credited, to some extent at least, the participation plans now found in nearly all women's colleges.

Additional examples of participation in higher institutions might be offered, but enough have been presented for our purpose here. From these early beginnings the practice has grown until now in practically all colleges and universities there are to be found three areas of responsibility, (1) the administration, legally responsible for policies, finances, property, personnel, and publicity, (2) the faculty, responsible for instruction and contributions to existing knowledge, and (3) the student body, through its representatives responsible for the organization, promotion, and handling of the many so-called "extracurricular" activities.

Quite obviously, student participation in the colleges has had a tremendous influence on practice in the secondary schools and, more recently, in the elementary schools. It was natural that the teachers in these schools should reflect in their work the ideals and practices of their alma maters.

The Modern Development of Participation.—Despite the facts already presented, it must not be assumed that all schools of an earlier day had student councils. Undoubtedly many schools about which we have no records did have them, but it is also certain that many more schools did not have such an organization. Several studies have been made which indicate that although the movement originated centuries ago its greatest growth has been quite recently.[1] A few examples of these investigations will illustrate.

In 1926, C. R. Dustin, in a study of 81 student councils in 35 cities, reported that about one-half had been in existence more than 5 years, the oldest for 13 years.[2] The same year E. U. Rugg reported that an investigation of 191 councils showed 68 per cent had been organized for 5 years or less and 32 per cent for more than 5 years, the median being in

[1] Probably the first national survey in this field was that of J. M. Brewer, reported in *Educational Review*, May, 1909.

[2] Dustin, C. R., An Investigation of the Scope, Working Practices, and Limitations of Pupil Participation in Government in the Secondary School, *School Review*, 34: 341–342, June, 1926.

the 4-year group.[1] N. R. Ringdahl in 1927 discovered that more than one-half of the 171 schools included in his survey had organized their councils since 1920.[2] In 1935, Galen Jones found that the median date of the organization of 132 councils was 1924, and that none of them existed before 1900.[3] H. C. Lent's 1938 investigation of 160 councils disclosed that the median age was 9 years, that the oldest had been in existence for 25 years, and that nine had been operative for at least 15 years.[4] The same year H. E. Patrick reported the median age of 74 councils to be 10 years.[5]

There are still other similar studies, but enough have been reflected to show that by now more than 50 per cent of American secondary school student councils date from about 1925.

The Present Status of Student Participation.—How many student councils are there in the elementary schools, junior high schools, senior high schools, junior colleges, colleges, and universities in America today? We have no accurate answer to this question, but we do have bases for rather intelligent guesses. Rugg[6] found in 1926 that of 191 schools selected at random, 90 per cent reported some form of student participation. In the study referred to on the previous page, Jones in

[1] RUGG, E. U., Student Participation in School Government, Chap. XI, "Twenty-fifth Yearbook," Part II, p. 133, National Society for the Study of Education, 1926.

[2] RINGDAHL, N. R., High School Student Councils, *School Review*, 36: 329–337, May, 1928.

[3] JONES, G., "Extra-curricular Activities in Relation to the Curriculum," Bureau of Publications, Teachers College, Columbia University, 1935.

[4] LENT, H. C., The Status of the Student Council in the Class A and B Junior and Senior High Schools of Michigan (unpublished master's thesis), University of Chicago, 1939.

[5] PATRICK, H. E., Pupil Participation in School Administration and Government in Eighty Secondary Schools (unpublished master's thesis), University of Chicago, 1938.

[6] *Op. cit.*, p. 135.

1935 discovered 132 councils in 269 secondary schools. In the 1939 Brogue-Jacobson investigation for the National Association of Secondary School Principals, 1,608 of the 1,992 schools that responded to a request for information (on a form enclosed with the regular mail of the Association) showed that 81 per cent had some form of student participation.[1] As a result of a questionnaire sent in 1940 to 5,000 schools of all types from the elementary school to the university, 1,801 replies (1,431 from junior and senior high schools and junior colleges) in which 1,549 schools had student cooperation were received. E. C. Kelley in 1941 reported that of 1,904,775 students in schools from which replies to his form were received 91.9 per cent were under some form of student participation.[2]

Of course, these and similar surveys have the weaknesses of (1) inadequate sampling, and (2) inaccurate representation; some schools having plans do not reply. However, they do represent some basis upon which a rough estimate may be made. Brogue and Jacobson suggest that "recent studies indicate that from two-thirds to three-fourths of all the schools have some form of student participation in school government."[3] We could easily guess that practically all junior high schools and junior colleges have student councils. These estimates may be a bit high, but if participation is to be found even in one-half of the secondary schools and colleges, probably a low estimate, and if it is recalled that very few of these plans were in existence 25 or 30 years ago, it will

[1] Brogue, E. B., and P. B. Jacobson, "Student-council Handbook," National Association of Secondary School Principals, March, 1940.

[2] Kelley, E. C., Student Cooperation—A Report of Student Government in the High Schools, National Self Government Committee, Inc., 1941. Mr. Kelley points out that because the mailing list was composed of school officials who at some time showed interest in student cooperation, it is "therefore more favorably disposed toward this goal than a list of all schools would be."

[3] *Op. cit.*, p. 16.

be seen that the movement has had a most remarkable development.[1] In any case, this much is certain, student participation is now established in American schools.

Factors Responsible for the Recent Development of Student Participation.—In addition to the influences of successful participation in earlier schools and to the permanent establishment of the democratic ideal in America, together with an increasing recognition of the responsibility of the school for preparing more directly for active citizenship, several other factors gave impetus to this movement.

1. *Local, State, and National Organizations.*—In 1903, Charles W. Eliot, then head of the National Education Association, asked Richard Welling, long a vigorous advocate of the participation plan, to address the Boston meeting of the Association on the subject of self-government as a means of civic training. This address resulted in such a flood of correspondence that the "School Citizens Committee," composed of well-known and highly respected educators and laymen, was formed. The original title, "School City Plan," was later changed to "Self Government, Inc.," and still later to "National Self Government, Inc."[2] For 40 years this committee has promoted conferences, meetings, and special lectures, published and distributed books, pamphlets, articles, and reprints, arranged and staged public debates, forums, and demonstrations, and given counsel and support. It organized, sponsored, and paid for the first course in extracurricular activities, "Teacher Training Course on Pupil Government as a Training for Citizenship," at New York University in

[1] Data on the growth of associations of student councils would represent additional evidence of this remarkable development. For instance, the first convention of the Illinois Association of Student Councils, held in 1936, showed an attendance of 25 delegates from five schools. At the eighth annual convention, held in Chicago in 1944, 1,048 delegates were registered on the first day of a two-day session.

[2] The address of this organization is 80 Broadway, New York, N.Y.

1910. During all these years Richard Welling, the winner in 1912 of the Owen Johnson Prize for the best essay on the topic, "How to Democratize the College," has been the efficient chairman of this committee. He was described years later by William McAndrew as "a well-known New York attorney, untiring wheelhorse in every campaign for good government since his graduation from Harvard, and intimate of Roosevelt, Strong, Goddard, Jerome, Low, Waring, Mitchell, and every New York fighter for a decent city."

The story of Welling's long fight for a more universal recognition and acceptance of the participation idea makes most interesting and inspiring reading.[1] Influenced by the writings of Aristotle, da Feltra, Catherine Beecher, Bronson Alcott, John MacMullen, and William R. George, and by personal contacts with William McAndrew, Oswald Schlocklow, Adeline Simpson, and Edwin Goldwasser—all pioneers in student participation—Welling persisted despite great opposition in his efforts to develop further this plan. His ideas were called "visionary" and "impractical" and he himself (a lawyer) "just an interfering layman who could not understand curricular demands." In order to ground himself more thoroughly in professional education, Welling attended New York University afternoons and evenings for 2 years, acquired a Master of Pedagogy degree, and then, for experience, taught in an East Side evening school. American education, especially that part concerned with the development of its major objective, good citizenship, owes much to the enthusiastic, tireless, and patient efforts of this eighty-six-year-old master teacher.

In April, 1927, while a student council adviser at the Roosevelt High School, Minneapolis, N. Robert Ringdahl conceived the idea of a nation-wide organization; and, as a direct result, the first meeting of the Conference on Student Par-

[1] See Welling's autobiography, "As the Twig Is Bent," G. P. Putnam's Sons, New York, 1942.

ticipation, planned for 75 persons and attended by 250, was held in connection with the June, 1927, Seattle meeting of the National Education Association. Ringdahl was elected the first president of this organization. Regular meetings were held at all subsequent conventions of the National Education Association until 1942. In 1941 the name of the conference was changed to the National Association of Sponsors of Student Participation in School Administration.

In 1931, student leaders, encouraged by Dr. Willis A. Sutton, Superintendent of Schools, Atlanta, Ga., organized the National Association of Student Officers which later was renamed the National Association of Student Councils. This organization also held its meetings in connection with those of the National Education Association. It was inevitable that the National Association of Sponsors of Student Participation in School Administration should very shortly assume sponsorship of the National Association of Student Councils. At Denver, in 1942, executive action was taken by these two organizations to have the National Association of Secondary School Principals become the sponsor for the National Association of Student Councils, and terms of understanding were formulated and approved in 1943.[1]

In addition to the above, there are a number of other organizations that promote council interests and activities. Some of these are affiliated with the national associations. These organizations may be classified as local (New York City, Detroit Metropolitan Area), district (Illinois, six districts plus the state organization, border cities of southeastern Michigan), state (Colorado, Indiana, Pennsylvania, West Virginia), and regional (Northwest Federation of Student

[1] A description of the plan of organization and operation will be found in Aiding Youth in Secondary Schools, *Bulletin of the National Association of Secondary School Principals*, Vol. 28, No. 120, pp. 71–74, February, 1944. The address of this association is 1201 Sixteenth Street, N.W., Washington, D.C.

Councils, Central States Federation of Student Councils, Southern Association of Student Government, New England Regional Association). Another somewhat similar form of educational setting is the "student leaders' conference" held annually by a number of colleges and universities.

These organizations have established and maintained an excellent and functional medium for the exchange of helpful ideas. Their meetings have resulted in clearer objectives, greater knowledge, and increased enthusiasm, all of which together have meant a broadened scope and an augmented importance. The attendant publicity of their activities has also added to participation's friends and supporters. Not a small part of their contribution has been the development of self-confidence. In short, these organizations have exerted a powerful and wholesome influence.[1]

2. *The Development of Extracurricular Activities.*—Although many of our modern extracurricular activities such as competitive athletics, clubs, debating, literary programs, special day celebrations, dramatics, and music, were to be found in the schools of ancient Greece, some of them, such as the yearbook, handbook, point system, thrift, and home room, are of very recent origin. In any case, the movement in America fully to recognize, organize, correlate, and capitalize these activities is only about three decades old. Since about 1910 they have multiplied and diversified until now the average school has a startling array of these settings and opportunities. This is proof that school people have found them to be educationally worthy.

The student council is usually considered to be one of the most important of these activities, if not the most important, because increasingly it has assumed responsibility for the

[1] A brief description of some of these organizations, and an excellent discussion of "suggestions for convention programs" will be found in Brogue and Jacobson, *op. cit.*, Chap. VIII.

development, supervision, correlation, and financing of them. Clearly it is provident that the council and these activities developed together, because they represent a perfect field of endeavor for it, and it, in turn, represents a nourishing and unifying force for them. In fact, it is quite improbable that there would have been a great student-council movement today had there not been a correlational development in the general-activity field.

3. *Leadership.*—Another influence responsible for the rapid recent development of participation is to be found in the many courses in extracurricular activities established in colleges and schools of education throughout the land. The great pioneer in this field was Elbert K. Fretwell, then professor of education at Teachers College, Columbia University, and now (1944) Chief Scout Executive, Boy Scouts of America. For more than 20 years, his classes were the mecca for teachers and administrators interested in the field, and his addresses, writings, and contacts, as well as the efforts of his students, many of whom like the author taught similar courses in other institutions later, all reflect leadership that has paid prodigious educational dividends. Other well-known teachers and writers in this field, Roemer, Allen, Terry, Johnston, Draper, Wilds, Jordan, and Roberts, to mention a few, have also helped to make for substantial progress of the movement.

4. *Literature.*—Still another influence is to be found in the literature published. In 1925 there was hardly a book in the general field of extracurricular activities.[1] During the following decade a dozen books, each of which includes a discussion of the council, and more than twice this number of books dealing with specialized activities, appeared. Several cities and states have published outlines, monographs, and bulletins

[1] In 1917, the author wrote a master's thesis in this field, and the expression "extracurricular" does not appear in it. In those days the term was "extra-class."

for distribution to their schools.[1] An examination of the periodical literature reveals only forty-seven articles published from 1900–1918, but at least 218 from 1934–1943.[2] For several years, *School Review* has published an annual descriptive bibliography prepared by Paul W. Terry. Further, there is a monthly magazine, *School Activities*,[3] which is devoted to this general field, and another, *Student Life*,[4] composed almost entirely of student efforts, relating partly to council interests and activities. *The Clearing House*[5] publishes numerous articles that concern general and specialized activities. *The Councilor*[4] is a four-page monthly issued jointly by The National Association of Student Councils, and The National Association of Sponsors of Student Participation in School Government. All this literature together has carried the story of the student council to the four corners of the nation.

5. *The Junior High School.*—The high school has long been dominated by its traditions and by the college and, similarly, the elementary school has long been dominated by its traditions and by the high school. The net result has been a rigid educational structure in which change has always been slowly and grudgingly made. Then about 1910 came the junior high school, a new institution without traditions, loyalties, or organized dominations, one which welcomed change and encouraged the expression of the more progressive policies both curricular and extracurricular. As one result, the junior high school today probably has a better organized and artic-

[1] Among those which the author has seen, one of the best is "Democracy in Action" (38 pp.), Michigan State Board of Education, Lansing, 1941. This board also issues a more inclusive general treatment (107 pp.), "Youth Learns to Assume Responsibility: a Handbook on Experiencing the Ways of Democracy in Schools," 1944. Both these publications could be imitated with profit by any state or school system.

[2] See p. 9.

[3] 1515 Lane Street, Topeka, Kans.

[4] 1201 Sixteenth Street, N. W., Washington, D. C.

[5] 207 Fourth Avenue, New York, N. Y.

ulated program of extracurricular activities (from an educational, not a public-show, point of view) than either the elementary school or the senior high school. Few are the junior high schools that do not have some form of student participation. Naturally, the junior high school's success with the council has had a wholesome and stimulating effect on both the elementary school and the senior high school.

The Modern Trend in Participation.—In completing this brief presentation of the origin and development of student participation, it is only logical to point out that in recent years has come a change in thinking about and planning for it. The ideals of such pioneers as Cronson, Wilson, and George found expression in the form of "republics," "states," and "cities," in which self-government was the predominant idea. Because experience was limited, most of these plans were rather complicated, and because school administrators were generally fearful or antagonistic, nearly all these plans were unsuccessful. These failures, although discouraging to enthusiastic and sincere originators and supporters, were really a blessing in disguise, because they demonstrated the necessity of recognizing limitations, proceeding slowly, and building soundly.

As a result, since about 1915, the trend has been away from imitative and complicated "self-government" plans and the use of this inaccurate and somewhat odious expression, toward the simpler and more practical "participation in school control" idea and more accurate and attractive designations such as "student council," by far the most popular of all titles.[1] This newer concept, as will be shown more in detail in Chap. II, recognizes important limitations in student experience, judgment, and maturity, as well as in areas of responsibility, and further, its designation does not imply conflict with those in authority. "School council" has replaced "student council"

[1] As a matter of fact, there probably never was "student self-government" in any schools except the universities of the latter Middle Ages.

in many schools, especially those in which teachers as well as students are elected. In such cases, the former designation is, of course, more accurate than the latter. However, the term "student council" is still used by some schools in which teachers are elected to membership.

It is interesting to note that recently the expression "student cooperation" has become increasingly common in the literature of this field. Perhaps "cooperation" is a smoother and more desirable term than "participation," a bit closer and warmer in its connotations. However, at the present time, at least, plans of cooperation are probably little or no different from plans of participation. In any case, these terms have all but crowded the expression "student self-government" out of professional literature.

Selected References

An Annual Conference of Student Councils, *School Review*, 46: 321–323, May, 1938.

Baker, G. E.: Student Councils in Illinois, *School Review*, 48: 771–780, December, 1940.

Bowden, A. O., and I. C. Clarke: "Tomorrow's Americans," Chaps. II–IV, VII, G. P. Putnam's Sons, New York, 1930.

Findlay, J. F.: Student Government, Medieval, Colonial, and Modern Style, *School Activities*, 11: 315–316, 350; 368–370, April, May, 1940.

Gibson, C. S.: A Project in Citizenship, *Clearing House*, 7: 351–353, February, 1933.

Hartshorn, C. B.: A Study of Pupil Participation in Iowa High School Government, *School and Society*, 38: 379–382, Sept. 16, 1933.

Jackson, N. A.: Pupil Government in Secondary Schools, *Education*, 42: 197–210, December, 1921.

McClure, W.: Morale by Rote, *School Review*, 27: 458–464, June, 1919.

Sheldon, J. A.: Pupil Participation in School Control in High Schools of Iowa, *School Review*, 43: 189–197, March, 1935.

Chapter II

The Objectives of Student Participation

IT HAS already been suggested that the student council is now well established in American schools. Obviously, it is only a part of a school's offering, hence, to understand it, it is necessary to examine the generally accepted objectives of education in order to appreciate just how this particular part fits into the scheme of things. Further, because education is based upon or built around certain methods of instruction, it is necessary to examine these also in order to understand how council procedures exemplify or utilize them. The first two sections of this chapter will provide these preliminary discussions.

The Main Purpose of Education.—It is a truism to state that a society organizes and supports a school system in order to perpetuate itself by training individuals for future successful membership in it. This membership in a democracy we call citizenship. Never has it been more important, and never before has there been such an insistent demand for this type of training by the schools. A brief glance at our educational history will show the reasons for this great present demand and so set the stage for a consideration of the means of meeting it.

In an earlier day, formal education, almost entirely private in organization and support, was largely concerned with religious and moral codes, creeds, and sanctions. Later, when the state began to organize and support a system of education these earlier emphases were to a considerable extent crowded out by a new emphasis, mental training. Because these mental activities were easily defined, classified, arranged, taught, and evaluated, the graded school with its very definitely organized curriculum emerged and before long became solidly established in America. It was bookish and "cultural" in nature and even in its more practical fringes of physical, social, and civic instruction its work was so academic as to be largely nonfunctional. In this century-long era the subjects were considered to be the most sacred things in education. "Passing on the noble heritage" became the school's slogan, and scholarship its ideal.[1]

About thirty years ago came (1) a new educational philosophy which held that the most important thing about the school is the child, not the subject, (2) a new educational psychology which emphasized the importance of individual interests, abilities, and differences, and (3) a happy combination of these two which stressed the advantages of "doing" over "learning about." During this same period the demand for a more useful schooling became so great that traditional education could no longer resist it and new ideals, subjects, motives, activities, materials, and methods came into the school. These centered about such areas as health, leisure, and vocation, all more or less included in the general category of good citizenship. So today it is widely recognized and accepted that the primary function of the school is to "turn out good citizens."[2]

[1] A number of investigations have been made of the relative later success of high school "scholars." One of the best of these is that reported by J. R. Shannon, The Post-school Careers of High School Leaders and High School Scholars, *School Review*, 37: 656–665, November, 1929. Three of his conclusions were: (1) "In general, it seems that the scholars are least successful in post-school life"; (2) "It seems that whatever it is that is necessary for success in high school is not the factor that is requisite for success in life"; and (3) "Whatever is required to excel in the extra-curriculum life of the high school seems to be the same thing that contributes most to success later."

[2] Descriptions of distinctive programs of civic education will be found in "Learning the Ways of Democracy," Educational Policies Commission, National Education Association, 1940.

However, in reality, the school cannot turn out good citizens because its students are not yet legal members of society; not yet being of age they cannot vote, they cannot own property, they cannot be taxed, and they cannot bring suit in court. In short, because they are minors they cannot become full-fledged citizens of their country. Obviously, then, the only thing the school can do is to give them training through subjects, opportunities, settings, and activities that will fit them for successful adult life.

Essentials of Effective Civic Education.—There are three elements that are absolutely essential to any kind of effective education: pertinent knowledges, worthy ideals, and functional habits. A brief discussion of these will indicate their importance and relationships and also their place in a system of student participation.

Pertinent Knowledges.—These are basic to all learning and to all living, but they do not, as many individuals apparently believe, constitute education; by themselves they are only a type of ornamentation. All the facts in the world have never, in and by themselves, accomplished anything; a knowledge of how never constructed a table, built a bridge, painted a picture, planted a tree, or wrote a poem. Knowledge is valueless until it is used. Similarly, a knowledge of how the good citizen acts and behaves does not mean that the individual possessing such information will choose to act accordingly. Knowledge of law is certainly no guarantee of its observance. It is only the foundation upon which intelligent observance may be built. Long ago John Dewey expressed this idea in these words: "There is nothing in the nature of the ideas *about* morality, of information *about* honesty or purity or kindness which automatically transmits such ideas into good character or good conduct."[1]

[1] DEWEY, JOHN, "Moral Principles in Education," p. 1, Houghton Mifflin Company, Boston, 1909.

In order to acquaint its pupils with the American way of life, the school has long stressed the importance of pertinent information. Through its various courses it has given the pupils a knowledge of our social inheritance, our heroes, inventors, authors, musicians, and statesmen, as well as important events now reflected in our schedule of holidays and anniversaries. Similarly, the school has taught the details of our democratic organization, its elements, relationships, responsibilities, traditions, and customs. All these are essential. However, far too often these important knowledges have been colorless and non-vital because they were acquired through the medium of formal school "work"; they represented lessons to be mastered, papers to be written, and examinations to be passed. Further, in many instances the pupil did not associate them with his own life because they stressed mystical and mythical elements and represented heights to which he could not aspire. Some of them were practically useless, especially those relating to civic and political organization, because they were not always accurate; they represented the ideal but not always the actual as the pupil knew it.

Appropriate Ideals.—A mental image or notion of the thing to be accomplished is the second essential element in the production of good citizenship or anything else because it supplies the motivation and also the standards by which achievement is evaluated. Of course, the clearer this mental image is the more easily will it become a reality. In an earlier day the school attempted to instill ideals directly by means of a memorization of mottoes, maxims, slogans, pledges, oaths, creeds, and similar material, and this method is still used to a considerable extent.[1] Perhaps the use of these devices can be

[1] It is the basis of a great deal of our present-day advertising, much of which is insulting to human intelligence. This is true especially of political advertising. Consider, for example, the compliment which the use of such slogans as "Keep Cool with Coolidge" and "Who but Hoover?" pays to a nation of supposedly sensible voters.

justified in the lower grades, provided they are meaningful, because these younger boys and girls lack the knowledge, experience, and maturity necessary for a recognition and appreciation of the many implications of an indirect presentation of the same idea.

However, this so-called "direct method" of establishing ideals fell into disrepute because it was ineffectual.[1] It represented formal lessons to be learned and recited instead of personal lessons to be applied and practiced. It lacked emotional appeal. Very often it was meaningless to the individual because it concerned the ideals of distant adulthood and not those of immediate childhood. Undoubtedly, too, often the individual understood the meaning of the ideal but for various reasons did not accept it as a guiding principle in his life.

What is said here is not an indictment of ideals, which are absolutely necessary, but is rather an indictment of the belief that because an individual knows an ideal he invariably reflects it in his thoughts and actions. Here again, a knowledge of an ideal is no guarantee of its acceptance. It is only the basis upon which acceptance can be and must be built.

Functional Habits.—The third essential of effective civic education is a set of habits which capitalize the knowledges and ideals in observable and positive actions. Good citizenship, like good reading, singing, swimming, or automobile driving, is composed of a group of highly specialized actions all properly integrated and correlated and directed toward the achievement of the appropriate ideals. It is important to note that there can be no good citizenship without these habits, just as there can be no good reading, singing, swim-

[1] A discussion of the direct and indirect methods of moral instruction—materials, advantages, disadvantages, and suggestions for use—will be found in H. C. McKown, "Character Education," Chaps. VI–VII, McGraw-Hill Book Company, Inc., New York, 1935.

ming, or automobile driving without the corresponding habits.

Until very recently the conscious development of actions through habit-forming activities was almost entirely neglected in moral instruction, character education, citizenship training, or call it what you will. This neglect was due largely to the assumption that the impartation of pertinent knowledges and the instillation of worthy ideals would inevitably result in the establishment of properly functioning habits. It is downright amazing that any educator of any age should make this assumption, an assumption which he did not make in the teaching of reading, writing, spelling, arithmetic, or any other subject. In these he very carefully provided for the practice which resulted in the proper habits.

With the modern increasing emphasis upon "doing" there has come a decreasing emphasis upon "being." In the progressive schools of today practicing the doing of the activities which the good, the honest, and the courteous individual does has replaced the earlier sermonics about being good, being honest, and being courteous. And this is the result of a logical recognition that the "being" is merely the end-product of the "doing," that one cannot "be" good, honest, or courteous except by "doing" the activities which together represent these. This idea is being reflected more and more in the replacement of the expression "the ideals of good citizenship" with "the habits of good citizenship," or "the ideals and habits of good citizenship," and this is a thoroughly logical and justifiable development.

Knowledges, ideals, and habits are equally essential to good reading, walking, kite flying, book writing, piano playing, window washing, or any other activity, including good citizenship; not one of them can be omitted. If the individual has the knowledges and the ideals but not the habits he is as functionless as a stationary locomotive. If he has the knowledges and the habits but not the ideals he is an automaton, a mere machine always acting in a predetermined manner. If he has the ideals and the habits but not the knowledges he is only an animal with no understanding or appreciation of the reasons why of all things. In the latter two instances he is incapable of intelligently adapting himself to a new situation.

Further, an individual lacking any one of these elements could not be said to be even moral. In the first illustration the individual lacks habits, and these are basic to morality. Morality also implies a conscious choice between the good and the bad, the right and the wrong, and neither the automaton nor the animal could make such a choice. To repeat, in a program for the development of good citizenship there must be adequate provision for the developing and utilizing of all three of these elements.

How Is Participation Concerned?—Recognizing that the traditional school's program of citizenship training was weak because it lacked provisions for practicing the necessary habits, the pioneer educators of the present century began to call for a setting within the school which resembled, to some extent at least, that in which the child would find himself when he became an adult. The very logical theory was that living successfully in his "here and now" would fit him for successful living in a somewhat similar setting later, and that under such conditions worthy school membership would become a functional preparation for worthy adult citizenship. For instance, years ago Dewey stated, "The school cannot be a preparation for social life except as it reproduces, within itself, typical conditions of social life," and "Except so far as the school is an embryonic typical community moral training must be partly pathological and partly formal. The child ought to be judged by the same standards in the school, as the adult in the wider social life to which he belongs."[1] And

[1] Dewey, *op. cit.*, pp. 1, 14.

again, "The school must be a community in all which that implies."[1] In this same vein Kilpatrick says, "The effective school in a democracy must give its pupils an intelligent understanding of the issues of democracy, make them well-disposed toward democracy as a way of life, and make them skillful in the cooperative activities through which democracy must function."[2]

Cubberley, in discussing the relationship of the school to a democratic government, writes, "Responsibility for good government under any democratic form of organization rests upon all, and the school should give preparation for the political life of tomorrow by training its pupils to meet responsibilities, developing initiative, awakening social insight and causing each to shoulder a fair share of the government of the school."[3]

The philosophy of student participation embraces the "embryonic community" idea, providing for common interests and activities and motivated cooperation through natural settings and opportunities. Thus, as will be shown more in detail in the following pages, all three basic elements of any education, pertinent knowledges, worthy ideals, and functional habits, are also basic elements in this practice school of democracy. This is ample justification for the student council.

Specific Objectives of Student Participation.—What is meant by objective? An examination of investigations of the purposes of student participation in school administration, as stated by those directly interested—administrators, teachers, and students—reveals a great deal of confused thinking which,

[1] Dewey, J., "Democracy and Education," p. 416, Houghton Mifflin Company, Boston, 1916.

[2] From notes taken by the author in Dr. Kilpatrick's classes.

[3] Cubberley, E. P., "An Introduction to the Study of Education," p. 159, Houghton Mifflin Company, Boston, 1925.

of course, might be expected due to the recency of this development. For instance, some individuals state these purposes in the form of more or less general objectives such as "to train for citizenship," "to develop intelligent leadership and followership," and "to give functional training in self-government," while other individuals indicate such objectives, usually designating them as "specific purposes," as "to promote noon-hour activities," "to seat pupils for formal assemblies," and "to supervise corridor traffic." Consequently, for our purpose here it becomes necessary to define the term "objective."

As used in the following pages, an objective represents a rather general and inclusive ultimate end to be attained, such as "intelligent leadership and followership," "increasing self-direction," and "respect for law and order." Under this definition such objectives as "promoting noon-hour assemblies," "seating pupils in formal assemblies," or "supervising corridor traffic" are not objectives at all; they are merely activities through which it is hoped the ultimate ends of wholesome noon-hour recreation, efficient auditorium seating, and orderly passing will be achieved.

Although at first glance this discussion may appear to be space-taking quibbling, a little more reflection will show that it implies a most basic concept, the difference between getting things done and getting things done with educative results. The council is not primarily, as has often been suggested, an administrative device. The school's administration can discharge most of the council's responsibilities more quickly and efficiently than it can, in exactly the same way that the teacher can solve the students' problems, write their themes, perform their experiments, and take their examinations more successfully than they. This is but another way of saying that very often working through the council represents a slow and indirect method of getting things done.

The Objectives of Student Participation

The main purpose of the council, like the main purpose of all other justifiable activities about the school, curricular or extracurricular, is to educate those who participate, either directly or indirectly. Naturally, the council's activities are important; if there were none of these there would be no council. It is also important that they be successfully carried out, but far more important, the members of the council and the students who elected them must profit educationally through these activities and projects. If no such profit results, the time and efforts spent on council activities are time and efforts wasted.

This point is worth emphasizing. Specifically, this means that such activities as "promoting noon-hour activities," "seating pupils in formal assemblies," and "supervising corridor traffic," are not ends in themselves but are the media through which the ultimate objectives are achieved. This holds true for all student activities. All of them must be justified solely on the basis of their direct and indirect educational contributions.

Basic Elements of Good Citizenship.—If the primary function of the school is to develop good citizenship, then the primary function of any and all of its parts is to assist in this development. Hence, assisting in the development of good citizenship is the primary function of the student council plan.

Now any thing, be it a definite object such as an automobile, painting, chair, garden, or book, or a less definite quality or trait such as courtesy, loyalty, sincerity, cheerfulness, or neatness, is composed of basic elements properly proportioned and articulated. Naturally, the way to produce this thing is to make and coordinate the elements which compose it, or which are responsible for it in its final form.

Good citizenship, too, is composed of elements which must be produced and articulated. Among the most important of these are (1) a knowledge of the theory of democracy, (2) sentiments of law and order, (3) intelligent respect for authority, (4) increasing self-direction, (5) leadership and followership, (6) cooperation, and (7) morale. Undoubtedly there are other important elements because citizenship is a many-sided and complicated structure.[1] However, a discussion of these seven will show the pattern which a program of civic education must follow, and will indicate also some of the possibilities of the student-participation approach.

1. *A Knowledge of the Theory of Democracy.*—As was pointed out earlier in the chapter, the public school has always imparted the knowledge of how a democratic form of government is organized and how it functions, or how it is supposed to function. It was also suggested that much of this information is academic and bookish because it concerns the interests and activities of adulthood. Naturally, this weakness in our program must be strengthened, and it can be, by supplementing theoretical instruction with practical application.

The student council represents an excellent device through which important knowledges of democracy can be made meaningful, colorful, and vital, not only because it is based upon democratic principles and procedures but, just as important, because its interests and activities are those of student life. Participating in an election campaign, evaluating the qualifications of candidates, voting, representing a group, discussing proposed policies, serving on committees, discharging assigned responsibilities—these and similar activities represent a practical and firsthand experience with democracy which gives real meaning to it.

2. *Sentiments of Law and Order.*—Everyone from birth till death, yes, and even before birth and after death, is ordered

[1] In her article, What Constitutes Good Citizenship?, *School Review*, 32: 534–536, September, 1924, Retha E. Breeze reported that an investigation of the opinions of four hundred men and women appearing in "Who's Who in America" resulted in a list of 212 different traits, thirty-eight of which were mentioned at least five times.

by established customs and legal enactments. The individual cannot eat his dinner, walk down to the corner, drive his car into the garage, or answer the telephone without observing or violating law and order. Because man's very existence depends upon law and order it is regrettable that this expression has become so formal and that often, apparently, it implies unpleasantness, restraint, and control, instead of reasonable mechanisms for establishing social welfare.

Naturally, where there is law and order there must be discipline to prevent breakdown and resulting lawlessness and disorder. In general, discipline may be of two kinds, external, which is based upon fear, and internal, which is based upon pride. Two illustrations will show the difference between these. Suppose a policeman, noticing an individual walking on a protected spot of grass, bawls at him, "Get off that grass or I'll put you off." This individual will probably get off the grass, realizing that if he does not the officer will put him off bodily. In short, he fears the officer. Probably he does not even reflect on the matter of his violation and resents being spoken to in such a manner. Now suppose that instead of an officer this individual's best friend sees him and says, "Jim, you should know better than to stand on that grass." He will get off the grass, this time without resentment, because he recognizes the impropriety and because he likes and respects his friend and wants his friend to continue to like and respect him. The first illustration represents the poorest of disciplines, while the second reflects the best.

It is well to remember, also, that externally and arbitrarily set rules and regulations often represent challenges. In the first illustration above the unexpressed attitude of many an individual would be, "I'll stand on this grass all I want to, and you can't stop me." Some of these individuals, after the officer had walked away, might even stand on the grass again in order to prove to themselves, and perhaps to their friends, that they were independent. How many are the teachers and administrators who have found that making threats in classroom and assembly hall have only increased their troubles, all because some students accepted their challenge and very likely "got away with it," to the further detriment of good order.

Another illustration. Several years ago the author, while visiting a school in which it was reported sentiments of law and order had been developed to a high degree, decided to make a test. He walked down the corridor while classes were passing, took a sheet of paper from his pocket, glanced at it, crumpled it up, threw it onto the floor, and walked straight ahead. In an instant there came a decided tug at his sleeve and he stopped and turned to face a somewhat irritated boy, perhaps a seventh grader, who said to him, "Mister, we don't do that in our school." Note that he did not say, "Mister, the principal does not allow that in his school." It was "we" and "our." Needless to state, this school passed its examination with flying colors.[1]

In no way whatever does this mean that school authorities should surrender their legal and moral obligations for effective discipline; in fact, they could not, even if they wanted to. Such an attempt was the weakness of the older forms of "self-government," a weakness which the newer conception of participation in control obviates. However, it does mean that wherever expedient, that is, wherever possible, wise, and justifiable from an educational point of view, the students should help to set the goal of efficient self-discipline and make serious attempts to achieve it. In such a setting the student has a clear conception of the laws needed, helps to set them, and because he has had a voice in making them, he is vitally interested in seeing them observed.

[1] A description of a plan in which every pupil of the school shares direct responsibility will be found in M. W. Wallace, Every Pupil a One-semester Sponsor, *Clearing House*, 17: 212–214, December, 1942.

Here is another most important area of student-council relationships. The promotion of systematic street and corridor traffic, of good order in the assembly and at games, of courtesy at parties and other social events, and safety on the playground and about the school, as well as the promotion of neatness and the proper use of school materials and equipment, to mention a few possibilities, all represent fields of council activity in which thoughtful respect for law and order can be functionally developed.

3. *Intelligent Respect for Authority.*—In every group there is recognized authority. This authority may vary all the way from a common acknowledgment of the relative importance of some bigger, more assertive, or older boy in an unorganized group of children to a formal acceptance of the laws and officers of some organized adult body. Certainly it must not be thought that all authority is in the form of regulations; some of it is in the form of traditions, customs, attitudes, and beliefs which have become established. For instance, the criminal's contempt for the "stoolie" or "stool pigeon," a fully completed development of the child's attitude toward the "snitcher" or "peacher," is based upon authority, even though unorganized and uncoded.

Authority may be accepted blindly or intelligently. In the case of the very small child it must be accepted blindly because he is too young to understand the reasons for it.[1] When this child becomes old enough to understand and appreciate these reasons, authority becomes more meaningful and his acceptance more intelligent. Such acceptance does not spring full bloom into being; it grows gradually and slowly.

[1] "Of all the undemocratic traditions in school and home, the hardest to escape is the worship of obedience as a virtue," is the opening sentence of H. S. Tuttle's article, Obedience: a Necessary Convenience, in *The Elementary School Journal* for February, 1943, pp. 343–346. This is an excellent and interesting article, which any teacher can read with profit.

Although intelligent respect may imply, to some extent, a questioning attitude toward authority, or the wisdom of its promulgations and actions, yet it does not mean that its every order should be debated and discussed by those for whom it is designed, because there would never be time enough for such logical reasoning. Intelligent obedience must imply some considerable respect for the purposes, abilities, and sincerity of those in authority. On the other hand, knowing something about the reasons for certain regulations and customs should mean that the individual will all the more appreciate the necessity for them and have a further interest in helping to observe them.

Further, intelligent respect does not mean usually that the individual debates the matter and then decides for himself just what he shall do. He must understand that authority was originated because it appeared to be logical and necessary, and then later it became permanently accepted because it appeared to be successful. Too, he must appreciate the fact that democratic authority was established on the basis of the greatest good for the greatest number and that even though occasionally it may restrict him, yet in the long run it will be beneficial to him. In other words, he must be led to realize that he himself cannot enjoy freedom and safety except through such established authority.

But intelligent respect means more than these attitudes toward authority, it means also that the individual should obey sincerely and conscientiously to the best of his ability. This is an important point which unfortunately is not often found in the discussions of this subject.

Specifically, just how is student participation concerned? It should be clear that the student who has seen corridor traffic become more orderly, recreation schedules become better organized, courtesy become more evident, assembly programs become more interesting, and financing become more successful through the efforts of his elected representatives in the central organization, can not only understand and appreciate the part played by the council, but can also get a thrill from helping to elect it and to support its policies. Because he recognizes himself as a part of the school's democracy instead of an isolated individual, his obedience to the rules of his governing body, even in those matters in which he may personally disagree, will tend to be all the more complete, because he appreciates the necessity for such rules for the good of the school as a whole. It would not be too much to expect that because of this direct and personal interest, his own observance will be pretty sincere and conscientious. What else is intelligent respect for authority?

4. *Increasing Self-direction.*—The life of the individual falls easily into two different stages or periods, childhood and adulthood. In fact, these are two different worlds because they represent such completely dissimilar settings. The first is the world of autocracy and the second the world of democracy. In childhood the individual is controlled and dominated by his parents, and rightly so, because he lacks the knowledges, ideals, and habits which make for social competency and independence. In adulthood he possesses these essential elements which make for self-direction.

However, it is quite impossible for the individual suddenly and successfully to step from the restricted world of childhood to the unrestricted world of adulthood. The learning, accepting, and practicing necessary represent a slow process of work. Assuming that social adequacy comes automatically with physical adulthood is as stupid as assuming that the individual can write legibly merely because he has attained physical maturity. Such an assumption and procedure, or rather lack of procedure, will always result in failure.

An excellent example of such failure is to be found in the case of the boy (or girl) who has been babied and over-mothered by fond but unintelligent parents and who suddenly finds himself away from home for the first time, say at college, where he is on his own. It is well known that those students who "break" first are the pampered pets who have never been allowed to grow up, who have never been allowed to develop self-reliance. They cannot live happily and successfully in an adult's world with only a child's training.

Training for effectual social living may come very naturally and easily through a miniature society in which the individual learns the pertinent knowledges, accepts the worthy ideals, and actually practices the habits necessary for successful membership. The student council idea is built around these three processes; through them the student becomes increasingly self-directive, irrespective of whether he is a member of the central body or only of the general organization that sponsors and supports it.

Further, this school setting provides for increasing self-direction, or development, in the matter of individual interests and abilities. One student has an interest and some native ability in originating, another in organizing, another in executing, another in expressing, another in publicizing, and another in evaluating, and the discovery and development of these potentialities are basic responsibilities of successful student cooperation because successful student cooperation depends upon them.

5. *Intelligent Leadership and Followership.*—In every group, from a disorganized and frenzied mob to an orderly and dignified legislative body, there are leaders, those who give direction to thought and action; and it is reasonable to state that the more intelligent and resourceful the leaders are, the more successful will their groups be.

In an autocratic setting leaders come into power because of tradition, custom, parentage, friendships, political favoritism, or some other influence that does not necessarily guarantee wise leadership. In a democratic setting, theoretically at least, leaders come into power through election, direct or indirect, on the basis of a recognition of their abilities. Naturally, then, because of their strategic positions it is of utmost importance that they be carefully selected. Successful democracy depends upon skilled leadership and this, in turn, must rest upon intelligent followership, the source of its authority and support.

Intelligent followership implies a double responsibility; first, a wise selection of leaders and, second, sincere and successful attempts to follow their leadership. Because this second responsibility was discussed in the previous section, only the first will be reflected here.

In order to avoid having leaders selected on the basis of friendship, sympathy, obligation, or for other purely personal reasons—all of which represent the lowest bracket of voting purposes because none of them comprehends the real objective of office holding and therefore none of them guarantees success in office—it is essential that the electors shall be trained to appreciate the importance of a deliberate and unbiased evaluation of the candidates' qualifications, and further, to vote upon the basis of the results of such reflection. Definite suggestions for this training will be found in Chap. VII.

Intelligent leadership and followership, like all other characteristics of good citizenship, must be developed; they do not spring unprompted into being. Because the school enrolls all the children of all the people, it is only logical that it should accept a considerable share of this responsibility. Nearly thirty years ago Thorndike suggested this when he raised and answered the very pertinent question, Is not special training in judging the qualities of leaders worthy of a place in democratic education?[1] In just what settings in the school are these

[1] THORNDIKE, E. L., Education for Initiative and Originality, *Teachers College Record*, 17: 405–416, November, 1916.

qualifications developed? To some extent the various subjects help to provide the bases of knowledge and ideals, and in a very limited way in specialized vocational and recreational fields, provide opportunities for some practice, but in the general area of democratic participation little is scheduled or accomplished through the curriculum.

Here again, the council idea provides natural settings for training in both leadership and followership. These are functional settings because they concern the student and his activities. For instance, an elected leader who is autocratic in his methods, arbitrary in his decisions, careless in his commitments, and erratic in his judgments will soon discover that he must improve or he will be replaced; and the follower whose home room, class, activity, or school suffers from his vote or his ineffectual attempts to follow good leadership will soon recognize that the fault is his own. In both cases it is almost inevitable that the student shall recognize the disastrous consequences of his unwise or careless efforts. And, just as important, later he will have other opportunities in which he can do something about it.[1]

6. *Cooperation.*—This is another important element of democratic living which must be developed because, although in man's original nature there is a desire to associate with others and share in their activities, there are no fully developed skills which result in effective cooperation. Cooperation means combined efforts for the common good. The cooperator will, usually, benefit from the united effort, but for the moment at least the immediate objective is a benefit for the group.

[1] Two good investigational studies of student leadership are G. C. Bellingrath, "Qualities Associated with Leadership in the Extra-curricular Activities of the High School," and M. Brown, "Leadership among High School Pupils," published, 1930 and 1933, by the Bureau of Publications, Teachers College, Columbia University, New York.

Is the student taught cooperation through his academic courses? Hardly. In fact, cooperation in English, algebra, history, language, and other subjects is usually frowned upon, the emphasis being, as almost every student has heard time and again, "get it yourself." Even in those subjects in which cooperation is talked about and the ideals set, such as some social science courses, very few are the opportunities in which actual practice is possible. We are not contending that anything else is desirable or possible, we are merely pointing out that as at present organized the curriculum offers very few opportunities for the functional teaching of cooperation.

In the extracurricular field there is an entirely different story. Note, for instance, that a dramatic cast, music organization, athletic team, assembly committee, or newspaper staff requires successful cooperation. Each member must practice it in order to retain his position and standing. Through the student-council organization, which represents all these and many other activities, there are hundreds of opportunities, large and small, for the practice of this important element of good citizenship.

However, there is another phase of cooperation. Far too many discussions of this topic stop with student-student cooperation; too few of them reflect student-teacher cooperation. This, too, is highly important. One of the unfortunate features of traditional school organization, especially in the large and highly departmentalized school, is that it separates the student from his teacher. In it the student learns to know his teacher only as an assignment-maker, a task-setter, a recitation-hearer, and an examination-giver, and rarely does he learn to know her as a well-educated, high-idealed, warm-hearted, honest-to-goodness human being. It is quite probable that what he might learn from her personally is as important as the facts that he picks up in her classes. The other side of the picture is just as true; only rarely does the teacher get to know the pupil personally.[1] The result is that in many schools there are two more or less conflicting bodies, the student and the faculty, each of which knows relatively little of the interests, ambitions, and problems of the other. Further, there are often strong emotional reactions, fears, prejudices, and jealousies which make for anything but a unified and harmonious school.

There are many opportunities in the extracurricular field for the development of better student-teacher relations and mutual cooperation, especially where the council promotes, unifies, and coordinates these activities, because each of them is usually sponsored by a teacher. In these nonacademic settings the teacher is no longer a task-setter, nor the student a task-doer; rather they work together for the common good, the students furnishing the drive, the student contacts, and the execution, the teacher providing the experience, the administrative contacts, and the judgment.

7. *Morale.*—Closely related to cooperation is group spirit or morale, which was once defined by a boy as "the feeling a team has when it knows it is good." Morale is essential to any kind of organized effort. An army without morale would be little better than an unorganized mob, and a school in which each teacher and student bustled around to his individual classes with little or no interest in his institution as a whole, not feeling himself as a vital part of the school, would not be a school worthy of the name. It would be as colorless as a factory in which the employees were war prisoners.

Two elements are basic to morale, something to be proud of or loyal to, and a feeling of personal responsibility. A team

[1] Developing desirable pupil-teacher relationships is one of the important objectives of the home room plan, another miniature democracy. For a detailed discussion of this purpose see the author's "Home Room Guidance," pp. 25–32, McGraw-Hill Book Company, Inc., New York; 1934. See also G. T. Lewis, Friendliness through Home Room Advisers, *School Review*, 48: 55–59, January, 1940.

whose record was poor could never have group spirit, and neither would it if its record were good but unfelt by its members or those closely associated with them. Every student in the school can thrill to his team's record even though he does not play on the team because he participates indirectly as a member of the school which his team represents. This idea of personal feeling is basic. If, in a school assembly, the cheerleaders arose and called for a yell for algebra, they would be laughed off the stage; but if they called for a cheer for the algebra team, they would get a rousing response. Not one of us has ever heard a cheer for football, but all of us have heard hundreds of cheers for football players and teams. Football is not "our" game, but the team is "ours."

The function of the student council is this connection is to develop and coordinate opportunities for many different kinds of participation, not only in games, competitions, programs, public events, publications, and similar activities but also in such projects for the common good as orderly corridor traffic, safely on the streets, neatness of lockers, thrift in the use of materials and equipment, courtesy to visitors, and friendly aid to new students. Every one of these activities originated and promoted for the school as a whole represents a morale-developing setting.

Conclusion.—It must not be assumed from the presentations of this chapter that the author believes that the student council offers the one and only medium through which good citizenship can be and is developed. He believes nothing of the sort. Other school and outside-of-school settings also contribute to this training, and should continue to do so in an increasingly effective manner. But he does believe that such a group properly organized and supervised offers the best of these opportunities because its objectives are educationally justifiable and its methods and procedures are psychologically sound. It is a motivated and functional miniature democracy, one which represents student interests and activities and all students, and a plan which more closely resembles adult democracy than anything now to be found inside the school. It is, in short, a practice school of democracy, a laboratory for citizenship.

Selected References

BARNES, M. C.: The Value of the Student Council at East High, Waterloo, Iowa, *School Activities*, 10: 400–401, May, 1939.

BOWDEN, A. O., and I. C. CLARKE: "Tomorrow's Americans," Chaps. I, III, VI, XIV, G. P. Putnam's Sons, New York, 1930.

BROGUE, E. B., and P. B. JACOBSON: "Student-council Handbook," Chap. II, National Association of Secondary School Principals, 1940.

CHARTERS, W. W.: "The Teaching of Ideals," The Macmillan Company, New York, 1927.

COE, G. A.: "Educating for Citizenship," Charles Scribner's Sons, New York, 1932.

DIEMER, G. W., and B. V. MULLEN: "Pupil Citizenship," Chap. I, World Book Company, Yonkers-on-Hudson, New York, 1930.

DOUGLASS, H. R.: Citizenship and the School, *School Activities*, 10: 332–334, April, 1939.

ESTVAN, F. J.: Democratic Processes in School Life, *Elementary School Journal*, 43: 143–150, November, 1942.

FAUST, R. M.: Pupil Self Direction, *Clearing House*, 8: 51–55, September, 1933.

FISHBACK, E.: An Elementary School Builds Citizenship, *School Activities*, 12: 195–196, December, 1940.

FRETWELL, E. K.: "Extra-curricular Activities in Secondary Schools," Chap. IV, Houghton Mifflin Company, Boston, 1931.

GILCHRIST, R. S.: An Evaluation in Terms of Pupil Participation, *Clearing House*, 7: 358–363, February, 1933.

GRAYBEAL, L. B.: Re-examining Our Democratic Concepts, *School Activities*, 14: 123–124, December, 1942.

HALL, D.: Democracy Begins at Home, *Journal of Higher Education*, 11: 360–362, October, 1940.

JARNIE, L. L.: Students Take Part in Policy Making, *Clearing House*, 13: 223–225, December, 1938.

JOHNSTON, E. G.: Internes in Citizenship, *School Activities*, 9: 61–62, 75–76, 103, October, 1937.

KELLEY, E. C.: Utilizing Student Power, *Journal of the National Education Association*, 25: 217–218, October, 1936.

KIRBY, B. C.: Pupil Participation in School Life, *School Executive*, 56: 151–152, December, 1936.

KIRKENDALL, L. A.: Is Your School Council an Effective Instrument of Democracy? *School Activities*, 14: 83–84, 86, November, 1942.

Leadership in Democratic Living, *Teachers College Record*, 40: 561–649, April, 1939.

MORGAN, R. E.: School Activities for School Morale, *School Activities*, 13: 331–336, May, 1942.

———: Student Democracies Can Function, *School Activities*, 12: 219–220, 234, February, 1941.

O'BRIEN, F. P., and I. M. SHEPPARD: What They Say about the Junior High Council, *School Activities*, 13: 339–340, May, 1942.

REAVIS, W. C.: Training in Cooperation through Participation in Solving Secondary School Problems, *School Review*, 50: 629–635, November, 1942.

RINGDAHL, N. R.: What Outcomes May Be Expected from Pupil Participation? *School Activities*, 7: 3–5, January, 1936.

ROEMER, J., and C. F. ALLEN: "Readings in Extra-curricular Activities," Chaps. I, II, VI, Johnson Publishing Company, Richmond, Va., 1929.

SALTZER, C. E., and J. H. HUSBAND: Student Government in the Guidance Program, *School Activities*, 14: 113–114, November, 1942.

SCOTT, M.: Creative Democracy, *School Activities*, 12: 301–302, April, 1941.

SMITH, W. R.: Educational Bases for Participation in School Control, *School Activities*, 5: 3–7, February, 1934.

STRANG, R.: "Group Activities in College and Secondary School," Chap. I, Harper & Brothers, New York, 1941.

TERRY, P. W.: "Supervising Extra-curricular Activities," Chaps. II–V, McGraw-Hill Book Company, Inc., New York, 1930.

VINEYARD, J. J., and C. F. POOLE: "Student Participation in School Government," Chap. I, A. S. Barnes and Company, New York, 1930.

WELLING, R.: Building Character for Democracy, *Better Schools*, January, 1942.

WILSON, H. E.: "Educating for Citizenship," McGraw-Hill Book Company, Inc., New York, 1938.

WYMAN, L. K.: "Character and Citizenship through Student Government," John C. Winston Company, Philadelphia, 1935.

———: Meeting the Challenge of the Times, *School Activities*, 9: 395–396, 442, May, 1938.

Chapter III

Principles Underlying Student Participation

THE policies relating to good organization and administration of student participation can be suggested in a consideration of the principles underlying them. Although the types of student-council organization vary widely, all of them rest upon about the same basic ideas. Those discussed in this chapter are based upon both logic and experience and reflect the opinions of directors, sponsors, and teachers who have had and are having successful experience with the student council plan.[1] Only the more general principles will be discussed here. Those relating more particularly to the initiation of a new council, sponsorship, constitution, organization, discipline, and financing will be found in the presentation of these topics.

1. The School Must Feel a Continuous Need for the Council.—The principle that participation should grow out of the felt needs of the school, instead of being forced upon the school, is presented on pages 97–106 in connection with the general discussion of how to start a council. However, this principle is as important after the council has been established as it was before it came into being. The feeling of need must be continuous because if the school comes to the point where it feels no need, there is no need, and so no justification for participation. In such a setting the council is merely an

[1] There are, of course, some differences of opinion concerning these principles. The Harvey-Allen and Kelley articles listed in the bibliography —both good—should be read together because the second is a "reply" to the first.

ornamental nonfunctional organization which enjoys the respect of no one about the school. The proper maintenance of this felt need requires constant study and adaptation as will be explained in detail later.

2. The Entire School Should Be Represented in the Council.—Generally speaking there are two main plans by which members are elected to the council—by such definitely organized groups as classes and clubs, and by the units of the school as a whole.[1] Usually in the latter type of organization the members are elected from the smaller unspecialized groups such as the home room.

The chief disadvantages of the first plan are the dangers that (1) not all students will be represented because not all of them will belong to the organizations allowed representation; (2) those who belong to more than one organization will be represented more than once; (3) petty politics will develop; and (4) the larger organizations, usually represented by more members than the smaller, will benefit at the expense of the latter. In a way the last two possibilities are but natural because in electing a representative a group obligates him to work for it. In such a setting the test of his value as a representative is to be found in the extent to which he is able to get concessions and favors for his group. In case of conflict, for instance, he could hardly be expected to vote against the wishes of his organization. The emphasis here is upon getting instead of upon giving. In short, under this plan there is a serious possibility of loyalty to group overshadowing loyalty to school.

The second plan, election by unspecialized groups, avoids the difficulties and dangers suggested above. All the students

[1] In some schools the council members are appointed by the principal and teachers. This form of organization violates the basic principles of democratic government and so will not be discussed in this book. The other forms will be presented more in detail in the following chapter.

are represented because all of them are in home rooms. In it the student represents his whole school instead of a particularized section of it and consequently sees all of its activities in proper perspective as elements of the entire picture. Under this plan attention can be centered on the weak places in the schedule, and unbiased efforts be made toward the development of a well-balanced and closely articulated program.

In some schools there is a provision for "honorary membership" in the council. For instance, famous alumni, soldiers, sailors, guests, speakers, and even the superintendent, principal, supervisor, or other administrative officers or respected retiring teachers are elected honorary members. There is nothing to be said in favor of this practice, and there are several things to be said against it: (1) the council is a working and not an honoring organization; (2) such members can never be, in a real sense, members of the council because they represent no school group or interest and attend few or no council meetings; and (3) it violates the basic principle that every member should assume some definite responsibility. This practice is a pretty gesture of affection but it is illogical, unnecessary, and confusing.

3. The Faculty Should Be Fairly Represented.—If the council is to represent a genuine cooperative school effort, then teachers as well as students should be elected to it. The usual practice is for the principal to appoint a sponsor, and while this plan has some obvious advantages, yet it really does not represent the ideal. Far too often the students consider an appointed sponsor a sort of spy or "wet blanket" whose duty it is to guide and control the council in accordance with the wishes of the administration, and this conception may not be entirely inaccurate. In any case, under such a plan the attitudes of both sponsor and council can hardly be one hundred per cent harmonious.

Logically, if the council is to represent the whole school, and the faculty is a part of the school, then the faculty members should be elected the same as the student members. In fact, there is no more justification for the principal appointing the faculty members than there is for the teacher appointing the student members. An equitable representation of the faculty, on perhaps a teacher-faculty ratio somewhat similar to a student-body ratio, through a regularly held election, adds to dignity and importance, and helps to prevent misunderstandings and petty jealousies. This subject will be discussed more in detail in Chap. XII.

4. The Average Student Should Feel His Representation.—It is but natural that the student who feels that he is represented in the council will have a more wholesome attitude toward it and a greater interest in its policies and programs than the student who does not so feel his representation. In plans in which specialized groups elect representatives to the council, the student who is not a member of any of these organizations will not be represented, and he need not be expected to be vitally interested in the council or its activities. For him there is actually little or no participation in administration; the setting is not wholly democratic. Nor does a palliative plan of allowing the election of a few members "at large" add much to such a student's interest. Usually the smaller the group represented the greater is the probability that its members will feel their representation, and, just as important, their own responsibility, and it is easy for the individual student to initiate an idea or action for consideration through his representative.

5. The Average Student Should Feel His Own Responsibility.—This principle grows easily out of that suggested immediately above. In many a school the average student's actual connection with the council appears to cease after he has cast his vote because he has no opportunity to assist in the development of school policies or plans. These he leaves to the body he helped to elect. Even listening to the reports of his representative as to what the council did at its meeting leaves him relatively unconcerned because he had little or no part in discussing the various items before the council acted upon them. Such a rubber-stamp state of affairs is not conducive to the development of school or any other kind of democracy. The council member should represent not merely his group but the thought of his group. In order to develop this essential felt responsibility in the school citizen, the council should encourage the discussion of pertinent problems in the home rooms or other groups represented, and, if practicable, in separate groups, even classes in civics and problems of democracy. The purpose of participation is to educate electors as well as electees; and this purpose will not be achieved unless suitable opportunities are provided for it.[1]

6. In General There Should Be No Restriction on Council Membership.—There are a number of possible restrictions on council membership, the principal ones of which are sex, marks, approval, reelection, and tax. A brief discussion of the first four will indicate the attitude which should be taken against all restrictions.[2] A complete general policy regarding these restrictions, applicable to all schools and to all situations, cannot be handed out by the author or anyone else, but enough of the implications may be indicated to assist a school to outline and define a justifiable policy.

Sex.—Should there be a requirement that a certain proportion of the council members be boys or girls? The author can see no justification for such a limitation. Certainly sex itself is hardly a factor in determining ability to represent a group

[1] An excellent article to read in this connection is R. W. Hallett, The "Gripe" Session; Home Room Bill of Rights, *Clearing House*, 16: 198–202, December, 1941.

[2] A discussion of the tax limitation will be found on page 241.

successfully. But even if there was such a restriction, how could it be enforced? For instance, if boys and girls were in the same groups, say home rooms, who would say which rooms were to elect girls and which boys? On the basis of what kind of democracy would he say it? This is rarely a problem because it usually solves itself, but anyway the above point is worth making.

Marks.—This restriction on council membership splits very easily into two parts: (1) should passing marks in all subjects be required? and (2) should higher than passing or average marks be required?

The usual arguments for the first type of restriction are that (1) the student who is not "up" in his work is not a good, completely respected school citizen and should not be allowed to hold a citizen's position of honor; (2) if he is "down" he may be motivated to get up, if he is not allowed to hold office; and (3) if he is down he should give first attention to his academic work. Probably there is considerable logic in requiring the council member to discharge satisfactorily his first major school responsibility, that of carrying his regular academic load successfully. We do not allow the athlete to represent his school if his work is unsatisfactory, so why should we allow the student who is not passing in his subjects to represent his group?

Should the council member be required to maintain a higher average than that represented by merely passing marks? The first argument for this practice is that the members will be more respected, a statement certainly not true or vital enough to be worth serious consideration. The second argument is that there is a high correlation between scholarship and leadership; consequently, limiting membership to the scholarship group will ensure a high quality of leadership in the council. It has long been assumed by classroom teachers that this scholarship-leadership correlation is high. This assumption has been proved fallacious but is still tenaciously held by these teachers, apparently because they are unfamiliar with the investigations, or are too deeply set in their ideas to change. There is no justification for requiring a better than passing or better than average mark for council membership. It is not required in any other activity in the school except the honor club, a highly specialized group in which the qualification for membership is scholarship, so why should it be required in council affairs?

Approval.—Some schools have a plan whereby a student must have the approval of his home room teacher, his adviser, the dean, the council sponsor, the principal, or the entire faculty before he is allowed to become a candidate for council membership. The theory is, of course, that the approver knows the student and can best decide whether or not he is suitable material for this body. The implication naturally is that student electors are incompetent, and that an inefficient council would result if there were no such restriction. This plan is entirely illogical and undemocratic. Really, it is but a reflection of the fears, jealousies, and misinformations of the faculty.

Moreover, such a plan is unsound educationally because it represents a denial of opportunity to learn. To take an extreme case, let us suppose that there was no such restriction and as a result the council was totally incompetent. Naturally, those who elected the council would suffer, and it is quite likely that in a very short time they would realize that they themselves were to blame. Further, it is reasonable to believe that at the next election they would be much more careful in their selection of members. This would be a most excellent lesson in practical citizenship, a lesson which would never be learned if the approval of candidates was required.

Reelection.—Should reelection be allowed? Here again the author can see no justification for restriction. Except in rare instances such limitation is not a part of the machinery of American democracy. A senator, representative, judge, mayor, or even the president can run for office as many times as he wishes. Certainly in no other activity in the school is such a limitation practiced; the athlete, actor, newswriter, or musician can belong to his organization for the full four years if he is "good enough to make it." In all likelihood, because of the frequent changes in the personnel of groups, reelection will rarely become a problem.

In summary, these limitations on eligibility for council membership or office holding are unjustifiable because they represent (1) faculty, not student body, ideals (and usually fears) which are the outmoded academic conceptions of the purpose of the school; (2) an unfair discrimination against such council membership or office holding, a discrimination which is not practiced against other school memberships and activities; and (3) faculty pressure to determine who shall represent the students. In a school with such restrictions the participation plan is only deceptive window dressing, it does not represent genuine democracy; it is, as Kelley aptly says, "a semblance of democracy without the fact."[1] In his investigation Kelley found such limitations present in nearly three-fourths of the 1,431 councils studied, and in 96.5 per cent of the councils in schools of more than 3,000 students.[2] Here, indeed, is one of the weak spots in our present plan of participation.

7. Each Member of the Council Should Assume Some Definite Responsibility.—The council which has no responsibilities will soon disintegrate. It can never have self-respect and morale because these are built through the successful

[1] Kelley, E. C., "An Evaluation of Student Participation in Government in American Secondary Schools" (unpublished doctoral dissertation), p. 122, Northwestern University.

[2] *Ibid.*, p. 105.

discharge of duties. In exactly the same way the individual member of the council must have responsibilities in order to maintain his interest, self-respect, and morale. He must feel a personal challenge.[1] Nor should this be a difficult problem despite the fact that occasionally there are members who, because of timidity, a feeling of incompetence, or a lack of interest, hesitate to accept personal responsibility. Certainly most of the members of a council will recognize their opportunities and want to shoulder responsibility. In the council and its subdivisions there are places for many helpers and many different kinds of skill. An important duty of the council is to ensure that these abilities are discovered and properly capitalized.

8. Each Committee or Subgroup Should Be Held Strictly Accountable for Its Particular Responsibility.—A committee without a definite responsibility is a handicap to any organized body because it will soon either (1) lose interest and spirit, or (2) impatient for action, trespass on the areas of other groups. This point cannot be overemphasized; the job first, and then the committee to do it, instead of the reverse. One good method of keeping committees alert is to require a report from each once a month or oftener. Any self-respecting committee will strive to have something worth bringing to the attention of the council and will consider a statement such as "the committee has nothing to report" as evidence of its own failure. A staggered schedule of these reports, so that not all of them come at every meeting, will help to prevent this order of business from degenerating into pure routine. Further, such a plan will bring a wholesome spirit of competition into the picture.

[1] The importance of accepting responsibility and a method of accomplishing it are described by F. B. Dixon in his article, Why Not Develop a Bill of Duties?, *School Activities*, 14: 13–14, September, 1942. See also, R. Fulton, Taking the Lag Out of Our Great Object, *Clearing House*, 17: 92–94, October, 1942.

9. The Council Should Be Neither Too Large Nor Too Small.—This is a somewhat witless statement, but the idea is important. A large council tends to be unwieldy in organization and scattering in its efforts because of the difficulty of handling discussion and business in an orderly manner, and of educating the members so that they will act most intelligently on the various items under consideration. The usual plan of superimposing a council-of-the-council or an executive committee arrangement has several weaknesses and disadvantages. Further, the larger the council, the greater the possibility and the probability that some of its members may be underloaded—some may even become "sleepers"—and a council member with no definite responsibilities is a liability to the participation plan.

On the other hand, especially in the case of the medium-sized and large schools, if the council is small, (1) the represented units will have to be so large that their members may not feel their representation, (2) some valuable student ability will go uncapitalized, and (3) the council members will probably be overloaded.

To summarize, the council should be large enough to provide felt representation, to include a variety of interests, abilities, and competencies, and to furnish an equitable load for all of its members; and be small enough to handle its business with efficiency and dispatch. This problem of proper size must, of necessity, be settled by the individual school.

10. The Duties and Responsibilities of the Council Should Be Specifically Defined.—Although discussion is basic to the efficient handling of the council's business, yet this discussion unfollowed by positive action is of little value to the school or anyone concerned. The council is a discussion group with legislative, judicial, and executive powers and duties and hence the boundaries must be set so that this body may develop to the proper edge of its area and at the same time stay within it. In a democracy the establishment of checks and balances is as necessary as the establishment of duties and responsibilities.

Clearly defining this area of council responsibilities may be a bit troublesome because it formerly belonged to the faculty and administration, and sometimes these give way grudgingly with half-hearted consent and acceptance. But it must be done in order to avoid detrimental bickerings and misunderstandings over possible conflicts in authority.[1]

These rights, privileges, duties, and responsibilities are only delegated by the head of the school, who cannot escape his own legal and moral responsibility. The delegation is usually through some form of properly authorized and formally adopted constitution. This subject will be discussed more in detail in Chap. VI.

11. The Principal Should Retain Veto Power.—Because the principal is legally and morally responsible, under the superintendent and board of education, for everything that goes on in the school, it is only reasonable that he should have final authority on any matter that concerns it. Capitulation is as unthinkable as domination. The entire school, teachers and students, must realize this, and that authority is not unreservedly given but merely delegated to the council. Such a recognition should not make the council less responsible, but more responsible, and also cause it to be more careful in its deliberations and its actions in order to avoid veto. Such deliberations should, in turn, reduce to a minimum the number of times which the principal should be forced to exercise his right of veto.

On the other hand, the principal himself has a considerable responsibility. In the first place, if he vetoes frequently he will discourage the council, and some of its members may take an

[1] A pertinent article is L. Shuster, Need a Student Council Worry Over Power?, *School Activities*, 7: 6–8, November, 1935.

unwholesome attitude toward the administration. However, occasionally failing to veto some measure which the principal knows will not be successful is educative for both the council members and those who elected them, because it places the responsibility squarely upon them.

In the second place it is reasonable that, if the council is charged with the responsibility for coordinating the various activities of the school, the principal should act through it; this is courteous and businesslike and proves the principal's confidence in this body. Naturally, his recommendations, suggestions, and contacts should be through the faculty members of the council. If he walks into a council meeting with a "now here's what I want you to do" attitude, his presence will probably be very properly and promptly resented.

12. The Council Should Not Be Considered a Trouble-shooting Body.—Unless intelligent and positive steps are taken to prevent it, there is a danger that the teachers and students may get the idea that the council is a sort of dumping ground for all the many little disagreeable tasks about the school, an organization whose main duties are largely those of trouble-shooting. Although undoubtedly in any council's schedule of activities there will be those that represent repairs, yet mending damage is only a part of its responsibilities. The council's main job is construction, plus the restoration that keeps the structure in good order.

This undesirable attitude, taken far more frequently by the faculty than the student body, is most likely to develop in a school in which the faculty has accepted the participation idea only halfheartedly, or less. Sometimes it is taken out of jealousy, the usual reaction being "Oh, that's the council's job," sometimes, in order to avoid responsibility for distasteful jobs and even the faculty's own failures, and sometimes, when jealousy is fully developed, it is taken deliberately to sabotage the council's efforts. Needless to say, such an attitude not only is unfair to the student body and the council but also reflects uncommendably upon the faculty and the administration that permit it to develop.

13. The Council Should Not Be Considered a Disciplinary Body.—Whether or not the council should be allowed to handle cases of discipline is a matter on which there is considerable disagreement, and this whole problem is so important that it will be reserved for a more detailed treatment in a later chapter. However, there should be no general disagreement on the question of whether or not the council itself should handle cases of discipline. It can, and probably does in some schools, but the weakness of this arrangement is the probability that the council will become so sidetracked on this activity that it will neglect more constructive projects. If the council becomes a disciplinary body, there is danger that it will be too busy to do anything else; if so, it will lose standing in the school. Handling cases of violations of regulations concerning student activities is probably an entirely logical and justifiable responsibility of the council, but it should be accomplished through a special committee or court instead of by the council itself. In such an arrangement the council may act as a reviewing body and probably should in cases involving major violations.

It is entirely possible that, because of some of its activities, the council may easily become considered by the school largely as a disciplinary body. For instance, the main job of some councils appears to be the organization and supervision of the corridor monitor system, and in such cases the students of the school can hardly escape the impression that the council's most important job is disciplinary in nature. In short, the school's mental picture of the council is, for all practical purposes, a real representation of this organization.

Incidentally, this type of monitorial system is facing increasing criticism because it (1) is uneconomical of the monitors' time, since dividing attention between a lesson and hall responsibilities will never result in the development of effective study habits; (2) overemphasizes watching for or guarding against violations; (3) stresses external authority rather than internal sense of responsibility; and (4) especially in the elementary school, tends to make bullies of the monitors, the older pupils.

Provisions for handling cases of discipline, if such provisions appear to be desirable and desired, should come late, not early, in the council's development. Many councils have disintegrated and been abolished because they assumed a sort of police function from the very beginning. Successful discipline requires an understanding and skill which inexperienced students do not possess—and even some experienced teachers, for that matter. Responsibility must be grown into slowly.

14. The Cooperative Aspects of Participation Should Be Continually Emphasized.—Everyone resents despotism and if, because of its autocratic and dictatorial attitudes and policies, the council comes to be considered a despotic body it is high time for a major realignment. However, this difficulty may be avoided if the council constantly reflects cooperation in both its activities and its talk. It need not harp continually on this ideal, but at the same time it should not entirely forget to talk about it. Actions speak louder than words, but there are plenty of times when words will help. In this connection it is imperative that the council understand and remember that there are two kinds of cooperation, (1) cooperation of the student body with the council, the type most frequently discussed, and (2) cooperation of the council with the student body, which is just as important.

15. The Council Should Not Attempt to Carry on All the Activities Itself.—Occasionally, a council assumes that it alone should be responsible for initiating, organizing, promoting, and handling all the activities of the school. This is a mistaken conception of the council's place and duty. Nearly all school projects can be carried out much more economically and successfully by the organizations to which they logically belong. The council's job is to suggest, stimulate, encourage, and assist in every way possible.

16. The Council's Financial Policy Should Be Well Organized and Closely Supervised.—The financial administration of activities represents one of the most bothersome problems in a modern school, not only because of the large total amount of money involved, but also because of the great number and variety of ways in which it is handled. Most of the criticisms of school activities have been due, directly or indirectly, to the loose handling of funds. Properly raising, handling, and disbursing funds are essential parts of any activity program—and these together represent a device which may be used effectively in developing the proper kind of program and giving it balance. This is true especially where the control of finances is centralized in the council. Even at best, finances are dynamite and hence should be most carefully handled and supervised. This topic will be discussed more in detail in Chap. X.

17. The Machinery of the Plan Should Be Simple.—In more than one American school a highly complex, pretty-on-the-chart organization of upper and lower houses, courts, cabinets, boards of appeal, etc., has been abolished because attention to the schedule of activities was hindered by official red tape and complications. How frequently has the author, after listening to some enthusiastic sponsor explaining a complicated system of participation, wanted to raise the very pertinent question, "When do you find time for council activities?" Usually these complex forms of participation are imitations or adaptations of municipal or federal organization, themselves very complicated, even to experienced adults. The idea here is not to get a pretty organization but an effective one. Irrespective of the type of plan developed or adopted, it should be simple enough to be easily understood and administered, and direct enough to be of immediate and appreciable influence. This means that the major part of the student effort should be spent on the program rather than on the machinery.

18. Council Meetings Should Be Held Regularly and on School Time.—Scheduling regular council meetings is in line with good business principles. Calling meetings only when "there is something to do" represents a poor and unbusinesslike policy necessitating extra work and causing inconvenience to all. Canceling or postponing meetings usually militates against effectiveness, and once begun the practice soon develops into a decidedly bad habit. Even when there is apparently no business to be discussed, and such instances should be rare indeed, the meeting should proceed according to the usual form and then be adjourned immediately. It should not be allowed to degenerate into an aimless "bull session." This same principle holds for any meeting; when the business has been completed, the meeting should be adjourned at once. Special meetings may be called at times convenient to the members when necessary.[1]

Further, it is logical to assume that if council meetings represent educationally important settings, and they should not be scheduled unless they do, they should be held on school time. Such scheduling will (1) guarantee the presence of all members, (2) officially recognize and sanction the program, (3) give it importance and dignity, (4) ensure good teacher and student attitudes, and (5) bring a correlative demand that the teachers' and students' time be well invested. The students

[1] In some schools with a two-house council, the houses meet on alternate weeks. An account of a daily council meeting will be found in F. J. Butrum, Our Student Council Meets Every Day, *Clearing House*, 16: 423–425, March, 1942.

will not take the council seriously unless the administration and faculty do.

Often council meetings are scheduled in the activities period. However, in some instances this is disadvantageous to the members because it prevents them from participating in the other activities during this period. Any member who would rather be somewhere else than in council meeting is hardly an asset to that meeting or body. It should not be difficult to schedule a time when all members can attend without conflict. This period should be kept sacred to council activities; no members should be excused for any other school purpose, curricular or extracurricular. Incidentally, about the poorest time and place for holding council meetings is in the evening at the home of some student or teacher. Such meetings will lack the necessary school atmosphere and will almost inevitably develop into social gatherings. The council is not a social club.

19. Council Meetings Should Be Open to All Who Care to Attend.—The student or teacher who helps to elect members to the council has as much right to attend the meetings of this organization as the adult has to attend sessions of congress, the state legislature, a court, or a municipal body to which he helped to elect members. The usual arguments given for the exclusion of visitors are (1) the limited size of the council room, (2) the unsuitability of the period for visitation, and (3) the possibility of interruptions caused by visitors entering and leaving. These arguments do not represent the real reason for such exclusion. The real reason is the council's fear of student and teacher reaction to what is said and done at the meetings. It is true that the size of the room and the time of the meeting will naturally restrict such attendance; hence, these arguments are illogical. If disturbances are caused this is the fault of the council itself. On the other hand, such visits should be highly conducive to the development of the interest and the education of the visitors. Occasionally, it may be advisable for the council to hold a closed session, but this practice should not be adopted as a general policy. "Secret session" is a term that is very foreign and distasteful to a democratic form of government.

20. The Necessary Facilities and Equipment Should Be Provided.—The council should have a regular place for its meetings. Holding the meeting in any room that for the period happens to be vacant is unbusinesslike, detracts from dignity and importance, dissipates student and teacher energy in hunting up the meeting place, and encourages interruptions. Similarly, a room that is inaccessible, or poorly lighted, equipped, and ventilated—a room that is available because it can be used for nothing except as a storage place or a council chamber—handicaps council activities and morale. The school office is about the poorest place in which to hold council meetings. A private file should be provided for the council's books, correspondence, notes, communications, forms, and reports. Other necessary elements of a business meeting are a gavel, secretary's and treasurer's books (a neat substantial book brings respect and encourages the keeping of neat and accurate records), paper, forms, etc. Having a permanent place for this material will make for efficient procedure in using it.

21. Continual Study and Adaptation Should Be Made. No school is a static institution; on the contrary, it is continually changing. Board members, administrators, teachers, custodians, and students come and go; educational philosophies, policies, and organization change; new subjects, activities, and emphases appear and old ones disappear or become less important; and even the utilization of buildings, material, and equipment varies from year to year. All these changes in the school must be reflected in the adjusted ideals, policies, and programs of the student council. No plan of participation can ever be permanent. Last year's council may not fit this year's school any more than last year's shoes will fit this year's student. Therefore these possibilities of change require continual study in order that (1) they may be recognized and understood, and (2) the necessary adaptations in participation machinery may be made.

This process is but a continuation of that suggested on "initiating the council" in Chap. V and it capitalizes much the same schedule of activities and procedures: (1) a study of new forms and ideas in the student council field, and (2) a continuous survey of local needs and materials, activities and leadership. A vital part of this program of evaluation and reconstruction is a study of failures and successes. This is so important that it demands a separate treatment.

22. The Reasons for Success and Failure Should Be Analyzed.—Often success brings an emotional thrill of encouragement, and little else; and often failure brings a feeling of discouragement, and little else. In both instances, something very important is missing. A mere recognition of success does not necessarily guarantee a repetition of that success, nor does a recognition of failure necessarily mean a future avoidance of it.

There are important reasons for student-council successes and failures, just as there are important reasons for success and failure in any other kind of organization or undertaking.[1]

[1] Recently, in two state conventions, the author heard the causes of council failure discussed. The major reasons given were; (1) the school—teachers and students—and the community were not prepared for the introduction of the council idea; consequently, they misunderstood its objectives and field of activity; (2) a suitable constructive program was lacking; the council busied itself with worthless projects, duplicated other services, or "bit off more than it could chew"; (3) the general school setting was not propitious; too undemocratic—a poor example for a body with democratic ideals and ideas; and (4) the sponsor was unsuitable. Four minor reasons given for council failure were: (1) a lack of suitable representation; (2) petty politics; (3) extreme formality; and (4) extreme informality.

Knowing the reasons for present success will help to make it permanent, and a success is a real success only when it can be repeated later. Similarly, knowing the reasons for a present failure helps to guarantee a future success. In reality, a failure is a failure only when it is not capitalized in the direction of a success; which is another way of saying that, where properly appreciated and capitalized, a failure represents one of the best educational opportunities there is. These points should be kept in mind by the members of the council. It is to be regretted that so few accounts of council failures are published. Although they might be discouraging to timid souls, they would undoubtedly be helpful to the braver pioneers who are attempting to discover the path to the heights of success.[1]

23. No Other Organization Should Be Allowed to Usurp the Council's Rightful Place in the School.—There are two organizations which may, unless prevented by wise action, usurp some of the council's power and place. These are The National Honor Society (The National Junior Honor Society in junior high schools and in the ninth and tenth grades in four-year senior high schools)[2] and The High School Victory Corps.[3] Neither of these organizations can ever be a substitute for the student council, and it was never intended that they should, but some misguided administrators and faculties have allowed such unjustifiable substitution.[4] Of course there are far more administrators and faculties which have made no such mistake, and in their schools these organizations and the council work together harmoniously. However, an explana-

[1] One such account is E. V. Jeter, What! No Student Council? *Clearing House*, 9: 118–121, October, 1934.

[2] Both these societies are sponsored by the National Association of Secondary School Principals, 1201 Sixteenth Street, N.W., Washington, D.C.

[3] U.S. Office of Education, Federal Security Agency, Washington, D.C.

[4] A few years ago a doctoral dissertation at a great American college for teachers urged that the Boy Scouts be assigned duties which are within the council's area of responsibilities.

tion is in order for those who misunderstand or misinterpret the functions of these groups.

The author has heard more than one school administrator say, "We don't need a student council; we have the National Honor Society." Such a statement clearly shows an appalling ignorance of both these organizations and of their proper places in the school. The membership requirements of the National Honor Society are scholarship, leadership, character, and service (plus school citizenship for the Junior Society), and these represent the best of educational ideals, quite in line with those discussed in the previous chapter of this book. As a result, a chapter of the National Honor Society usually includes at least some of the best all-round ability in the school. However, (1) it does not represent the democratic ideals for which the council stands, its members (incidentally, many more girls than boys) being named by the faculty, not by the students; (2) many worthy school citizens miss election by very small margins (membership is limited by set percentages); (3) its membership comes from only the top three semesters of the senior high school; (4) its members represent no organization and no activity; and (5) it is an honoring and not a service organization at all, even though it is supplied with a program of suggested activities. It is in this program of activities that conflict with the council may develop. And it is just here that the council should ensure that such conflict does not develop. The school-wide activities of the society should be authorized and supervised in exactly the same way that the school-wide activities of any other organization or club are authorized and supervised. The National Honor Society is not a competing organization and should not be allowed to become one.[1]

[1] A pertinent article is E. B. Brogue, Are Student Council and National Honor Society Competitive?, *School Activities*, 12: 139–140, December, 1940.

Nearly all of what has been said about the place of the National Honor Society can also be said about the High School Victory Corps, a recently organized war activity which, if controlled, represents a worthy addition to the school's activity program. But the current enthusiasm for the successful prosecution of the war may very easily bring an off-focus view of the place of this corps. It is, after all, in spite of its outside source and support, a school organization and, like any other organization or activity of the school, should in its school-wide contacts be under the student council. And in case of conflict between these two, the more important student council should be given preference. Only a misguided administrator would ever allow the Victory Corps to prevail over the council.

24. The Local Council Should Affiliate with Council Associations.—As indicated on pages 16–19 there are now a number of local, state, regional, and national associations of student councils which hold conferences, distribute literature, provide speakers, and in other ways work for the common good of their members. They represent an excellent medium for the exchange of helpful ideas and give deserved publicity to the participation idea. The local council should belong to the appropriate organizations and participate in their activities. The small expense of membership will represent an investment very much worth while.

25. Too Much Should Not Be Expected of the Council. If, after more than a century and a half of development, adult American democracy is still "a great experiment," as a noted federal judge recently designated it, the teacher or administrator who expects to democratize his school in a few months, or semesters, or even years, is certain to be disappointed. After all, students are but children, inexperienced and immature, and it is unreasonable to expect adequate self-government at their hands. As Dean Kerr pointed out in 1925, "Student government is not an end, but a process; it never will be, nor can be, expert government."

The individual who expects too much and who loads the council with responsibilities far beyond its ability is not only unintelligent but unfair. In such an instance, and there have been many of them, neither the students nor the participation is to blame. This is not saying that there should be and will be no failures—as suggested above, often these are good educational settings, provided that they are properly capitalized—but it is saying that too many or too serious failures will discourage an interested teacher or student, and will add more voices to the "it may be all right in theory but it won't work in practice" chorus.

26. The Council Should Give Continuous Publicity to Its Ideals, Activities, and Problems.—The fact that a school's population is constantly changing means that there should be a continuous program of education designed to acquaint the new teachers and students with the theory of the plan and its local application. In addition, such a program will reemphasize these to the older teachers and students and establish them more firmly in the minds of the council members themselves. This program of education can be promoted through the home room, assembly, bulletin board, exhibits and demonstrations, and the school publications. An impressive installation service represents a fine device for this purpose.

Not only is the school constantly changing but so also is the community, and a continuous program of education is necessary in order that the parents and patrons understand and appreciate what is being attempted. This program of community education is absolutely essential when participation is first being planned, but it is also important after this organization has been effected. Community support must not only be won but also be maintained. Most of this program of education will come indirectly through the attitudes and activities of the students themselves. But occasional direct reflections of the participation idea can be made through public programs, and school and community publications.

SELECTED REFERENCES

CALVERT, M. M.: Recipe for Student Government, *Clearing House*, 18: 156–159, November, 1943.

FINDLAY, J. F.: An Administrator Speaks to Student Council, *School Activities*, 11: 275–276, 290–291, March, 1940.

HARVEY, C. C., and C. F. ALLEN: The 20 Questions on Student Government, *Clearing House*, 18: 67–71, October, 1943.

JOCKUMSEN, E.: Activity of a Publicity Club, *School Activities*, 14: 135–138, March, 1943.

KELLEY, E. C.: Too Many Safeguards Kill Student Government, *Clearing House*, 18: 68–71, 195–197, December, 1943.

MEYER, F.: Exhibiting Student Government to Parents, *School Activities*, 12: 99–100, November, 1940.

MEYERS, G. C.: Self-government Has Limits, *Journal of Education*, 120: 230–231, May 3, 1937.

PETTY, H.: Interpreting the Student Council, *School Activities*, 11: 323, 351, April, 1940.

SHUSTER, L.: Need a Student Council Worry Over Power? *School Activities*, 7: 6–8, November, 1935.

STARR, G. G.: Preparation Precedes Participation, *School Activities*, 10: 243–244, 278, February, 1939.

TAYLOR, R. E.: An Integrated Student Council and Activity Program, *School Activities*, 8: 3–5, September, 1936.

TOMPKINS, E.: Publicity and the Activities Program, *School Activities*, 9: 175–177, December, 1937.

TUTTLE, E. M.: Student Government: Why Ours Worked, *Clearing House*, 17: 135–138, November, 1942.

Chapter IV

Types of Council Organization

PROBABLY no two council organizations are exactly alike, and this is reasonable because no two school settings are exactly alike. This means that there are nearly as many different kinds of organization as there are organizations. Consequently, it is not possible to describe in detail these many types of council. Even if it were possible such a procedure would not be wise, because many of these organizations are so similar that they are easily classifiable together, while others represent unusual settings.

Student councils may be classified on three bases: (1) source of membership, (2) responsibilities assigned or accepted, and (3) general structure or organization. A critical study of a few of the possibilities under each of these headings should help to set the standards of good council organization.

TYPES OF COUNCILS ACCORDING TO SOURCE OF MEMBERSHIP

Representation of Specialized Interests.—In this, one of the older forms of council representation, very commonly found before the appearance and development of the home room, and still popular in small schools, the members are elected from particular organizations such as classes, clubs, or activities. Usually the extent of representation is determined by the size or importance of the activity represented.

Theoretically, this type of organization appears to have a logical basis because, if the council is to coordinate and supervise the various activities of the school, these activities should have the right to elect the members of the group which is to control them. Further, it is a natural outgrowth of the participation plans of the represented groups, especially classes or clubs, and hence it can capitalize experience gained in these somewhat similar settings. In fact, one logical method of developing a participation plan for the entire school is to begin with the smaller plan in a more limited group such as a club or a class.

On the other hand, there are several very serious objections to this plan. The first of these is the great possibility that, because he feels his obligation to the organization which elects him, the council member's main interest will concern his own group, not the school as a whole. As suggested in an earlier chapter, in such a setting the best representative is the one who gets most. And, often, as in adult politics, "logrolling" and "mutual backscratching" develop. Those organizations which are best represented will tend to receive the lion's share of help and attention, or lack of attention if this appears to be more desirable.

A second objection to this plan is that some activities may not even be represented. This may be true either (1) in fact, as when small and relatively unimportant activities or organizations, on the basis of membership, may not be allowed representation, or (2) in effect, as when small organizations may be allowed only proportional representation, often too small to be of any real significance in the competition for serious council attention.

Further, some students may not be represented. Unless special provision is made, those students who are not members of the organizations allowed representation will, of course, not be represented in the council. Sometimes, in order to overcome this difficulty, a few members-at-large are provided. But even these, in an organization which is based upon the representation of groups, will probably have little standing or influence, except as attractive "bait" for the representatives of groups which want particular favors and votes.

Another objection is the above somewhat in reverse. The student who belongs to several organizations is really represented several times in the council.

A fifth objection to this plan of representation is that its democratic ideals and standards are limited both in number and scope. The emphasis is not upon an entire school program but upon specialized parts of that program, not upon giving but getting, and not upon a smoothly coordinated cooperative program but upon competition between organizations for council patronage.

In a more complicated form of this type of organization there are several councils, one for each of the major activities, such as, for example, a council on clubs, each school club being represented in it. Similarly, there may be a council on athletics, another on publications, another on classes, another on service or civic activities, and another on social activities. Often there is a top council designed to coordinate all these various councils and also to provide for miscellaneous interests and activities not encompassed by the programs of the other councils. In addition to being subject to the objections previously raised, this organization is likely to be cumbersome in structure and scattering in its efforts.

About the only setting in which representation by specialized interests is justifiable is in the small non-home-room school, where the representatives are elected from classes. Each class, of course, represents a much more democratic organization than any specialized activity because it includes all kinds of interests. If the school is small, general school interests loom larger than class interests. Preferably, in the junior and senior high school, all classes should be represented, the upper and smaller classes being allowed additional representation in order to balance that of the larger and lower classes. Another setting in which specialized interests, especially classes, may be allowed representation is in the case of the two-house council, in which the larger body is composed of representatives of the home rooms, and the smaller body of representatives of classes. This possibility will be discussed more in detail later.

Automatic Representation.—Generally speaking, there are two forms of automatic representation, on the basis of (1) office already held, and (2) academic or citizenship records, or both.

In the first form, officers, usually presidents, of the bodies represented (classes, home rooms, or activities) automatically become members of the council without further election. The two main arguments in favor of this plan are that (1) it results in the formation of a good council, one composed of competent and recognized school leaders, and (2) because each of these representatives is directly and officially responsible to his group, close cooperation between the various groups and the council will be assured.

The arguments against this plan are that (1) too much responsibility is concentrated in too few students; (2) it greatly limits the number of participation opportunities, those of both electors and electees; (3) it does not capitalize the abilities of non-president students; (4) it tends to overload these representatives; (5) it is no more logical than would be the plan whereby city mayors automatically became members of the state legislature, and governors, members of congress; and (6) probably only one side of any question, that favored by the president, would be presented to the basic group. Obviously, the second argument in favor of the plan is very weak because it assumes that only the president of a group is able to represent it adequately. Although this plan or variations of it is rather widely used, especially in smaller schools, it has little to commend it.

In the second plan mentioned above, those students who have the highest records in academic work, or citizenship, or both, automatically become members of the council. There is nothing whatever to be said in favor of the first of these two variations, or for any variation which includes it. As suggested in Chap. III, academic-minded teachers have long assumed that there is only one kind of intelligence, that which is reflected in the ability to do academic work; further, they have assumed that this academic intelligence guarantees success in all other phases of man's life and activities. This false notion allows no place for social, civic, political, service, or similar intelligences which are the essentials of good citizenship. Nor does good citizenship necessarily recognize that brilliant scholarship is an important element. The council represents an organization for service, not for honor, and consequently it must be built around the ideals and competencies of service, not around the ideals and competencies of scholarship.

In another variation of the second plan, those students who have achieved good records in school citizenship automatically become members of the council. Occasionally, too, the members of the National Honor Society constitute the council. Obviously this plan elevates to the council those students who are most competent in leadership, character, and service. However, while it may result in the formation of a rather competent central body, it does not provide educational opportunities for those students in the school who (1) are too new in the school to have achieved such records or memberships; (2) may be quite worthy but who missed the proper rating or election by very narrow margins; (3) may have real ability which is not capitalized; and (4) only elect and serve under their representatives. Further, (5) neither this plan nor that of automatic election on the basis of scholarship makes any provisions for the development, in the average student, of a vital interest in the affairs of the council or in the general welfare of the school because he has no direct and personal contact with the council. The plan is not democratic because the students do not choose their representatives.[1]

Either of these last two objections is enough to prohibit the use of this form of automatic election. As an adult, the student will live in a democracy in which he will have voting privileges and responsibilities, and this plan of automatic election robs him of an important educational opportunity in which intelligent voting could be taught. There is a little more to be said in favor of this plan than that which is based upon scholarship alone, but it is a very little, and not enough to make its use justifiable.

Representation by Principal or Faculty Appointees.—In some schools the principal or the faculty, or both together, appoint the council members. In a few schools the result is the so-called "informal council," a group of students being merely called in by the principal and handed some job, or asked to suggest some project, and, perhaps, commissioned to do it. In other schools the council is formal, being definitely internally organized along the usual lines. Because this form of representation, or lack of it, so completely violates all principles of representative government it will not be discussed further. It is mentioned here in order to emphasize that, despite the fact that it actually exists, it in no way comprehends the ideals and practices of democratic government.

Representation by Student Leader Appointees.—This plan, in which the president or chairman of a class, club, home room, activity, or organization appoints the representative to the council, is no more justifiable than that discussed immediately above. Representative government is based upon elected, not appointed, officers.

[1] See also reference to the National Honor Society, pp. 68–69.

Representation of School Alumni and Board of Education.—This form of council organization provides for the representation of two groups outside the school. Although it is desirable to obtain and maintain the support of these two groups, yet there is a real danger that such representation will be decidedly detrimental. The plan is faulty because it brings in representatives who are not necessarily competent, and who do not necessarily owe allegiance to the present school and its administration. Consider, for instance, the trouble that might arise because of some one conceited troublemaking alumnus, or one board member who happens to be at odds with the principal or superintendent. Because of their positions, independence, reputations, physical size, or even just their ages, they could carry entirely too much weight. There would also be the practical difficulty of arranging council meetings so that all could attend. Very few schools and principals would ever approve such a council organization, and none should.

Representation of Unspecialized Units of the School.—In this plan the representatives are elected from the home rooms or similar groups or, in the case of small schools, from the classes or from the school at large. Sometimes there are combinations of these plans, but specialized interests as such are not definitely represented.

This plan has far more to commend it than any of those discussed above. It (1) provides representation for every student in the school; (2) therefore tends to interest each student and make him feel his individual responsibility; (3) represents unspecialized interests, therefore all activities, or the school as a whole, consequently providing for proper development, balance, and coordination; (4) provides unrestricted opportunities for every bona fide member of the school to vote and hold office; (5) allows for an equitable proportionate representation of the various units; and (6) is simple and easy to understand.

It may be argued that in large schools such a plan, especially if it were based upon home rooms, would result in too large a council, and if it were based upon classes, too small a council. However, this is a possible objection only to the form of organization, not to the type of representation involved. As such it will be discussed later in this chapter.

Civil Service Types.—In this form of council organization there is no recognized representation of any group or groups about the school, but rather a representation of the school as a whole. No council members are elected; they are appointed, usually by the faculty, on the basis of their records in activities and the marks made on formal examinations in school ideals, activities, procedures, and relationships. The main advantages of the plan are that (1) the group represents the entire school, not specialized groups within it; and (2) only students whose activity and examination records are good become members of the council. The arguments against it are that (1) it does not necessarily result in competent council members, since a knowledge of the pertinent facts does not necessarily guarantee the possession of the proper ideals or the ability to handle school affairs; (2) it is too cold and formal, too far removed from individual groups and students; (3) it tends to represent faculty and not student opinion; and (4) it is very difficult to develop suitable examinations and to score them accurately. This civil service plan has been tried out in a number of schools but has never achieved popularity, and it is extremely doubtful if it ever will.

TYPES OF COUNCILS ACCORDING TO POWERS

A second possible method of classifying councils is on the basis of what they are allowed to do, or the direction and extent of their authority. Such powers, of course, vary widely from school to school, ranging all the way from discussion only to rather complete control of all student activities. A consideration of these powers, as represented by organization, shows four types of councils which, for our purpose here, we shall call informal, forum, service, and general. Although a few councils represent a combination of two or more of these types, most of them are easily classifiable into one of these groups. It is well to emphasize that this section, like the preceding and following sections of this chapter, is designed only for the purpose of assisting in the development of a picture of a good type of council organization.

Informal Council.—This type of council is not a student elected body, but merely a group of students, usually juniors and seniors, who are called in by the principal. He assigns the group some project, or discusses some task with it and then perhaps commissions it to do the job. Generally, the group is not organized; it has little or no authority, and few or no definite powers; it has no established policies, no program, and allows for little or no student initiative; it is responsible to no one except the principal; and it offers few and very limited educational opportunities.

In no way does such a group represent democratic ideals or practices. In reality it can be little else than "the principal's flunky gang," as the author heard one disgusted student evaluate such a "council." It is not a council and never can be, even though occasionally such a group appears under this heading in the newspaper or yearbook. This type of "organization" is most common where the principal is extremely jealous of his authority, is fearful of student mismanagement or adverse community sentiment, is ignorant of the participation idea, or cannot distinguish between paternalism and democracy.

The Forum.—This is merely a discussion group. It may be elected, invited to come, or come of its own choosing. Usually the principal calls the meeting in order to determine student opinion, supposedly so that he can better understand the students' viewpoint and so be guided in his policies and actions. The group has no legislative, executive, or judicial authority. It is not a student council in any sense of the word.

Occasionally one finds a school that is just initiating a participation system using either of the above plans to make a beginning. In such instances this procedure is entirely justifiable. The group discussions will interest the students, give them opportunity to face some of the pertinent problems and difficulties, help to develop the proper school attitude, and perhaps bring some little experience. But such a procedure should soon develop into a more definite form of organization.

Specific Service Council.—In this type of student participation an elected or appointed group is assigned responsibility for the initiation, development, direction, and supervision of some particular activity such as corridor traffic, social events, newspaper, study hall monitoring, assembly programs, or intrascholastic athletics. In some schools there are several of these councils, unrelated to each other and unsupervised by a central organization. In reality, they are not councils at all, merely activity committees.

This plan has the advantages of a definite assignment of duties and a capitalization of specialized student abilities, and both of these are important. However, it has serious disadvantages and dangers. Intercouncil conflicts and duplication of efforts will inevitably develop because the program is uncoordinated, and a poorly balanced program will result because some activities are certain to be overemphasized, while others just as surely will be neglected.

The plan does represent an excellent first or second step in initiating and developing a council. Accepting and discharging responsibility, gradually growing in experience, judgment, and self-confidence, and educating the school to the possibilities of the participation idea represent natural and essential elements in a council-developing program. However, if this development ends with separate, uncoordinated, and unsupervised committees, there has been no growth toward a justifiable system of participation. The plan is still in its childhood.

General Council.—This type of participation organization is that usually meant by the expression "student council." It is a general central group of students and teachers which represents the entire school. It has final responsibility, except for the principal's veto, for the initiation, development, coordination, supervision, and evaluation of all the organizations and activities of the school which, according to the constitution, have been assigned to it. It is a single body, although it can be and should be composed of various kinds of elements: committees, subcouncils, house and senate, etc. This is the ideal form of participation, one in the direction of which the informal, discussion, and specific service types should develop.

TYPES OF COUNCILS ACCORDING TO ORGANIZATION

Councils vary widely not only in source of membership and extent of powers but also in form of organization. Here, as before, the purpose is not to describe and evaluate all kinds of council organization—that would be impossible—but rather to describe and evaluate a few of the basic types so that a rather accurate general picture can be given of particular forms of organization.[1] Not all councils can be classified into the three groups indicated because there are also many combinations of these types and a few can be classified in either

[1] In Chaps. V–VII of his book, "Extra-curricular Activities in Secondary Schools," Houghton Mifflin Company, Boston, 1931, E. K. Fretwell briefly describes more than thirty junior and senior high school councils, good, bad, and indifferent.

the first or the second group. However, for our purposes here such a classification will be satisfactory.[1]

These types of organization show all forms of representation and all degrees of power, which is another way of saying that the source of membership and the extent of authority are rarely or never a determining factor in the adoption of a council plan. Because these sources and powers have already been critically evaluated, little mention will be made of them in this section.

Single-house Council.—In this, the simplest form of council organization, there is but a single central body, the size of which usually, but not always, depends upon the size of the school. This type of organization is found most frequently in the upper grades of the elementary school, the junior high school, and the smaller senior high school, but it is also found in some larger schools. In fact, it is to be found in schools that elect representatives from more than one hundred home rooms. In size and powers the single house varies all the way from a small group, committee, or cabinet having responsibility for a single activity such as assembly programs, traffic police, or social events, to a large highly organized group responsible for all the activities of the school.

Naturally, the larger councils are organized very completely into departments, divisions, or standing and special committees, and often with an executive committee or cabinet at the top. This executive committee may be composed of the officers of the council, the heads of the departments, the chairmen of the standing committees, or members specially elected by the council or the school. Sometimes this committee is

[1] In addition to these types there is also an interschool or all-city council, composed of representatives from the councils of the various schools. In general, such an organization could be classified in either the first or the second group indicated. Accounts of this type of council will be found in the references at the end of the chapter.

staffed by a combination of these methods. This plan does not represent a two-house council system, but a legislative-executive combination in one body. The executive committee possesses no legislative functions, being responsible merely for executing the wishes of the council and for expediting its business. Hence, the contact between these two bodies, composed as they are of about the same members, is very close.

The advantages of this single-house plan of council organization are easily seen: (1) it is simple and direct, involves no complicated procedures, and therefore fosters efficiency in organization and work; (2) it is easy to understand and consequently no time need be lost in making explanations, interpretations, or adjudications; (3) because responsibility is definitely placed, there can be little or no "passing the buck"; (4) it provides for a direct and close contact between the council and represented groups; and (5) meetings are easily arranged.

About the only possible disadvantages of this type of council are that in large schools (1) it may be unwieldy; (2) where there are many activities it may not be able to give careful attention to all of them; and (3) its size may militate against free and complete expression by all its members. However, the organization of departments or important standing committees for the handling of the major phases of its work should obviate most of these dangers, as well as capitalize practically all the abilities represented in the group. In any case, however, even if the plan does represent some disadvantages due to the size of the council, these are outweighed by the directness and efficiency of its work. Of course, in the smaller and medium-sized schools even these suggested weaknesses will not be present.

Multihouse Councils.—In order to provide for the necessary felt representation and for the direction of the numerous activities, many larger schools have various forms of councils in which there is more than one main body. Although the most frequently used plan is of two houses or bodies, councils composed of three, four, and even five separately organized groups are not at all unknown. All of these many plans are unlike in source of membership and extent of power as well as in the details of general organization.

Two-house Council.—This is the most popular form of the multi-house council. Usually it is somewhat imitative of typical upper and lower house legislative organization, though often this distinction is not indicated. It goes under a wide variety of names such as school congress, school legislature, council and cabinet, senate and house of representatives, senate and council, council and advisory board, council and executive board, council and subcouncil, assembly and council, and council and legislature.

An examination of a dozen of these plans taken at random will reveal that no two of them are alike and, very probably, nowhere nearly alike. Neither the source of membership nor the degree of authority appears to determine any particular form of organization. Members of either or both groups are elected or appointed in all possible ways and in combinations of these ways. Similarly, legislative and executive powers and judicial powers, where included, are designated for both types of houses in different schools. For example, in one plan the upper house makes the laws but the lower house approves them; in another plan the reverse of this procedure is true; and in still another, either house may pass legislation independent of the other. In one plan the lower house is the legislative body and the upper house is the executive group; in another the opposite is true; and in still another, both houses legislate and execute. Often, too, there is no clear distinction between these legislative and executive functions.

Nor do the constitutions always give a clear idea concerning the specific responsibilities of the two bodies, although all of these instruments explain the details of election and internal organization. About one-fifth of the constitutions studied showed no definite distinction between the duties of the two main bodies described, nor their interrelationships. In fact, some of the constitutions do not even mention responsibilities, powers, or duties. In general, such organizations are duplicates without checks on or connections with each other. Further, some of these councils appear to be the result of the practice of adding on and adding on, with the inevitable result: legislative, executive, and judicial monstrosities.

The author is not intimating that all plans should be alike—far from it—nor is he suggesting that there is one and only one plan of organization that is suitable for all schools. What he is indicating is that a great deal of confusion is reflected in plans of multihouse organization. In fact, after studying a considerable number of these, especially those composed of two houses, he is convinced that some of them are rather slavish imitations of existing state or national organizations, and he has a sneaking suspicion that some of them are designed largely for show purposes. Of course, he is certain that some of them represent honest attempts to achieve the desirable ideals of felt representation and a competent handling of the school's activities. At the same time, he cannot escape the conviction that many of them evidence far more attention to the development of pretty machinery than to the development of efficient machinery.

As has been suggested several times previously in this book, it is not the intention of the author to present a ready-made plan which will fit any school or all schools; however, it is his purpose to suggest the possibilities which appear to be justifiable and from which the individual school can select those elements which seem to be most suitable. With this in mind let us briefly consider the elements which must be considered in the development of a two-house organization.

Name.—The name by which the plan is known is relatively unimportant; however, such a name should be accurate and dignified. It need not be fancy, certainly not foolishly fancy. In the following discussion "lower house" and "upper house" will be used to indicate the larger and smaller bodies, respectively, of the council. Even these designations, though commonly used, might be undesirable if allowed to become derogatory.

Representation.—Any justifiable basis for the selection of members to the council, as suggested in the first part of this chapter, is satisfactory. Usually, if the lower house is the larger, its members are elected from the home rooms or similar unspecialized groups, while those of the upper house are selected from units other than those represented in the lower house—classes, activities, or at large. Such a plan provides the felt representation necessary and also opportunity for council-group contacts and relationships.

Responsibilities of the Lower House.—In the majority of constitutions the lower house is described as being "advisory" in general intent and purpose, the implication being that it does not have very definite duties and responsibilities. For instance, one constitution states that the members of this group "present to their advisories (home rooms) the issues of the school as determined by the council." Most certainly this is a poor policy because if the group's main job is only to listen or talk, or both, or if it is only a rubber stamp, its members will soon realize the unimportance of their positions, lose interest in the participation idea, and probably quit in disgust, as they should. This sad state of affairs should be and can be avoided.

Because it is rather difficult for a large body to handle business affairs expeditiously and efficiently, and because of the setting made by the method of election, the larger group of the council should be charged with general legislative activities. This group represents all of the students of the school and it has direct contacts with relatively small electorates, and hence it is in position to reflect student opinion much more accurately than the smaller upper house. Therefore it is in better position to formulate policies and legislation. Further, it is in better position to reflect, explain, and interpret council deliberations and problems to the school, thus assisting in the proper development of a sound public opinion. It should offer free and unrestricted opportunity for discussion and exchange of ideas, but this exchange should result in some form of definite action.

In addition to initiating and approving legislation, the lower house may recommend the granting of charters and the making of appropriations; formulate policies for the organization, direction, supervision, and coordination of the various school activities; accept and consider petitions; pass emergency legislation; elect such school officers as historian and marshal; and in other ways represent the school in all matters that are largely legislative and policy making in general character and intent. And, as suggested above, it can carry back to the school reports of the council's business.

Responsibilities of the Upper House.—The relatively small size of the upper house ensures ease of calling special meetings, rapid and pointed discussion, and swift handling of business; hence the powers of this body should be largely executive and judicial in nature. It may, either upon or without the recommendation of the lower house, grant charters to clubs, associations, and societies; enforce these regulations and, if necessary, revoke them; approve legislation; interpret the constitution and adjudicate disputes; authorize and make appropriations; appoint, confirm, and recall officers; review court trials; administer the point system; appoint or confirm standing and special committees; elect managers, editors, and department heads; make resolutions effective; and in general assume rather direct control over the activities of the school. If desirable, it can initiate and pass legislation, especially emergency legislation, although probably a better procedure is for it to recommend such legislation to the lower house, the recognized legislative body. In short, the upper body is a sort of get-it-done clearinghouse for the council's business.

Relationships between the Two Houses.—Neither house should be the rubber stamp of the other, nor should one be recognized as "the talker" and the other "the doer." This means that each group must have particular clearly defined areas of responsibility which are respected by the other group, areas which represent supplementation rather than duplication. At the same time, in order to have a reasonable system of checks and balances, it is logical that in the larger and more general areas of responsibility there should be a plan of mutual approval. Although this may often be a form of routine or courtesy approval, it need not always be; each group should have the power to improve the acts of the other, or at least to suggest improvement. Just here, unless prevented by constitutional controls and a wholesome spirit of cooperation, conflicts of authority may result, conflicts which will always be detrimental, especially if they degenerate into pure retaliation. Such conflicts are almost inevitable if either group forgets the meaning and the importance of unified control or attempts to eclipse the other in importance and prestige. The ideal of a two-house organization is complete coverage of activities, no lost motion, and harmonious cooperation. In order to achieve this ideal, the necessary specifications of relationships must be definitely established in the constitution.

Other Multihouse Councils.—Occasionally a three-house form of council is found, a type in which all three branches of the federal government are represented, legislative, executive, and judicial. The responsibilities of the judicial branch are usually rather definite: (1) the interpretation of the constitution and its various elements; (2) judging the constitutionality of proposed amendments; (3) the handling of cases of violation of constitutional provisions, "civil" cases in which there are conflicts between school bodies over their rights and privileges; and (4) the handling of "criminal" cases which represent violations of the council's legal enactments. Sometimes there is a rather complicated system of courts, common, appeals, and supreme, although this is probably unnecessary. In general, however, this three-house type of organization is not very common, the judicial function being handled by the upper house or court of a two-house legislature, and by a special committee or court in the one-house type of council.[1]

Less frequently found examples of three-house, four-house, and five-house councils are those in which each of the major areas of school life elects its own council, for instance, athletics, publications, clubs, general school activities, boys' interests, and girls' interests. Each of these is separate and distinct from the others and usually there is no general coordinating body over them. Obviously, there is little to be said in favor of such a type of organization because the emphasis is entirely too much upon glorified specialized representation. In an approved type of council all of these interests and activities would be provided for through important standing committees or departments of the council, and just as important, they would be properly coordinated.

In one of the constitutions studied, the third house of a three-house organization was made responsible for "all legislative and executive powers not otherwise herein delegated." Apparently the school *just had to have* a three-house council, even though such an organization was not needed. So this third house was merely tacked on as an afterthought. One

[1] See Chap. XI for a discussion of the student court.

cannot help wondering (1) what this third house does, and (2) about the effectiveness of the entire plan.

The School-city.—This form of council may be either single-house or multihouse in organization, but it is usually the former. In an earlier day, owing to the efforts of such pioneers as Gill and Cronson, as well as such facts as (1) the nearness of the model, (2) the study of municipal organization in civics courses, and (3) the general appeal of the plan, this form of participation was quite popular. Although it is not nearly so popular as it once was, it is still to be found in American schools, especially, in adapted form, in elementary schools.[1]

This plan follows the main outline of the local municipal organization. In small schools the rooms or classes represent the wards, and in larger schools the floors, or sections of the building, assembly, or classes, represent the wards, and the various individual rooms the precincts of these wards. The city council is composed of aldermen elected by the wards. The mayor, burgess, or city manager, chief of police, chief clerk (secretary), and treasurer, and the other major officers or commissioners are usually elected by the "city" and the minor officials are appointed or elected by the council. Such departments as Health, Finance, Welfare, Streets, Parks, Recreation, Organizations, etc., are provided and into these are incorporated the corresponding activities of the school.

The advantages of this form of organization are that (1) all students are represented; (2) responsibility is clearly defined and placed; (3) it is motivated because it is imitative of a close real life model which can be studied firsthand at any

[1] For two accounts of this plan in elementary schools see M. Wright, The City of Make-believe—a Program in Character Building and Citizenship, *Elementary School Journal*, 26: 376*ff*., January, 1926; and L. R. Kelly, Education through Real-life Experiences, *The Instructor*, November, 1935. See also *School Review*, 44: 4–6, January, 1936.

time; (4) it can capitalize the interest and efforts of municipal officials; (5) it provides functional training in natural settings and activities; and (6) parents, recognizing that soon their children will be the citizens and officials of the community, and also appreciating the practical training this plan offers, readily support it.

The chief disadvantages are that (1) the more complete and elaborate forms of municipal administration are difficult to reproduce, and (2) any failure to reproduce them more or less accurately may be considered evidence as a sort of failure; (3) in a school some activities, such as assemblies and athletics, do not lend themselves readily to municipal function classification; (4) attempting to duplicate municipal machinery may detract from the more important aspects of participation; and (5) there is some possibility that for various reasons a local municipal administration may not be worth imitating.

Conclusion.—It has been pointed out in this chapter that, although councils may differ widely as far as type of organization is concerned, in order to be successful they must be built upon the basic principles of (1) equitable representation, (2) a clearly defined internal division of a reasonable schedule of nonprofessional duties, and (3) structural efficiency. A glance through the foregoing pages will indicate that there is still plenty of room for improvement in all of these elements of student council relationships. It is actually quite probable that, despite the stated opinions of concerned administrators, sponsors, teachers, and students, no council is entirely satisfactory. Probably no council should ever be considered entirely satisfactory, at least for any length of time, because educational ideals, materials, organization, and procedures are constantly changing, and participation in school control represents one phase of instruction. Constant readjustment is not always uncomplimentary; on the contrary it is often very complimentary, one of the earmarks of progressive thinking.

The Student Council

A fair criticism of participation in America is that most of the student associations and councils are overorganized; they are too complicated. Perhaps this is only natural in a country and in an age in which people appear to have a sublime faith in organization. In any case, it cannot be overemphasized in this connection that pretty machinery does not necessarily mean efficiently working machinery and that the final test of an organization is not to be found in what it resembles or how attractively it appears when written up in a formal constitution or newspaper account, or when pictured in a graphic representation. The final test is to be found in what it accomplishes, which will depend to a large extent upon the sagacity that was used in building it originally and in redesigning it as need arose. It is well to remember that the failure of one important element will probably cause the entire organization to misfunction.

Selected References

Brogue, E. B., and P. B. Jacobson: "Student Council Handbook," pp. 30–65, National Association of Secondary School Principals, March, 1940.

Calkins, F. M.: A Model-city Government, *School Activities*, 11: 51–52, 70–71, October, 1939.

Durfee, E. G.: An All-city Council, *School Activities*, 9: 303–304, February, 1938.

Forman, W. A.: A Parent-teacher-pupil Council, *School Activities*, 7: 5–6, March, 1936.

Fretwell, E. K.: "Extra-curricular Activities in Secondary Schools," Chaps. V, VII, Houghton Mifflin Company, Boston, 1931.

Gernant, L.: Kalamazoo's Venture in an All-city Council, *School Activities*, 8: 408–409, May, 1937.

Harriman, P. L.: The Student-faculty Congress, *Journal of Higher Education*, 8: 413–416, November, 1937.

Hayward, B. W.: Organization of Student Council of Neighboring Schools, *School Activities*, 11: 379–380, May, 1940.

Types of Council Organization

LEDERMAN, R.: New Rochelle All-city Student Council, *School Activities*, 10: 154, December, 1938.

RABEHL, F.: A Student Council on a State Government Plan, *School Activities*, 7: 10–11, January, 1936.

Student Government at Cornell University, *School and Society*, 48: 679–680, November, 1938.

TERRY, P. W.: "Supervising Extra-curricular Activities," Chap. IV, McGraw-Hill Book Company, Inc., New York, 1930.

Chapter V

Initiating the Council

THE maxim "Well begun is half done" is nowhere more true than in the development of a plan of student participation. How many are the discouraging failures which have occurred in American schools all because the plan was not properly initiated, and how much damage has been done through the discrediting effects of these failures. Further, how infrequently have the reasons for such failures been analyzed, and how rarely has the blame for them been properly placed.

The usual result of an unhappy experience with a council is an unexpressed or expressed final-word attitude of "It may work somewhere else but it won't work in my school." It is reasonable to believe that if the plan is successful in one school it should be successful in another school which is similar, and most schools are similar. In one way the handling of the participation idea is like the handling of an automobile; the car may be driven through a plate-glass store window by one driver and safely along the street by another. Yet it is a rare occasion when the first driver would blame the automobile itself, or the plate-glass window for being in that particular spot. In student council affairs the administrators and teachers who take the attitude indicated above apparently do not realize how thoroughly illogical it is; nor do they recognize that such an attitude only reflects their own ignorance or bungling.

Like an automobile, a council must be properly designed and equipped, but just as important, it must be properly started and kept going. How to initiate the council is the subject of the present chapter.[1] How to keep it going successfully is the subject of the various other sections of the book. The necessary steps and the logical order in which they should be taken will be discussed in the following pages.

The Necessity of a Felt Need.—Many student-council failures are due to the fact that the system was planned largely by the principal, or the principal and the sponsor-to-be, with relatively little or no assistance from the students, and in response to no direct demand from the school as a whole. For twenty years the author has taught courses in extracurricular activities, always including a discussion of participation, and several times a course on this topic, and he knows it is often very difficult to prevent enthusiastic students from rushing right home and starting a council. How many are the constitutions and plans which have been shown to him or sent to him by teachers and administrators, constitutions and plans largely copied from other schools and from the literature of the subject, usually accompanied with some such statement as, "Here's my plan for our student council, what do you think of it?" These individuals do not recognize the foundation upon which democracy rests. Their interest and enthusiasm are highly commendable, in fact, absolutely necessary, but these alone will never guarantee a successful plan of participation.

The foundation of democracy is consent of the governed. A democratic form of government cannot be imposed from without; it can come only in response to a definite demand from within the group. Such a demand must be based upon a thorough understanding of the purposes and details of the plan and an appreciation and acceptance of the duties and obligations which it will bring. No administrator, teacher, or even small interested group of students, can ever successfully

[1] See also C. E. Erickson's Questions Which Every School Should Ask Itself Before Starting a Council, *School Activities*, 8: 408, May, 1937.

force a council upon a school, because no such individual or group can ever give the intelligent consent necessary. Although it is unreasonable to expect that this demand will ever be entirely unanimous—it never has been in our American democracy, and it never will be in a school democracy—it is reasonable that it must be and can be a solid majority. Further, it is reasonable to suggest that this need should be something more substantial than a shallow desire to have a new or novel organization, or a halfhearted, "Well, we might try it" attitude. Without adequate support the plan is doomed even before it is introduced. In summary, the need and then the council is much more logical than the council and then the need.

Strange as it may seem, this felt need will have to be originated and developed. In traditional organization there is no felt need for participation because the school has not favored it and has offered no instruction designed to promote it. How can this need be developed? Through education, and again, strange as it may seem, by beginning with a study of the participation idea itself.

In the following discussion it is assumed that the classes, clubs, and home rooms have been organized along democratic lines. Where they have not been so organized, they should be, because the proper place to begin a school-wide participation plan is in these smaller quite similar settings. Each of these represents a miniature, but none the less real, democracy in which are provided the opportunities for the functional learning of the pertinent ideals and the practicing of the appropriate habits. From such settings, properly capitalized, it is comparatively easy to effect a smooth transition into the larger unit of the school as a while.[1]

[1] Discussions of these smaller settings will be found in any standard book on extracurricular activities. Longer treatments of clubs will be found in the author's "School Clubs," The Macmillan Company, New York, 1929, and

In addition to the above-mentioned settings there are two others which should be capitalized, social studies and English classes. The average civics or problems of democracy class all too frequently tends to degenerate into an uninteresting memorization and recital of organizational forms and functions, all little related to the life of the student, and the net result is perhaps a limited knowledge about, but not an interest in, democracy. The student-council idea represents a topic through the discussion of which democratic principles and concepts may be made clear and personally accepted. Similarly, theme-writing in English classes can contribute to an understanding of this subject and to an interest in it. Undoubtedly, many students would find such immediate topics much more intriguing and at least as functional as some of the teacher's traditional topics.

Education of the Faculty.—Because the modern conception of participation is new and somewhat out of line with the school's traditional policies and practices, administrators, teachers, students, and parents cannot be expected to know a great deal about it. Probably most of them have heard about it, and perhaps some of them have had a little experience with it, but even where such knowledge exists doubtless most of it is inaccurate and incomplete. Further, there may even be undesirable faculty attitudes, such as a feeling that the teachers are already overloaded (as they may be), indifference, a desire not to have to make troublesome readjustments, and

---

of home rooms in his "Home Room Guidance," McGraw-Hill Book Company, Inc., New York, 1934. Other discussions of the home room will be found in M. E. F. Detjen, and E. W. Detjen, "Home Room Guidance Programs in the Junior High School Years," Houghton Mifflin Company, Boston, 1940; I. C. Good, and J. M. Crow, "Home-room Activities," Professional and Technical Press, New York, 1930; and J. Roemer, C. F. Allen, and D. A. Yarnell, "Basic Student Activities," Chaps. II–V, Silver Burdett Company, New York, 1935.

opposition due to previous experience. In addition, the teachers may lack the proper educational philosophy, and some of them may lack the personal qualifications for successful voluntary group leadership. Therefore it is reasonable that a most serious study of the plan should be made before any attempt at actual introduction and organization is undertaken. This educational preparation will include attention to the ideals, objectives, implications, details of organization, activities, evaluation, and other related elements.

A favorable attitude on the part of the faculty is essential to the success of the plan because every teacher will have contacts with it and will be in a strategic position to encourage or discourage it. The faculty need never be expected to be one hundred per cent in favor of either the idea or the plan as finally worked out by the school, but it can be expected that by a good majority the faculty will be well disposed toward these. This favorable attitude must be built upon a basis of comprehensive knowledges and accurate appreciations; it can never emerge from a principal-imposed or student-group-imposed system. Free discussion and fair disposition of objections on the basis of facts and logic, instead of upon the basis of seniority, bias, or position held, should help to make for acceptable and accepted ideas and a fully matured sentiment.

A quite proper method of beginning this program of faculty education is for the principal to appoint a committee of those teachers who, on the basis of training, experience, personality, and open-mindedness, are most competent to give the subject adequate and fair consideration. In a small school the entire faculty may compose this committee. This group collects constitutions and handbooks of other schools and pertinent literature in the form of bulletins, books, and magazine articles, and makes a serious study of them. In addition, it may arrange visits to and from other schools; hold conferences with recognized and experienced authorities, and with both leaders and followers in other schools; take university courses which reflect the participation idea; attend student-council conferences and conventions; and in other ways cover the ground rather completely and deliberately.

The second step in this program is the education of the entire faculty. The committee assumes responsibility for this. Committee materials, as well as the results of the group's study, may be made available to the faculty. This program must be unhurried, and ample opportunity for free discussion both for and against the plan should be provided. In no case should the faculty be made to feel that the principal or the committee is forcing action on the issue. At the same time it should be able to understand and appreciate the significance of participation, and also catch some of the enthusiasm of the committee's members.

After the faculty has learned something about and, presumably, to some extent accepted the participation idea, it will promptly face the practical question, "Just how would it work in our school?" Undoubtedly, during the discussion, all or nearly all the teachers will have been thinking about, and perhaps giving expression to, possible local applications, and this question will therefore not be startlingly new. The answer to it will necessitate a survey of the local setting, including such elements as precedents, prejudices, and past experiences; faculty interest and approval; teacher and student leaders available; community approval; equipment and material available; school activities which might be concerned; necessary limitations of authority; delimitation of fields of activity; proper approval by educational authorities; sponsorship; details of representation, organization, meetings, etc.; and the methods and materials of desirable publicity.

This survey should be carefully made, preferably by the entire faculty instead of by the committee alone. Of course the members of the committee will have been thinking and talking about local applications but if this group attempts to hurry the matter it will probably shorten the faculty's period of learning about the idea in general. A superficial idea of the plan can only mean a handicapped application of it. A second reason why the entire faculty should participate in this survey is that, especially in a larger school, it is in better position than the committee to know conditions and students. A third reason is purely psychological, because if all teachers have an opportunity to suggest possibilities, and probably the majority of them will, they will feel much more interested in the plan. Participation in the discussion cannot help bringing an increased interest in the subject. Fourth, undoubtedly there is some competent training and experience which is not represented on the committee.

This procedure of educating the faculty first is thoroughly sound because every teacher in the school will have to take an attitude toward the plan and answer students' and patrons' questions concerning the general idea as well as possible applications of it in the school. This is a much better foundation than can be built on the interest of the principal and a few student leaders, or one or two teachers and such a group.

All education, including that of teachers, is a very slow and tedious process, and this program should not be rushed. It should be continuous and progressive so that the interest of the faculty may not be lost, and momentum may be capitalized, but it should be unhurried. The average teacher in any school is seriously interested in education, and is willing to learn methods and materials which will increase the general efficiency of her school's program. In a not too hasty program of education she will appreciate her own responsibility, and the administration's thoughtful consideration, much more than she would if the plan were just dumped into her lap as another formal assignment. Further, it is entirely possible that the teacher who is a bit hard to convince will, when once won, make an ideal supporter of the plan. This program of faculty education may require a whole semester, or even two or three semesters but, if carefully designed, it will represent time well invested.

Education of the Student Body.—After—not before—the faculty has become thoroughly acquainted with the ideals, materials, and procedures of the participation idea and has considered the possibilities of its local application, comes the education of the students themselves. But whereas in the case of the faculty this was a dual program, with the student body it is three-headed: the education of a smaller group of student leaders, the education of representatives of the various democratic units of the school, and finally, the education of these units through their representatives. In general, the procedures utilized are about the same as those suggested above for the faculty.

Student Leaders.—A group composed of recognized student leaders, not too many, is called together by the principal, or by the faculty committee with the principal's official approval, and this group, led by the committee, makes a study of the idea of participation, the various plans of organization, activities, and other details. The committee does not "lecture" the group but in an informal manner discusses the idea with it. This committee outlines the purpose of the meeting, arouses the curiosity of the students, and then makes available the material which had been collected and used earlier with the teachers. The students are asked to read this material carefully, think about it, and come prepared to discuss it at the next meeting, say a week later. As before, the main objective here is to acquaint the students with the participation idea, and not until this acquaintanceship has been established is the discussion allowed to center around the local school.

This group should make visits to other schools where its members can sit in at council meetings and talk with teachers and students. Occasionally it may be possible for the group to attend a district or state convention of student councils, a most excellent place in which to widen its knowledge. Because the group is relatively small such visits and trips should be comparatively easy to arrange. If they are made on school time and the expenses are paid by the school, the group will be all the more obligated to bring home something substantial. The entire faculty committee need not always accompany the group, but at least some of the members should go with it. Such a plan will give added importance to the trip, offer convincing proof of the faculty's interest, make for easy and official entree, and provide adult leadership.

Following this period of theoretical instruction, the attention of the group is directed to the local possibilities along the lines suggested previously. Of course, no definite organization is planned. However, out of these discussions should begin to emerge a pretty clear idea of what might be suitable and what might be unsuitable.

Student Representatives.—The second step, once the enlightened enthusiasm of this group of student leaders has been developed—and, incidentally, it will probably be more difficult to restrain than to develop it—is to arrange a series of meetings between this group, the faculty committee, and the representatives of the major democratic units of the school, say the home rooms. These representatives need not be specially elected; probably should not be because no definite organization yet exists. They may be the presidents or other ranking officers of these units, those who have already been recognized as leaders. In general, the education of this group follows the lines suggested for the other three groups, faculty committee, faculty, and student leaders, centering largely around informal discussion. Because of the size of this group, visiting other schools, attending conferences, interviewing authorities, and even studying the available material may be more difficult. It should not be difficult, however, to bring in representatives from these other schools as well as other speakers. This group will probably be rather large and hence more formal meetings may be necessary, but it is well to remember that an important part of such sessions is ample opportunity for asking questions and discussing freely. Here, too, the order of business is the general idea first, and the possibilities of local application second. Still further, as before, these discussions should not be forced. The aim is not only to interest and enlighten the representatives, but also to make them competent missionaries when they return to their own units.

Student Units.—The third step in this process is the education of the entire student body through the representatives. This step should not be undertaken until the representatives, like the student leaders, the faculty, and the faculty committee in turn before them, have become familiar with the purpose and general details of the plan so that they are equipped to lead wholesome discussions of it. Opportunity for free discussion is again provided. Visits, trips, conferences, interviews, and firsthand experience with councils, as well as individual study of available material are, of course, largely out of this setting, which is all the more reason why the representatives should be well prepared. However, the meetings of the councils of other schools may be presented to advantage in the school assembly. Finally, as before, when the group has been grounded in the basic ideas, it is led to think in terms of local application.

This plan is perfectly logical. It offers a progressive program of training and thinking, sets the stage for a localized demand for such participation, and provides the material out of which the demanded project may be organized. If wisely planned and conducted, this educational campaign capitalizes interest at the time when it has been developed to its peak. Further, the plan is not only logical but it is workable; it has worked before and it will work again.

At the beginning of this chapter the point was emphasized that the school must feel a need for participation. How the above program develops this need should be apparent. Before this educational campaign the school did not feel a need for participation because it knew nothing about the idea and so of course could not envision its possibilities. Following the campaign as outlined above, the school cannot help understanding the participation plan and also appreciating how it would fit into the local setting. This understanding and appreciation naturally result in a demand for it, and this demand is the felt need required.

Education of the Community.—The third main group which must be educated in the participation idea is that composed of the parents and patrons of the community. Too often in school affairs this group is neglected and the result, especially if some rather new proposal is being promoted, is either an apathetic attitude or downright opposition, both of which are detrimental to school morale and to the plan being suggested. Community support is necessary and in the case of the new, this means enlightened support.

Such understanding and support can be developed through the programs of the Parent-Teachers Association, bulletins from the principal, school and public newspaper articles, special assembly programs to which parents and patrons have been invited, and the students themselves. The value of this last device is obvious; a student who explains the participation idea to his parents will, in the majority of cases, be a supporter of it and hence will make a serious attempt to convert his parents. Any average parent would be impressed by an earnest and enthusiastic explanation and justification, and any student who made such an explanation would be all the more convinced of the value of the plan.

Developing the Constitution.—After the school has been brought to an understanding of the basic idea of participation, and the necessary felt need has appeared, inevitably there will come a demand for the adoption of the plan. Hence a sort of blueprint must be drawn, and this blueprint is the constitution. In it the areas of the council responsibility are staked out, organization is described, and authority is officially given and recognized.

The entire school will serve under this constitution and therefore the school should have the right to participate in its development, as well as the right to adopt it. But the school as a unit is too large and cumbersome and consequently a smaller group of students and teachers should have the responsibility for leading this development. This group may well be that which sponsored the education of the school in the participation idea, together with representatives of the various units, if there are not too many of these. If it appears more desirable, the various units may elect delegates to a constitutional convention. Probably the first plan is the better because it utilizes the interest and knowledge which have already been developed. The entire group studies and discusses the various possibilities, decides upon the basic features of the plan, and then commissions a smaller group to put these into definite form as a tentative constitution.

The constitutions of other schools, and suggested outlines from such books as this, will have been studied and these will help the group to plan a general form. Again it is well to emphasize that such models should not be slavishly imitated, because none of them will exactly represent the local situation, and practically all of them to some extent will be faulty. The job of this group is to write a constitution that is complete in coverage, simple in organization, and clear in style.

Once in definite form this tentative constitution should be shown to the principal, the final authority, before it is further discussed or made available to the various units of the school. In all probability, because the faculty members will have been familiar with his wishes and point of view, the principal will have few changes to suggest. In any case, his final reaction and decision should be obtained before the tentative constitution is given further consideration. Obviously, there is no such thing as adopting a constitution over the principal's head.

The group might also submit its plan to some authority in the field, although this is not very desirable because authorities differ in their opinions and because such an individual is rarely close enough to obtain an accurate picture of the local setting and its needs. His suggestions are almost certain to be general rather than specific.

Another possibility is for the group to ask some friendly and interested lawyer to look over the proposed constitution and see if it represents good form and organization. Such a procedure may result in a better instrument, but at the same time there is danger of a too close imitation of the constitutions of adulthood with their confusing terminology and complicated expression. Further, there is also a possibility of conflict of ideas because of the attorney's lack of understanding of the basic ideals and ideas involved in student participation.

After the tentative constitution has been developed by the group and approved by the principal, it should be taken to both the faculty and the student body for further discussion. Because it is practically impossible to study the document when it is read orally, it should be mimeographed and distributed. The representatives should take it to their various groups, explain it, and invite criticisms or objections, which means, incidentally, that these representatives must be thoroughly familiar with its contents and their various implications.

Probably few serious criticisms or objections will be made because of the previous group and unit discussions, but, at the same time, it is not at all impossible that some important items may have been overlooked. If constructive suggestions arise they are noted by the representatives and carried back to the central group where they are given serious consideration. In case of important changes the constitution, or the amended sections of it, is again returned to the units for final discussion before adoption.

In order to avoid later amending, this consideration process should not be hurried. Amendments to a constitution should not be impossible, but too frequent amending is evidence that the plan was not completely and clearly thought out originally. It requires less time to amend a tentative instrument than it does the final document, and such early change may save a great deal of confusion and trouble.

Adopting the Constitution.—When the tentative constitution appears finally to be in good shape, it is then ready for adoption by the school in a special election. This election should be an important and dignified event. Formal printed or mimeographed ballots should be used, and no such voting procedure as "say 'aye,' " "stand," or "raise your hands" should be scheduled or permitted. A public adoption in the general school assembly does not represent good practice, nor is a similar formal acceptance after adoption necessary or logical. Suitable publicity, officially designated polling places (perhaps the rooms of the various units) ballot boxes, and election officials will help to make it a real event in the life of the school. Such a procedure will increase school interest in the plan, and give it worthwhile publicity outside the school. The final results may be announced in the assembly or posted on the bulletin board. As soon as practicable after adoption, the constitution should be printed in an attractive booklet and distributed to the students and teachers.

Initial Organization.—The constitution has now been adopted but as yet there is no official student organization, so effecting one becomes the next order of business. This initial organization is directed by the original faculty-student group.[1] According to the provisions of the constitution, the necessary election of council members, or council members and school officers, is held, if necessary being promoted by the ranking student officers of each unit, or by temporary chairmen appointed by the teacher responsible for each unit. These elections should be as definitely formal as they will be when the organization is really under way. Such elections should not be scheduled immediately; sufficient time should be allowed so that the necessary campaigns within each unit may be organized and conducted.

When finally named, the council members assemble at the call of the president, if he is elected by the school, or that of the central faculty-student group, if the president is to be elected by the council itself. In the latter case a temporary chairman is appointed to handle the council's election of its president. Upon election the president proceeds at once with the election of the other officers, or, if the council is large, postpones this election until the group has had ample opportunity to study its material.

It is unlikely that the president will be able to appoint his committees immediately because, in all probability, he will need time to study the constituency of his group, confer with the various members, and evaluate the abilities represented in it. Further, the appointment of these committees will, to some extent at least, depend upon the activities to be first undertaken by the council. The council's initial meeting or

[1] Sometimes the civics or problems of democracy class assumes charge of this election. However, because such groups (1) probably include students who do not rate high in leadership and school respect, and (2) do not include some key leaders, this plan is not advisable.

two can be used in discussing the various possibilities and in deciding upon first projects.

Installation of the Council.—Shortly after being elected the council should be appropriately installed in a special program to which, if desired, parents and patrons are invited. This ceremony should be formal and dignified so as to make an impressive appeal to the student body. Nothing should be allowed to cheapen it in any way. The program may be somewhat as follows:

Processional	Council members
Explanation	First faculty member
Introduction of council members	Second faculty member
Delegation of authority	Principal
Administration of oath of office	Principal
Inaugural address	President
The school song	School

A prayer is not necessary because this is not a religious service. A recessional is too duplicative of the processional to be effective or inspiring.

Administering the Oath.—The oath may be administered (1) by the members reciting or reading it in unison, or repeating sections of it as these are read by the principal, or (2) by being read by the principal in the form of a question to which the members make a simple two-word response, "I do." The first method is always weak because (1) reading from a card or paper is an unattractive form of public presentation; (2) accurate memorization by all members of the group will be next to impossible; (3) effective group reading or reciting in an auditorium is difficult, if not impossible, due to differences in pitch, phrasing, modulation, rate, and pronunciation; (4) the ever-present mistakes and slips are disconcerting and sometimes downright laughable; (5) comparatively little of read or recited material is clearly understood by the audience; and (6) "repeat after me" material not only has nearly all the disadvantages suggested above, but also breaks continuity of thought. Having the oath administered in the form of a question is preferable because it avoids all the weaknesses and difficulties of the other plan. Even the possibility that some of the students may respond "I do," others, "We do," and still others, "Yes" is unimportant; at its worst, such a varied response will be only a short and small "growl," while reading or reciting the oath will represent a long and loud "growl."

Having each officer individually take the oath is unnecessarily repetitious and adds nothing of value. The somewhat common practice of administering an oath to the entire school is also unnecessary because in adopting the constitution the school agreed to abide by its provisions and to support its officers. No oath should be administered by a student. The ranking officer in the school, the principal, should perform this duty.

The oath, or oaths, in case the officers and members are sworn separately (a good practice), should be simple. The author has seen more than one installation ceremony made ludicrous by the use of high-sounding and flamboyant atrocities. Such oaths as the following are quite satisfactory:

> Do you, the officers of the Blankville High School Student Association, pledge yourselves to support the constitution and discharge to the best of your abilities the duties of the offices to which you have been elected?
>
> Do you, the members of the student council of the Blankville High School pledge yourselves to develop and support worthy school policies, promote the best interests of school activities, and faithfully discharge specific responsibilities individually delegated to you?

Other Possible Weaknesses of the Installation Ceremony. 1. The service may become tedious. This is especially possible where the oath is administered individually to the various officers and members, where outgoing or incoming officers talk at length, or where the program is too slow or too long drawn out. A program does not have to be long in order to be impressive. A twenty-minute ceremony is preferable to one two or three times as long, because it can maintain interest.

Such items and activities as a pledge of the faculty, a pledge of allegiance to the flag, the presenting of books to the secretary and treasurer and of a copy of the constitution to the president, and armbands or other insignia are unnecessary, and detrimentally clutter up what might otherwise be a dignified, simple, and effective program.

2. The ceremony may be too formal and complicated. This is especially possible where all sorts of dramatic features are used. Unless performed smoothly and effectively, dramatic features are disconcerting. In order to be performed smoothly and effectively they must be presented by students with dramatic ability, which is not a requirement for council membership or officership. In addition, they must be rehearsed and rehearsed and rehearsed, and what is gained by such rehearsals may not be worth the time and effort expended. Further, there is a possibility that the dramatic appeal of the event may detract from, rather than enhance, the main idea of the occasion.

3. The program may become feminine in general plan and appeal. Kneeling, bowing, carrying and passing lighted candles, and wearing robes hardly represent masculinity and can easily become most ludicrous. They may be suitable for a girls' school, but they are not appropriate for a boys' school or a coeducational institution.

4. The symbols used may be inappropriate. An ax, hatchet, mace, or sword carried and handed over as the symbol of authority is too militaristic to be suitable, while a representation of the Roman fasces (a bundle of rods containing an ax) is too ancient a symbol and has unpleasant modern connota-

tions. The gavel is the modern symbol of group leadership, and this may be suitably presented to the president either by the principal in the case of a newly formed council, or by the retiring president in the case of an already existing organization.

First Work of the Council.—Once the council has been properly elected, organized, and installed, it should begin some constructive piece of work immediately while school interest and enthusiasm are still high. A favorable school and community sentiment toward the council is absolutely necessary to its success, and because the body is closely watched by these two groups, its first efforts are most important.

The newly organized council is much more likely to err in attempting to do too much than it is in attempting to do too little. Naturally, the group wants to demonstrate its ability immediately, not only because it honestly feels its responsibility but also because it realizes that if it does not accomplish something rather promptly it will lose standing in the school and jeopardize the entire participation plan. Such a feeling of responsibility is highly desirable; the council which does not have it is not worth the name. However, there is a very real danger that the group will attempt to do too much and spread its attention and efforts out so thin that the results will not be clearly seen. One small well-done job which is easily recognized by the school is worth more than a dozen jobs only partly or ineffectually completed. Because of their greater maturity and judgment, the faculty members of the council will probably have to assume the responsibility for putting the brakes on youthful ambition. This can be done without dampening enthusiasm by stating and proving the point just made, a point which the council members will easily see and appreciate.

The first few tasks of the newly organized council should be small, very definite, and easily recognized and appreciated by the school. Fretwell says in this connection, "The council should begin with concrete activities where definite success is possible. More difficult problems may be taken up as the pupils and teachers, working through the council, gain ability to handle them."[1] Needless to state, each of these projects should represent an important felt need of the school. In order to illustrate this type of "concrete activities where definite success is possible," two such tasks will be described in detail.

Bicycle Parking.—In nearly all communities, many of the students ride their bicycles to school. In some of these schools, no provision whatever is made for parking them and as a result they are leaned against the building, trees, railings, and playground equipment, or thrown carelessly on the ground. Often perhaps they are moved out of the way by students or employees, sometimes borrowed, and occasionally stolen. In any case the picture is not pretty, and just here is an excellent opportunity for a concrete, useful, and practicable project for the council.

After proper authorization by the school authorities (principal, superintendent, or board of education) the council builds or has built a suitable bicycle rack, which may, if practicable, be roofed into a sort of shed or house. All bicycles are officially registered and each is assigned to a particular stall. If it appears to be desirable, all bicycles may be made secure from molestation by the simple expedient of running an iron bar or chain through the wheels and locking it. If this is done, an appointed officer may lock and unlock the bicycles at the proper times. Improperly parked or unparked bicycles are officially "arrested" and locked up, and can be repossessed by their owners only after a bit of discouraging formality. Other suitable activities in connection with this

[1] Fretwell, E. K., "Extra-curricular Activities in Secondary Schools," p. 193, Houghton Mifflin Company, Boston, 1931.

project are those suggested on page 176 in the description of the responsibilities of the Bicycle Committee.[1]

Care of School Trophies.—In some settings the school's athletic, dramatic, music, forensic, and other trophies are not attractively cared for and exhibited. Often these cups, plaques, and flags are scattered indiscriminately about the building, piled up in the principal's or coach's office, or placed in unlighted, unsuitable, and unattractive cases in the corridors, in the study hall, or on the stair landings. The author has even seen them used in the office as files for papers and documents, and he saw one that was used in the board's room as a cuspidor. Often some of them, especially old-time silver and gold-plated ones, are tarnished where the shellac has peeled off, and usually all of them are dusty or downright dirty. In such an instance, imagine what an appeal they must *not* make to the former athlete who visits school, thinks over old times and friends, and again inspects the prizes he helped to win!

Here is another fine opportunity through which the new council can establish itself in the school and the community. It can either make or buy or promote a campaign for the purchase of an attractive, well-lighted, enclosed trophy case. It can renovate all trophies, cleaning and polishing them, and reshellacking those which are tarnished, arrange them tastefully, and identify each with a small typed or printed card which designates or describes the event at which it was won, and, if practicable, lists the names of the members of the group or team which won it. A small plaque giving proper credit for the idea and the date of the project may be attached to the case. This case may be dedicated in an assembly program

[1] An interesting project which included the inspection and registration of bicycles (95 per cent of some 500 bicycles were found defective) and the education of the riders in safety is described by W. A. Gardell in Reducing Bicycle Accidents, *Safety Education*, 15: 86, 89, December, 1935. See also the references to Brooke, Browning, and Moog on pages 192–193; Lorenz, Susterich, and Tredennick on page 201, and Lawson on page 299.

built around the theme, "Our School Trophies and How They Were Won." Undoubtedly it would be possible to arrange, as a part of this program, presentations (talks, interviews, group discussions, etc.) by some of those athletes of former years who helped to win these trophies. An appeal by the president for the school to strive to add others to the collection is a logical conclusion to this program.

Other First Activities.—Additional appropriate first activities of the student council are:

Installing and maintaining a bulletin board[1]
Installing an electric basketball scoreboard[2]
Organizing and managing a lost and found department[3]
Collecting and printing songs and cheers for the school's use
Providing and caring for the school flag or flags
Sponsoring a visiting day or school night[4]
Compiling a short illustrated history of the school
Organizing and managing a candy counter or school store
Planning campaigns—safety, courtesy, punctuality, speech[5]
Designing and awarding school insignia, honors, or trophies
Developing an official school emblem, seal, or plaque
Maintaining a question or suggestion box[6]
Promoting the acquisition of pictures, plants, statuary
Organizing and conducting contests and competitions[7]

[1] See Bulletin Board Committee, page 176.

[2] For a description of one such project see J. Surak, and F. Rabehl, An Electric Basket Ball Score Board as a Club Project, *School Activities*, 8: 257–258, February, 1936.

[3] See Lost and Found Committee, page 181.

[4] See the author's "Extra-curricular Activities," rev. ed., pp. 115–116, The Macmillan Company, New York, 1937. Two other descriptions are McDougald, J., Open House Day Observed in School Centers, *Educational Method*, 17:12–15, October, 1937; and McMurray, J. F., Open School Night, *School Activities*, 6: 5–7, October, 1934.

[5] For suggestions, see pages 178, 179, 182, of this book.

[6] See page 183.

[7] See page 178.

Promoting a "Come to High School Day" for eighth graders

Organizing and supervising corridor and street traffic

Developing exhibitions—pets, hobbies, art, club, athletic

Organizing and arranging home room program exchanges and visits[1]

All these activities meet the specifications of a good first project: they are definite, they are not too complicated, they offer probability of success, and they are instrumental in developing capacity and desire for additional and more complex tasks. It is well to emphasize again that not many of them should be scheduled immediately. If the council does one or two of them well during the first term, and another one or two during the second term, by the end of the year it will have to a considerable extent established itself. Final establishment may require even two or three years, but when it comes it will be complete.

Appraisal of Efforts.—No project is really completed until the final result has been evaluated. Such an appraisal will indicate the points, procedures, materials, organization, or emphases which, because they appear to be successful, strong, or good, should be remembered and repeated in later activities, and those which appear less successful, weak, or bad, which should be remembered and avoided the next time. Although such an appraisal is important in all council work, it is especially important when the council is just getting under way. Detailed suggestions for making such evaluations will be found in Chap. XIII.

A New Start for an Old Council.—Occasionally, there is a situation in which, for various reasons, the student council is recognized as a failure by all concerned. What should be done in such a case? There are two possibilities: (1) remodel the plan, or (2) abolish it and start all over again. Either of

[1] See the author's "Home Room Guidance," pp. 58–59, 137.

these procedures, depending upon the seriousness of the failure, is entirely justifiable.

The advantage of the first procedure is that the better features of the plan—and all plans have some commendable features—represent a framework around which the new model may be built. These features, plus the contacts made and the experience gained, should be capitalized if at all possible.

If the whole machine is in such a deplorable state that it cannot be rebuilt, the best thing to do is to discard it entirely and begin to plan for a new start a year or two hence. A very important part of such abolishment is a very careful written analysis of the reasons for failure, an analysis which should be filed away for later use. This study should be made at once while the school is still close to the situation and before the personnel of the student body, faculty, and administration changes and sources of direct information are lost. Pertinent emotional reactions can also be reflected then much better than they can at some future time.

It requires courage to attempt to capitalize on a failure, and such an attempt is complimentary to those who make it. Conversely, making no such attempt is uncomplimentary. Upon more than one occasion the author has heard some principal say, "We tried it and it was a failure, so we quit." Such an individual is inconsistent. He would not take such an attitude in learning to swim, play golf, ride a bicycle, or talk. Even in learning to administer a school he had plenty of failures, but he did not allow these to discourage him; instead, he capitalized on them. He did not "quit." But some administrators, especially those who were not originally "sold" on the participation, are easily discouraged; they "quit" and become "quitters" in the nasty connotation of these words. Of course, in using the word "it" they are only showing the extent of their ignorance of the idea. There is no one and only one "it." The participation plan is composed of dozens and dozens of "its" in each of its divisions, such as organization, administration, supervision, program, financing. These "its" in different forms as well as in different combinations represent a potentially practicable plan for any school. In short, the principal should practice in council affairs the old adage which he has probably taught time and time again, "If at first you don't succeed, try, try, again."

Selected References

Bowden, A. O., and I. C. Clarke: "Tomorrow's Americans," Chap. IX, G. P. Putnam's Sons, New York, 1930.

Branford, W. W.: Reorganizing Student Government, *School Activities*, 12: 64–65, October, 1940.

Crawford, C.: Student Council Reorganization, *School Activities*, 12: 15–16, September, 1940.

Dorff, J. A.: Growth of Student Council, *School Activities*, 13: 179–181, January, 1942.

Erickson, C. E., F. B. Dixon, and L. E. Barthold: "Pupil Participation in School Life," Chap. III, Lucas Brothers, Columbia, Mo., 1942.

Fretwell, E. K.: "Extra-curricular Activities in Secondary Schools," Chap. VI, Houghton Mifflin Company, Boston, 1931.

Hyatt, W. S.: Introducing a Student Council to a Small High School, *School Activities*, 14: 55–56, October, 1942.

Kennedy, E. G.: Getting the Council Under Way, *School Activities*, 12: 5–7, September, 1940.

Meyer, F.: You Want to Establish a Council? *School Activities*, 13: 5–6, 17, September, 1941.

Rankin, O.: How to Begin a Student Council, *School Activities*, 13: 91–92, November, 1941.

Teeter, V. A., and W. W. Norris: Organizing the Student Council, *School Activities*, 13: 9–10, September, 1941.

Tuttle, E. M.: Student Government: Why Ours Worked, *Clearing House*, November, 1942.

Chapter VI

Constitution and Bylaws

IN A democratic form of government the purposes of the plan, the sources of authority, the rights, privileges, duties, and responsibilities of both electors and electees, and the organization, powers, and activities of the central group must be designated, described, or defined, and these ends are accomplished through a formally accepted and adopted constitution or a constitution and bylaws.

There is a great deal of confusion, not only among younger, but also among older, individuals, regarding the difference between constitution and bylaws, and a word of explanation may be in order. In general, a constitution is the fundamental or major law of an organization, while bylaws are supplementary regulations or minor laws, more specific working directions of the plan. Obviously, these bylaws must not contravene or conflict with any part of the fundamental or organic law. To illustrate: for our purpose here, on the whole we have included in the discussion of the constitution those items which the school itself should decide upon, such as purposes, name, powers, and organization. In the bylaws, we have included those items which refer more directly to the procedures of the meetings and activities of the council, such as order of business, parliamentary authority, quorums, reports, and special committees. This represents an ideal, but not always a possible, method of classifying items, but despite difficulties, it is satisfactory in the present connection.

Really, in student associations it may be relatively unimportant whether the basic instrument be called a "constitution," "constitution and bylaws," or just "bylaws." It is entirely possible that a constitution might be made so complete that a set of bylaws would be unnecessary; conversely, it is possible that a set of bylaws might be made so complete that a constitution would be unnecessary. The important thing is to see that all essential elements are included, irrespective of just how they are classified. However, constitution is a dignified and formal term which quite properly appeals to all individuals.

As a part of his preparation for the writing of this chapter, the author examined 217 school constitutions from all parts of the country. As might be expected, he found these instruments to vary greatly in size and complexity, and to show considerable variation in terminology and in the classification of materials. The majority are called "constitutions" or "constitutions and bylaws" but such other designations as "rules of organization," "procedure and regulations," and "rules of order" are used. These constitutions include nearly one hundred different subjects, usually designated both as "articles" and "sections," and sometimes only numbered, not headed. Of course nearly all these topics are classifiable into a few major groups. These constitutions also list the subjects in all sorts of order.

It is not the purpose of this chapter to offer a ready-made constitution because subjects, provisions, and arrangements, may, quite properly, vary from school to school. However, it is the purpose here to indicate general constitutional form, the major elements, and a suggested arrangement of these elements, which, incidentally, with one or two exceptions, is of relatively little significance. In order to be concrete, much of the material of this chapter will be based upon a critical examination of articles and sections taken from constitutions. Detailed discussions of the principles and procedures relating to the material of these articles—plan of organization, officers, committees, financial administration, etc.—will be presented later. Here we are interested largely in the form of the constitution. This general form will be reflected also in the organization of the present chapter.

PRINCIPLES OF CONSTITUTION CONSTRUCTION

1. Every Participation Plan Should Be Based upon a Written Constitution.—The author can see no reason whatever for a constitutionless form of student participation in control. He knows that in some schools for various reasons such as small size, fear of killing interest and informality, and faculty apprehension and jealousies, there is no written constitution. The council's area and organization is then defined and understood by "tacit agreement," but even this "tacit agreement" represents a constitution, although an unwritten one. Because this is true, there is no real reason for not putting this constitution into definite form. If it is written, needless discussions and misunderstandings over authority and responsibility will be avoided, a better knit organization will be developed, and standing and distinction will be given to the plan.

2. The Constitution Should Fit the Local Situation.—Nearly all student participation constitutions are imitations of those of other schools. There is some justification for this, because it would be very difficult for a group of inexperienced students to develop such an instrument without the proper base of fact and form. However, for a school group to copy bodily a constitution and plan of some other school is no more logical than for one student to copy exactly the suit of clothes of some other student. It might fit, but it is much more probable that it would not. A school may justifiably imitate the general form of constitution, but the details of the plan should represent the needs of the local setting.

3. The Constitution Should Be as Simple as Possible.—Often school constitutions so closely imitate municipal, state, and federal instruments with their legal and technical verbiage that they are cumbersome and confusing. Frequently, in such instances, the main order of business seems to be "amending the constitution." This is true especially where the constitution is considered a specifically detailed legislative statute instead of a more flexible enabling act. Obviously, the size and type of the constitution depends upon the size and type of the organization planned. It should be complete enough to cover all necessary details, but simple enough to be easily understood by the average student. Short sentences, sections, and articles, each confined to a single idea, and numerical designations for each article and section, help to give the impression of simplicity. A number of shorter articles and sections is preferable to fewer longer ones. All articles should be properly titled or headed. It cannot be overestimated that, like the council itself, the constitution is not an end, but a means to an end.

4. The Source of Authority Should Be Indicated.—Very few of the constitutions studied indicate the source of their authority. These are, in a way, unconstitutional; certainly the omission of their source of authority is entirely illogical. In short, because the participation plan rests upon delegated authority, the source of this authority should be indicated in the constitution.

5. The Constitution Should Be Positive, Not Negative. The author has read constitutions which appeared to be composed largely of "shall not" statements. In one of these, he counted seventeen sentences beginning with "No," such as "No student . . . ", "No action . . . ", and "No appeal . . . ". The occasional use of such expressions may be justified in properly defining powers and areas of authority, but if too much use of them is made the constitution will become a set of formal, cold, and impersonal commandments.

The too frequent use of such expressions as the following, nearly one-half of which were taken from one constitution, gives an incorrect and deleterious impression:

Within the limits of the restrictions imposed
Shall vote to oust the officer
In case of neglect of duties
In case of removal by recall, resignation, or incapacity
Pronounce judgment and sentence
Disqualification and removal of representative
Incompetence, laziness, and willful disobedience
No appeal shall be made
Adjust difficulties between faculty and students
Punishment and chastisement

To repeat, the constitution should give the impression of positive and constructive policies instead of the opposite. When negative ideas are necessary, they should be expressed in clear but not too harsh terms.

6. Serious Study Should Precede Final Adoption.—The constitution is not something to be written out and handed to the school in a "here's your constitution" manner. Because it represents the entire school, all students and teachers should have an opportunity to study it, criticize it, suggest changes, and in other ways attempt to improve it. This can be done properly through the various organizations which are, or are to be, represented in the council.

A good procedure for the development of this instrument is the election or appointment of a central committee, or even a constitutional convention, although the size of this group may militate against its effectiveness, to make a survey of the local needs and a study of typical constitutions. A proposed instrument is then drafted and distributed to the school for study and criticism. When advisable, the necessary modifications are made before the constitution is offered for final ratification.

Some schools even try out the constitution for a semester or two before finally adopting it. This procedure will help to avoid embarrassing and confidence-destroying errors and weaknesses. Frequently amending the constitution not only takes valuable time and efforts which might be better spent on other activities, but also is not complimentary to the group which originated the instrument. At the same time, when amendments become necessary they should be promptly made.

7. The Constitution Should Be Published.—Publishing the constitution in an attractive little booklet and making it available to all the members of the school will give it dignity and significance, make the school more participation conscious, and clarify thinking on purposes, organization, and responsibilities. This booklet should include a table of contents, chart of the plan, and, if rather long, a topical index. Except in small schools, printing the booklet is preferable to mimeographing it. If the school publishes a student handbook, the constitution may very properly be included in it.

ELEMENTS AND FORM OF THE CONSTITUTION

Name

Nearly three-fourths of the constitutions examined include the name of the organization, and these names fall easily into the following types.

1. A designation of the central governing body.

Student council	Executive committee
School council	Central body
School cabinet	Self-government committee
School congress	School organization officers
School legislature	Student senate
School executives	Welfare committee
School city council	Civic council
Board of governors	Representative assembly

2. A designation of the entire organization, of which the central body is only a part. Practically all these designations include the name of the school; all of them should.

Student association	Activities association
General organization	The school democracy
Student associates	Self-government association
The citizens' league	School city
The school union	School citizenship league
The school republic	Citizens association
Associated activities	Cooperative association
Civic association	United home rooms

Because the constitution concerns the entire school, the use of the second type of name is preferable because it is more accurate. The constitution is not a constitution of the student council any more than our national constitution is a constitution of Congress. It is an instrument which represents the entire organization of which the council is only the official head. The rules and regulations which govern the handling of the council's business are usually designated bylaws, and these, as will be explained later, may be officially adopted by either the entire organization or the council, or both.

Purpose

In general, there are two types of purpose-statements, as indicated below. Less frequently used designations for "purpose" are "objectives," "objects," and "aims."

1. A single, simple, and usually short but general statement.

To promote the general welfare of student activities.

To unify and coordinate the activities of the school in order to preserve and maintain the good name and traditions of the school.

To cooperate with the faculty in promoting better citizenship by fostering scholarship, high ideals, and school spirit.

> To promote the efficiency of all school activities through a unification of control.

Occasionally a longer purpose, composed of several of these statements, is used. This type of statement is usually numbered as a regular article of the constitution and its several sections numbered and set off from each other.

2. A longer and more formal statement, usually called a preamble. Generally this statement is not a numbered article of the constitution, being more in the form of an introductory paragraph.

> We, the students of the Selma Junior High School, desiring to promote our own interests through closer cooperation with our school, do hereby form ourselves and those who follow us into this association to promote student participation in the organization of our school.

> We, the citizens of the Hannah Penn Junior High School of York, Pennsylvania, desirous of showing more loyalty to our community and country through the enrichment of our ideals of citizenship, in order to form a more perfect community in which no partiality shall be shown so that there may be opportunities and justice for all, do establish this constitution for the Hannah Penn Junior High School.

> We, the students of Central Junior High School, in order to cherish and perpetuate Centralism; to maintain laws of good order; to maintain high standards of cooperation, loyalty, and fair play; to prepare to meet the problems of school and adult life; to set a high standard of citizenship; and to encourage and support all forms of student activities—do establish this constitution.

This second type of purpose-statement is probably preferable because it sounds more official, is more attractive in style, and reminds the students of the preamble to our national constitution. What is more, the use of such expressions as "we, the students," and "do hereby ordain" helps the average student to feel his place in the plan.

Membership

Because the student council idea is based upon the participation of the members of the school, the constitution should include a statement of the qualifications of this membership. There is considerable confusion concerning this matter; some constitutions do not include this basic idea, and some of them refer only to membership in the council itself. This point needs to be clarified and emphasized; "membership" refers to membership in the entire student organization, not to membership in the council. Membership in the council is properly a section of the article on the organization of this body. If there are such membership requirements as citizenship ratings, cards, registration, or taxes, they should be indicated. If the faculty members of the council are elected by the teachers, the faculty should also be included in this article. The following examples show several methods of expressing this idea:

> The membership of the Newton High School Associates shall consist of all bona fide students of the school.

> All teachers and student members of the student body and faculty of the Holland Junior High School shall be citizens of this Republic.

> All teachers and students of the Theodore Roosevelt Junior High School holding student body cards are members of this organization and are entitled to all the rights and privileges of the organization.

> Every citizen at the time of his or her registration as a member of this school shall automatically become a member of this

Community and remain so until his or her promotion to the Senior High School or until he or she shall discontinue his or her connections with our school. All members of the faculty shall also be members of this community.

Powers

This area is the heart of the participation plan, and consequently a great deal of care should be used in defining it and also in describing it in the constitution. The powers and responsibilities of the council may be indicated in two ways.

1. Through a general statement such as the following:

> This council will have the right and power to develop policies, set standards, and to make and enforce any rules necessary for the betterment of the school's life, interests, and activities.

2. By specifically indicated and numbered sections of the article.

a. To develop and adopt such bylaws as may be necessary, provided they do not conflict with the elements and spirit of this constitution.

b. To organize, promote, and supervise general and special elections; provide certified registration lists, polling places, ballots, officials, and all other necessary equipment, material, and personnel.

c. To create, authorize, supervise, and coordinate committees for specialized activities or services.

d. To issue, renew, and, if necessary, revoke organization charters; and to promote and coordinate organization activities.[1]

[1] Many constitutions list and briefly describe the responsibilities of the more permanent committees such as assembly, clubs, publications, athletics, and finance, in separate articles or as separate sections under a main article headed "Committees." Provision is made, of course, for the appointment and discharge of such other committees as may be necessary. Often this latter provision is entitled "Temporary Committees" and the former, "Standing Committees."

e. To initiate and approve necessary legislation.

f. To encourage and limit participation in extracurricular activities by means of a point system.

g. To develop and establish sound centralized financial policies and procedures.

h. To establish and enforce regulations for assembly, study hall, corridors, cafeteria, school grounds, social events, and public functions.

i. To consider, upon being properly petitioned, policies, activities, and changes recommended by students and teachers.

j. To appoint necessary officers or committees to interpret the various provisions of the constitution.

k. To develop and administer a system of awards.

l. To promote respect for school and private property.

m. To authorize, sponsor, and supervise drives and campaigns.

n. To appoint survey and investigation officers and committees.

o. To provide for referendum and recall elections.

p. To pass such emergency measures as may be necessary.

q. To recommend to the attention of the faculty and administration matters which are outside its own area.

r. To investigate and report on matters especially referred to it by the faculty and administration.

s. To originate and formulate any policies in the area of student activities which will make for more wholesome school citizenship.

t. To give school and community publicity to the council's policies and activities.

The main advantage of including a list of specialized powers can be easily seen. These responsibilities will have to be defined at some time or other anyway, and deciding upon them beforehand and including them in the constitution will mean fewer conflicts and misunderstandings than if they were developed after the constitution was adopted. Such specifications will also help to clarify the status and function of the council in the minds of all concerned.

Organization

Plans of participation vary widely and consequently their constitutions show a great variety of elements and structure. This is particularly true of the article on organization. For instance, some constitutions include the requirements for membership in the council, others do not; some show only the organization of the council, not that of the student body; some include discussions of the officers and committees, while others list these in separate articles; and there are numerous other variations. Perhaps, in general, this matter of what should be included under "organization" is not of really great significance, provided that the important elements are included somewhere in the instrument. However, it is logical that this article should include at least three sections, (1) organization of the entire student body, (2) qualifications for council membership, and (3) general organization of the council itself. A brief explanation will indicate the material of these three sections.

1. *Organization of the Entire School.*—This should state the basis of representation, the groups, classes, clubs, activities, wards, home rooms, etc., from which council members are elected.

2. *Qualifications for Council Membership.*—This section indicates who may be elected and under what conditions. If limitations are imposed, these should be described. Even if there are no restrictions on council membership, this section should be included.

3. *General Organization of the Council.*—This refers to the major divisions such as houses, sections, bodies, courts, boards, subcouncils, etc., their membership, responsibilities, and relationships.

If this article on organization is not too long or complicated it may include discussions of the officers and committees, appointment, membership, terms, and duties. If this article is rather long and complicated, or if this inclusion would make it so, the discussion of officers and committees should be provided in separate articles. On the whole, this second plan is preferable anyway because it simplifies the form of the constitution.

Officers

In some constitutions, the list of officers and committees and the details of their qualifications, election, terms, and duties are included in the article on "Organization." However, in nearly all instruments this material constitutes a separate article (sometimes in the bylaws) and, as suggested above, this is probably a better plan. The article should include information on the following topics:

1. Title or designation of the officers
2. Tenure or term of office and reelection
3. Eligibility for officeholding
4. Procedures of nomination and election
5. Vacancies
6. Recall procedure
7. Duties and responsibilities

Very often topics 1 and 7 are combined, the duties and responsibilities being listed immediately following the naming of the officers. In general, this represents good form.

Committees

This article can follow the outline suggested above for officers. It should not only reflect standing committees but also include a section providing for the creation and authorization of such temporary committees as may be necessary.

Bylaws

Most constitutions include a section on bylaws, and these will be discussed later. Often, the constitution grants the central body the right to develop and adopt such bylaws and rules of order as may be necessary for the conduct of its business. A statement that such bylaws shall not in any way conflict with the provisions of the constitution might well be included in such an article of authorization.

Ratification

Very few of the constitutions examined include an article on ratification. While it may not be necessary from a practical point of view, such ratification is necessary from a technical point of view. Where not included it is, of course, assumed that a majority vote ratifies the constitution. If such an article is included it should definitely state (1) the ratifying source or sources of authority, (2) the proportion of votes necessary, (3) the necessity for a special election for this purpose, and (4) the time when the constitution becomes operative. It may well include, in addition, a statement to the effect that the constitution should be placed in the hands of the voters far enough ahead of the election to allow time for study and discussion. Incidentally, a unanimous vote of approval is never required because in such an instance one individual could prevent ratification. The following articles on ratification illustrate these points, or the lack of them:

> This constitution shall become effective upon ratification by the faculty committee on student affairs, and approval by the principal.

This article makes no provision for a student vote, hence the plan represented is not democratic. If the faculty member of the council is elected by this group, as he should be, provision for a faculty ratification vote should also be included.

> This constitution shall become effective when ratified by the student council and approved by the principal and faculty.

This article is indefinite because it does not specify what vote is required of the council and faculty for ratification. Further, it makes no provision for a vote by the student body.

> This constitution shall become operative immediately after having been approved by a majority of the members of the council and the principal, and ratified by a two-thirds majority of the faculty and the general student body voting in a special election called for this purpose.

This article is satisfactory because it includes the necessary elements, except that concerning time for study of the proposed constitution, which is less important than the others, and because it places the procedures in the proper order.

VETO

The principal's power of veto should be included as a main article of the constitution or a clearly indicated section of such an article. The following three articles were taken from student-association constitutions. A brief comment about each will help to indicate the requirements of a justifiable statement.

> Since the principal and the faculty are directly responsible to the superintendent and the board of education for the welfare of the school, it is expressly understood that all student powers herein set forth are delegated by the principal and the faculty and may be revoked at any time.

This statement is not exactly a veto clause, although it is so designated, because it refers to the powers of the council rather than to any of its decisions or proposed measures.

The expression "may be revoked at any time" is harsh and discouraging.

> Any regulation passed by the council concerning the junior or senior high school may be vetoed by the principal with the option of making a counterproposal or giving a satisfactory explanation to the council.

The first clause of this statement is quite satisfactory, but the second, beginning "with the option" is entirely inappropriate. As stated, this means that the principal is required to either make a counterproposal or satisfactorily explain his veto in person to the council. Neither of these demands is reasonable because the council can legally and morally demand nothing from the principal. We also wonder what would be the result if the principal were to neglect or refuse to make a counterproposal or appear personally and explain his veto to the council's satisfaction. What would a "satisfactory explanation" be? Who would enforce this enactment, and how? The impression given is entirely out of keeping with the spirit of the participation idea.

> Since the powers of the student council are delegated to it by the principal, he shall have the right of veto over any measure which the student council proposes.

This is a good statement; short, clear, and to the point.

Amendments

No constitution can ever be considered a perfect and completely final instrument, so provisions must be made for officially amending it. These provisions must be included in the constitution or, technically speaking, it is not amendable. A good general policy is that amendments should be rather difficult to make, but not impossible. Here again, an examination of constitutions will reveal a great deal of looseness. In fact, very few of the constitutions studied incorporated good amending articles, and some of them did not include this important element at all. A critical examination of a few of these articles will help to indicate the proper content and form.

> A petition for an amendment to the constitution may be presented to the student council after having been signed by two-thirds of the student body.

This article is weak because it does not (1) specify who shall vote on the amendment, and (2) indicate in what way the amendment shall be made. It can be assumed that the council makes the amendment by a majority vote, which would be wrong unless the council adopted or ratified the constitution originally, but these details are not set forth. In other words, in this article there are no provisions for amending the constitution, hence this constitution cannot be amended.

> This constitution may be amended by a three-fourths vote of the members.

Members of what? The student council? The student body? The faculty? What kind of a vote? This constitution can really be amended by three-fourths of the members voting "No."

> This constitution may be amended if the amendment is passed by a unanimous vote of the council, approval of the principal, and has been approved by all the home rooms.

Why a unanimous vote of the council? One member, for any reason whatever, can outvote the entire school. Further, this article represents very poor expression.

> Amendments to the constitution or bylaws may originate in the executive council, legislature, or associates (student body) and shall be ratified by a three-fourths vote of the legislature,

> the executive council, and the approval of the Honorary President.

This article has the good point of indicating the possible sources of amendments but does not indicate the proper procedure nor provide for a student vote. Its main weakness is the requirement for the approval of the "Honorary President," a student. There is no reason why any one member of the central body should be allowed to block the proposed amendment. Even if this provision were included, there should be another providing for passing the amendment over his veto.

> Whenever one-third of the student body shall propose an amendment it shall be brought before the student council for ratification. A majority vote of the council is necessary for the ratification of the amendment.

This procedure is in reverse. The student body, not the council, should ratify the amendment, after it has been approved by the council. Further, one-third of the student body is not a sufficiently large proportion; ratification should require at least a majority vote.

> This constitution may be altered or amended by two-thirds vote of the members of the Student Association present at any lawful meeting of this Association, provided that such notice shall be given at least one week in advance of the time such amendment will be voted upon, and that such amendment shall have been previously approved by two-thirds vote of the council.

This is, in general, a good article, although it does omit the source of amendments and the principal's approval.

> Amendments to this constitution may be made, upon a signed petition of 10 per cent of the registered voters of the Association, by a two-thirds vote of the council, followed by the approval of

the principal, and the ratification by a majority of the home rooms.

This is the best of the articles presented. It includes all the necessary elements in proper order, and is concisely stated.

Summary.—An article of amendment should include the following items:

1. *Source of the Proposed Amendment.*—This may be any individual or group in the school upon the basis of some specified number or proportion of school citizens, say 10 per cent.

2. *Approval by the Council.*—This should probably be only a majority.

3. *Approval by the Principal.*—This may be unnecessary because of the article which delegates his authority to the council. However, because it helps to avoid misunderstandings and gets the principal's viewpoint before the trouble is taken to hold an election, it represents a wise procedure.

4. *Ratification by the Student Body.*—The council should have no more right to amend the constitution that it has to adopt it originally. This is a prerogative of the school as a whole. The voting should not come until at least a week has elapsed after the amendment has been made available for study and discussion.

5. *Effective Date of Amendment.*—The time at which the proposed amendment becomes effective should be indicated. Usually, an amendment becomes operative immediately, but not always.

Because an amendment is a part of the constitution, it, together with the date of its ratification, but not the numerical result of the vote, should be appended to and included in all subsequently issued copies of this instrument. Proposed but defeated amendments should not be so appended, although several such were found in the constitutions examined. Records of defeated amendments should, of course, be made in the minutes of the secretary of the council.

BYLAWS

The constitution must (1) establish the necessary bylaws, or (2) authorize the council to establish these, or (3) do both. This last procedure is the most common. Even where a council has as yet not been organized or elected there is in essence a council—the group which is sponsoring the development of the constitution—and this group is in position to decide, to some extent at least, upon the bylaws which should govern the ultimate council's deliberations and actions. The most important elements of bylaws are those indicated below.

Quorum

A quorum is a stated proportion of the council members who must be present before business can be officially transacted. Usually this proportion is "a majority" of the membership of the body, but often it is "two-thirds," and occasionally "three-fifths," or "three-fourths."

Meetings

The article on meetings should include the following items, although not all of these need be listed as separate sections of the article:

1. *Regularity and Frequency.*—These items are properly a part of the constitutional regulations which should be officially set by the student body, not by the council.

2. *Time and Place of Meeting.*—These items are not definitely specified in the constitution; it merely authorizes the council to set a time and designate a place which will be convenient for all council members.

3. *Continued Meetings.*—If, for lack of time, the topic under discussion has not been completely disposed of, the presiding officer may call a continued meeting for the following period,

some other period, or even some other day at which time the business is resumed.

4. *Special Meetings.*—The council through its presiding officer is authorized to call special meetings whenever necessary.

5. *Postponed and Canceled Meetings.*—The council, but more usually the president, is authorized to postpone or cancel meetings in the absence of a quorum or for other good reasons.

Election of Officers

In most instances, and especially where the council elects its own officers, the procedures of nomination and election are specified in the bylaws. Where these officers are elected by the school at large, these procedures are indicated either in the constitution or in the bylaws.

Order of Business

The order in which the various items of business are considered may be established by the "rules of order" adopted, or it may be set by the council itself. Usually, this order of business is somewhat as follows:

1. Call to order
2. Roll call
3. Reading and approval of minutes
4. Receipt of communications, bills, etc.
5. Report of standing committees
6. Report of special committees
7. Old business
8. New business
9. Adjournment

Rules of Order

A business meeting must follow established parliamentary procedures and the authority for these rules of order should be specified. A simple statement, such as "The meetings of the council shall be conducted in accordance with Roberts' Rules of Order," is all that is necessary. Often a parliamentarian is appointed to straighten out confusions and difficulties which may arise in the conduct of the meeting.

Voting Procedure

The method of voting, whether by secret ballot or by open ballot, show of hands or acclamation, should be indicated. This method may vary with the type of business being conducted; secret balloting is usually used in elections and open balloting in the handling of ordinary business meeting affairs. A roll-call vote in which the record of each member's vote goes into the minutes, which may later be read to the home rooms or other groups, enables the constituents to know how their representatives represented them. But the form or forms should be indicated, or authority given the council to establish these as it sees fit.

Reports

There are several different kinds of reports, such as those made to the council, to the principal, faculty, student body, and to other individuals and groups. The bylaws usually authorize a demand for these reports, often specifying the necessary details of form, time, and place.

Fees, Dues, and Assessments

Where fees, dues, and assessments are required or authorized, the details of amounts, procedure of collection, handling, etc., are usually set forth in the bylaws.

Insignia

In schools in which official insignia are worn by the members of the council, the specifications of these (type, size, shape, color, material, etc.), as well as the methods of wearing them and the occasions upon which they may be properly worn, should be indicated in the constitution or the bylaws. The matter of insignia for special committees or groups of the council, such as traffic police, should be decided by the council itself on the basis of an article or section authorizing them.

Amendments

Bylaws are not made once and for all; they must be changed as new occasions and demands arise. Hence, there must be provision made for amending them. As suggested in connection with the constitution, they cannot be legally amended unless a provision for amending them has been formally adopted, either by the council or by the student body, depending upon the form of the constitution.

Selected References

Brogue, E. B., and P. B. Jacobson: "Student-council Handbook," pp. 41–65, National Association of Secondary School Principals, March, 1940.

Castell, S.: A Study of Constitutions of Pupil Government Organizations in High Schools, *Bulletin* 24, January, 1929, pp. 153–155, National Association of Secondary School Principals.

Ramey, G. V.: A School Constitution as a School Activity, *School Activities*, 11: 204–205, January, 1940.

Chapter VII

Nomination and Election Procedures

AN ORGANIZATION is no better than its officers. It may be based upon the finest of ideals, be structurally sound, and have an excellent program of activities, and still be a miserable failure because its leaders are incompetent. In a way, an organization is like an automobile; it is useless or worse than useless unless and until it is driven competently by a good driver. This is as true in the case of student participation in control as it is in the case of any other form of organized effort. Therefore the election of able and capable representatives and officers is one of the most important problems of participation.

In this connection it must be remembered that the main objective of the student council plan is not merely to get things done, but to get things done with maximum educational benefits for all concerned. Similarly, the main objective of an election is not merely to put good leaders into office, but to put good leaders into office with maximum educational benefits for all concerned, both electors and electees. The individual who votes blindly or with no serious thought about his own responsibility profits, educationally, but little, while the voter who gives careful consideration to the qualifications of candidates, works conscientiously, and faithfully accepts his own responsibility receives educational benefits well worth the efforts involved.

Elections Committee.—A school election involves numerous and varied elements—ideals, ideas, materials, and procedures—and in any except the smaller schools it should probably be put in the hands of a committee or board which specializes in this phase of participation activity. This non-political group, composed of council members, or council members and a few competent students from the school at large, is responsible only to the council. It develops plans which will reflect the activities suggested in the following pages and, after obtaining official sanction for its program, proceeds to organize and supervise election procedures.[1]

Formal vs. Informal Procedures.—The methods of nominating and electing council members and officers vary all the way from a simple "stand up and nominate" or "raise your hands and vote" procedure to a highly organized system, imitative of the corresponding adult-life events and processes. Which type of procedure is preferable, the formal or the informal? The answer to this question will depend upon the local setting, including the size of school, organization of units, age of students, the participation plan's structure, traditions, and the faculty's evaluation of the educational opportunities involved.

There are those who believe that the closer the resemblance of school to adult-life procedure the more realistic, important, and valuable the event becomes. On the other hand, there are those who point out the shallowness and cheapness of some of the elements of adult-life political campaigns, the disorganizing effect they may have on the school, the "emotional debauches" they tend to produce, and the excessive cost in time and effort.

Here again, the determining factor in the selection of an election procedure should be a discriminating evaluation of the educational opportunities it represents. It is probable that, in most instances, the use of either the formal or the informal plan would result in the election of about the same group of

[1] A discussion of the methods of election, restrictions on candidacy, time of election, and term of office, will be found in Chaps. III and VIII.

council members and officers. Hence, the main point at issue is to determine which of these plans has the more to commend it from an educational point of view.

The formal plan appears to be more desirable. It gives dignity and weight to the event, brings vital interest, has a strong emotional appeal, and is realistic enough to be functional as preparation for later adult activities. Naturally, it should not be allowed to degenerate into a maudlin and boisterous affair which results in the detrimental effects which its antagonists fear or prophesy, and keeping it on a high plane is not at all impossible.

The main purpose of this chapter is to suggest the practices which will help to keep an election on a high plane. For the most part it will concern the election of officers by the school, instead of the election of officers by the home rooms or other smaller units. However, most of the procedures suggested are equally applicable to these smaller settings.

Nominations.—Candidates may be nominated in three ways, from the floor, by a committee, or by petition.[1] A brief discussion of each of these will indicate its suitability for the school situation.

Nomination from the Floor.—This is the simplest and most direct method of making nominations. The chairman merely indicates the office to be filled and calls for nominations, and anyone in the group may nominate any other member, or even himself. Depending upon the importance of the event and the time available, this form of nomination may range all the way from a simple statement to a short address in which the speaker gives the reasons for his nomination. Although it is a common practice to second a nomination, this procedure does not follow good parliamentary usage. A second is not necessary. An individual nominated immedi-

[1] A fourth possibility, by the faculty, is not included because it violates the basic principle of the student participation idea.

ately becomes a candidate. A nominee can, of course, ask that his name be withdrawn, and it probably will be if he so desires it, but this request does not necessarily eliminate him as a candidate. Such a request will in all probability reduce his vote, maybe even to zero, but on the other hand, it is entirely possible for him to be nominated despite his request. Such nomination is, of course, undesirable.

This plan has several serious faults: (1) it usually allows little opportunity for a discriminating evaluation of the potential nominees; (2) temporary emotional reactions due to some recent event, such as a touchdown at a football game, may outweigh intellectual considerations; (3) it allows for little in the way of organized efforts in behalf of potential nominees; (4) often too many candidates are nominated, confusion results, and an extra election, a primary, must be held in order to reduce the field; (5) frequently, if no primary is held to reduce the number of candidates, the less worthy ones are nominated because of a split vote; (6) occasionally, even, some smart aleck nominates a student who is completely undesirable and incompetent, thus cheapening the event and embarrassing the nominee; and (7) such nominations may be unduly influenced by friendly relationships and the desire to maintain them; such a nomination is, of course, not secret. In short, except probably in very small and informal groups, the use of this plan of making nominations is hardly justifiable. About the most illogical use of it imaginable is in the general school assembly.

A variation of this plan is the informal ballot in which each member of the group writes the name of his candidate on a slip of paper. These slips are then collected and the names are posted by the secretary. In this system all the names, not merely those with the greatest number of votes, are posted, and all these students become candidates. If desired, the group may vote again upon the basis of these names and so nominate its candidate or candidates. This has the advantage of secrecy, but it has several of the disadvantages mentioned above and, in addition, it is a time-consuming procedure.

Nomination by Committee.—In this plan a central nominating committee, composed of properly appointed or elected representatives, makes a slate of candidates, often naming two candidates for each office. The advantages of this plan are (1) it represents a variety of interests and contacts; (2) it centers attention on a serious study of potential candidates' qualifications; (3) it limits voting so that there is little possibility of some less desirable candidate "slipping in"; and (4) it is not necessarily restrictive or exclusive; usually it provides for the nomination of additional candidates if individuals or constituencies so desire. A possible disadvantage is that it limits participation in nominating procedure to relatively few students.

Nomination by Petition.—In this plan a formal authorized petition is made up and passed around among the voters. The proper number or percentage of the voters who must sign it before it can be officially considered is usually set by the constitution. Generally, the larger the unit represented in the election the greater the number of petitioners required. The main advantages of this plan are that (1) it is democratic —any bona fide member of the school may, upon being properly petitioned, become a candidate for an office; and (2) it gives some little actual experience with a procedure very common in adult elections. The possible disadvantage that too many candidates may be nominated is made improbable by the requirement of a considerable number of signers.

Generally speaking, either of the last two methods of nominating is better than the first suggested, and either is quite satisfactory for the school election. Sometimes there is a combination of these two, provision being made for the nomination of candidates in addition to those named by the committee. There is nothing wrong with this procedure. It provides for competent group choices and also for consideration of any other individual the group may have overlooked, or, because of the limitation on the number which it could suggest, was unable to name.

Commonly Made Parliamentary Errors.—In order to clarify nominating and electing procedures, it is pertinent to consider a very few commonly made parliamentary mistakes.

1. *Accepting the Report of the Nominating Committee and Declaring the Candidates Elected.*—Often, following the report of a nominating committee, some member will make a motion that the report of the nominating committee be accepted and, upon proper seconding and group approval, the chairman will declare the candidates elected. This procedure is wrong. This motion merely means that the individuals named in the report are accepted as candidates, and it means nothing more. They must still be voted upon. Too, the chairman should ask for any additional nominations before calling for a vote.

2. *Moving for a Unanimous Vote.*—In case there is only one candidate, a member may move that the president cast a unanimous or a one-vote ballot for this individual, thereby electing him. This is an incorrect procedure, and if the constitution specifies, as most constitutions do, that the vote must be taken by secret ballot, it is illegal. Although such an election may represent a mere formality, yet it is parliamentarily correct to vote for this one candidate in exactly the same manner as if there were more than one.

3. *Moving for a Unanimous Vote by the Defeated Candidate.*—Frequently, upon being defeated, a candidate moves that the vote be made unanimous in favor of the winner. Obviously, such a motion represents a fine attitude, but it is only a pretty gesture; it is not according to accepted parliamentary practice. Naturally, no candidate can give away the votes he did not cast. In fact, it is hardly possible for him to give away

even the vote he did cast. Nor is it necessary, because the winner has already been declared.

4. *Withdrawing from Candidacy and Giving Votes to Another Candidate.*—Sometimes, when there are not enough votes to elect any candidate, one nominee withdraws and turns his votes over to some other candidate, and so causes him to be elected. As suggested above, no candidate can give away the votes cast for him. In such an instance of an incompleted election, another election is necessary.

The Election Campaign.—The political campaign in school serves the same purposes as the corresponding political campaign in adult life. It (1) interests the voters and arouses enthusiasm; (2) educates the voters and clarifies political issues; and (3) mobilizes support for school improvement. The general form of the campaign will depend to a considerable extent upon the general form of the school's political organization, or lack of it. Nearly all major school campaigns run about a week or ten days.

In most of the smaller and medium-sized, and in many of the larger schools, there is no political party organization of school citizens. In other schools there are various forms of officially recognized political party organizations, always at least two. These parties go under such names as "People's Party," "Progressive Party," "Square Deal Party," and "Citizens' Party." Only rarely are they called "Republican" or "Democratic" parties. In a few schools each of the classes is organized as a separate party; thus, in a four-year school there would be four separate and distinct political parties.

In the party type of organization each group selects a campaign manager; nominates its own candidates, often through a special nominating convention; outlines a platform; makes speaking schedules for its candidates and workers; organizes for personal service; holds pep meetings; stages parades, snake dances, and bonfires; develops and distributes handbills, tags, dodgers, cards, posters, blotters, etc.; utilizes blackboard advertising; collects and spends money for campaign purposes (schools or councils usually limit the amount a party may raise and spend); and in other ways attempts to whip up enthusiasm for its candidates. In a nonpartisan school a number of these devices may similarly be utilized by the friends of the particular candidates, but usually less outright rivalry is developed. Which plan is preferable?

The arguments in favor of the party plan are quite evident; it (1) makes the election a real event in the life of the school; (2) tends to produce good political platforms and good candidates because of the intense competition it engenders; (3) provides an opportunity for wholehearted enjoyment and fun; (4) gives all participants some very realistic training and experience; and (5) is traditionally established.

The main disadvantages of this plan are: (1) the campaign may develop into a cheap, school-disorganizing debauch; (2) the party, not the school, receives major attention; (3) voting "a straight party ticket" will probably result in the nomination or election of some undesirable officers; (4) support of a party may unduly obligate that party; (5) the "good platform" argument mentioned above in number 2 is not too strong because both parties will usually, in essence, have about the same platforms; and (6) argument number 5, "it is traditionally established," is very weak.

The main argument in favor of the nonpartisan method of election is that the attention of the school will be centered only on the positions to be filled and the candidates' qualifications. The school will not be influenced by the name or prestige of a party or by showmanship. In this nonpartisan organization, the school, not the party, ranks first in importance. A second argument is that petty politics is far less likely to develop in this setting than it is where two or more organized bodies are competing for supremacy. The chief arguments against nonpartisan organization are that (1) it may not result in an exciting or thrilling school event, and (2) it is not realistic because it does not resemble adult campaigns. This last argument is not entirely true, because in many cities and some states there are nonpartisan elections.

The final answer to the relative values of these two plans will depend upon (1) the local setting, and (2) the extent to which the advantages of each plan are enhanced and the disadvantages are minimized. Specifically, this means that in the party plan the school must loom over the party in importance and the campaigns must be dignified. In the nonpartisan plan, the election must be so organized and promoted that it becomes an event of prime importance in the life of the school.

Campaign Speeches.—Speeches are as much a part of an organized political campaign as the ballots themselves. Making such an address requires the candidate to think through the possibilities of school improvement and also gives the audience an opportunity to evaluate him as a candidate. It is not always true that a fine speaker makes a fine organizer and administrator, or that a poor speaker makes a poor organizer and administrator; the reverse of these propositions may often be true. However, in general, speaking ability is required of presiding officers because they must educate their constituencies, win support for their programs, and handle meetings satisfactorily. It is not so essential that secretaries and treasurers be effective speakers because their work requires less of this activity and more of specialized record and account keeping, responsibilities entirely different from those of the presiding officer.

A good campaign speech does at least four things: it (1) interests the listeners; (2) outlines the needs or opportunities for improvement; (3) suggests remedies or improvements; and (4) obligates the speaker to provide these remedies or support these improvements. Such an address should be skillful in expression and convincing in argument. It should be dignified, specific, and short, instead of cheap, general, and long. It should concern vital topics, and it should be sincerely made. Typical "political oratory" with its mud-slinging, smearing, and excessive criticizing should be taboo. The address should not contain ridicule because, even though it may be interesting or humorous in a sordid sort of way, it can be "sunk" by a single sentence: "My opponent uses ridicule, and this is proof that he has no good arguments of his own." In short, the emphasis should be constructive about a candidate instead of destructive about his opponent.

There are a number of settings about the school in which campaign speeches may be made, such as in the assembly, in broadcast form, in the home rooms and corridors, and out of doors. A brief word about these will show their relative suitability.

Assuming that the speeches are to be made to the entire school, the assembly is the best of all the settings indicated. The situation is natural because the auditorium is designed for purposes of public presentation; therefore it tends to guarantee an interested and attentive audience. It offers opportunity for the voters to see as well as hear and it provides fair and equal chances for all speakers. It also tends to guarantee extra efforts from the candidates. If the school is large, several of these programs may be scheduled.

In order to give all candidates a fair opportunity to make their presentations, the chairman of the assembly program should announce and enforce, if necessary, two rules of courtesy: (1) no applauding during an address, and (2) no booing or other boisterous conduct. If campaign placards and signs are used these should not be taken into the assembly because they not only hinder hearing and seeing but often lead to downright disturbance. If left outside or at the rear of the auditorium they should be stacked according to party and each stack be guarded by some of the members of that group.[1]

A broadcast from the central office is not nearly so good as speaking in the assembly because the setting is cold, formal, and unreal; it is unappealing alike to both speaker and audience because neither can see the other. Usually, it does have the advantage of requiring the speakers to prepare carefully composed speeches, from an expression point of view, because it allows these addresses to be written out and read. Even this advantage may not be worth while, because only in rare instances later will the elected officer follow such a procedure in addressing a school group.

The home room as the setting for political addresses has the advantage of being a small group and allowing for questioning and discussion, but it lacks the audience atmosphere a larger group would have. The number of home rooms in the average school would necessitate a rather strenuous speaking schedule for the candidates, and in the case of the large school, this schedule would be impossible. Of course, using substitute speakers represents a weak technique.

About the poorest setting for campaign speeches is the school corridor. This picture is far too common in American schools: a candidate will climb onto a box or chair or stand on the stairs and begin to speak with the hope of drawing listeners around him. Obviously, owing to lack of complete attention, hallway traffic, acoustic difficulties, and the interruptions and wise-cracking that are certain to come, speaking

[1] In one school's plan which has had a bit of publicity, the auditorium is darkened and on the stage each candidate is spotlighted while his autobiography is being read by another student. Such a plan may be novel and interesting but it is probably valueless or worse as a candidate-judging opportunity because it embarrasses the student, distracts attention from competency, and overemphasizes the dramatic.

in this setting is ineffectual. In fact, the school should not even allow it, because it represents a "soapbox" type of political oratory that will cheapen the whole event.

Outside of school settings, such as on the lawn, on the sidewalk, or around the front steps, are similarly not conducive either to good listening or good speaking. They do not offer fair opportunities to anyone concerned. They, too, should be ruled out of the school's campaign.

Election Officials.—A formal election requires a number of different officials such as those suggested below. In some schools, because of size, organization, or procedure, not all of these may be needed, and some of them may be combined. However, this list will suggest the possibilities.

Doorkeeper.—Prevents the admission of any student who is not properly qualified to enter the polling place. Enforces the rule against loitering, electioneering, or "party watching."

Clerk.—Checks the voter's name on the registration list, or writes his name on a list, and hands him a ballot. Or, if desirable, two clerks may be used, one to attend to registration and the other to initial and hand out the ballots.

Ballot Box Guard.—Presides at the ballot box and sees that each voter drops in his own ballot.

Judge.—Settles any difficulties or challenges that may arise. Often is in charge of the polling place.

Page.—Where each room votes as a group according to a time schedule, this official goes to the room and leads its members to the polling place at the proper time.

These officials, or members from the central elections committee, examine the ballot box before the voting and then lock it. Sealing is not necessary if a lock is provided. After the polls are closed the judge and clerk take the box to the central committee, or, if this plan is used, open it at the polling place, count the votes, prepare the necessary report or tally sheet, sign it, and take it to the committee. In order that there will be no confusion, election officials usually vote first. All officials are, of course, formally sworn in.

Instruction of Election Officials.—Before any election the officials in direct charge of the polling place should be properly instructed in their duties. In case of emergency, or where the polls are open for a considerable period of time, it may be necessary for the judge to reassign responsibilities. Each member of the group, therefore, should be familiarized with the duties of every other member. One good method, after the group has examined the forms, ballot box, sample ballots, and other materials and equipment used, is to hold a rehearsal of the event, each official not only performing in turn the duties of the other officials, but also voting. A most important part of this instructional program is an emphasis upon the seriousness of the occasion. It is easy to see how a little unintentional looseness or a bit of boisterousness or horseplay can vitiate the event. A similar explanation and demonstration to the entire student body will be found helpful.

Election Materials and Equipment.—All election materials and equipment, ballot boxes, registration lists, ballots, forms, "Polls Open" and "Polls Closed" and other signs, should be kept by the central committee, and be issued before and collected after each election. A careful inventory following each event will help to ensure that these items are available for the next election. It is a good plan for the committee to keep a few copies of the ballots, voting instructions, and other forms for use in planning a later event. Further, as suggested at the end of the chapter, a critical examination or evaluation of the election should be made and filed for future use.

Ballot Box.—The use of a regular ballot box will help to make the event more dignified and also prevent trouble due to loose handling of ballots. Probably nothing detracts from the proper appeal of actual voting so much as the use of some hurriedly prepared cigar box, shoe box, wastebasket, or paper sack for a ballot box. A tight, attractively stained or painted wooden box, with a slotted and hinged top, and equipped with a small hasp, staple, and padlock, can be easily made in the school shop or by some of the boys at home. A metal handle at the top or, in the case of a larger box, a handle at each end, will make for convenience in transportation. Rodded glass windows, often found in adult boxes, are not necessary. Such a box can be used time and again, and it makes a nice piece of permanent election equipment.

Ballots.—A good ballot meets two specifications, simplicity and completeness. The ballots should be either mimeographed or printed, preferably printed. However, if mimeographed, they should be expertly prepared on white, not on yellow, paper. Sample ballots are sometimes mimeographed on yellow paper and distributed a day or two before the election. A mimeographed ballot which is defectively typed, smudged, poorly organized, or inaccurately cut, detracts from the significance of the event.

The ballot may be either "write-in" or "mark." In the former type the voter writes the name of the candidate on the proper blank; and in the latter he merely marks the box in front of the typed or printed name. In the latter case a blank is usually provided in which the voter may write the name of some other candidate. The "mark" type of ballot is preferable to the "write-in" type; and it is just as easy to prepare.

The ballot should clearly indicate the number of candidates to be voted for. It should be small and convenient in size. It should not include the school biography of the various candidates. Requiring that pen and ink, instead of pencil, be used is unnecessary, confusing, and impracticable. Often an adult-election type of ballot is made with a perforated numbered corner or end to be torn off before the vote is cast. Explanation of such a ballot is, of course, necessary, as is also an alert clerk to ensure that the proper part is deposited in the box.

Generally, ballots are official only after they have been initialed by the proper election official at the time of voting. In the interest of a genuine "secret" vote, the ballots should be folded by the voter before being dropped into the ballot box. Folding the ballots before they are handed out will encourage the voters to fold them after they have been marked. After the votes have been counted the ballots should be returned to the box, locked up, and placed in some safe spot for a few days before being finally destroyed. Such a precaution may save trouble, or even another election, in case serious disputes, challenges, or other difficulties arise. Incidentally, a screen or simple booth does much to help make the voting "secret."

Registration of Voters.—The answer to the question, Should voters be registered? will probably depend upon (1) the size of the school and (2) the restrictions imposed upon voting. In a large school there must be a number of polling places and in order to expedite voting, and also prevent voters from "repeating" at another polling place, such registration lists are probably necessary. Even in a small school a record should be kept of those voting so that there will be no repeating, and checking off a name on a registration list is simpler and faster than writing down the voter's name. If there are restrictions, such as tax receipts, voting permits, polling place assignments, or residence requirements,[1] registration lists are necessary in order to prevent those who do not qualify from voting.

Instructions to Voters.—If an election is to be orderly and systematic it must follow certain regulations or procedures, and the voter must be familiarized with these. A good plan

[1] In many schools, voting in the general election is denied to entering students on the theory that they are too unfamiliar with the school to vote intelligently.

is for the committee in charge of the election to develop a simple set of "Instructions to Voters," mimeograph or print this sheet, and send it to the home rooms for posting, distribution, and study. In small schools these instructions may be written on the blackboard or posted on the bulletin board. In whatever way offered, they should be complete, simple, and clear. They should include such information as the following.

Event.—Name, purpose, or other designation of the election.

Date.—This should include the day as well as the date.

Who May Vote.—Any restrictions on voting should be stated.

Time of Voting.—The hours at which the polls are open. If a "school period" is used, the corresponding clock time should also be indicated.

Place of Voting.—In larger schools there may be several polling places and not only these should be indicated, but also the voters (rooms, floors, grades, etc.) who may use each. If special arrangements for group passing and voting are necessary, these will be described.

Method of Voting.—This section briefly describes or pictures a sample ballot and indicates how it is to be used, covering such items as number of candidates to be voted for, writing in or marking the names, folding, secrecy (no signatures on the ballot), and depositing it in the ballot box. In the case of voting by groups, the necessary directions concerning entering, seating, voting, and leaving the room will be included.

Other Material.—Often the set of instructions to voters includes some such appeal as this:

> Consider very carefully the qualifications of the candidates. Remember that you are voting for a leader of the student body who, if elected, will serve for an entire year. Such a leader should be a student who can preside at council meetings with poise and dignity, well represent your school in interschool

affairs, and be successful in helping to organize and supervise your program of activities. Make sure that you vote for such a person.

Some of these instruction sheets go even farther and not only list the names of the candidates but also give a brief résumé of their school life, including class, offices held, honors, and achievements. Unless marks are a recognized restriction on office holding, they should not be included. Such records should be entirely factual and should include no recommendations, opinions, or other comments. Nor should they reflect out-of-school interests or activities. These names should be listed alphabetically.

Often these instructions include a statement to the effect that electioneering or loitering around the polls will not be permitted. This rule includes "party watchers" and workers. Under certain conditions, making, publicizing, and enforcing such a rule might be very well worth while.

Probably, in order to forestall questions and to avoid misunderstandings, the subject of absentee voting should be mentioned. Although in adult elections provision is often made for such voting, in the school election it is unwise because of the necessary confusion it brings, and also because only rarely would this absentee vote be large enough to make any significant difference in the final result.

Setting Standards for Officers and Representatives.—Perhaps, in general, it may not be necessary for the central committee to suggest the qualifications required for the successful discharge of the duties of the various officers. These qualifications, especially in the case of organized campaigns, are quite likely to emerge from the public discussions of the various candidates. If the group is relatively small, however, or if there is no intense rivalry between parties and constituencies, it may be well for the committee to develop such a set of standards and distribute it to the various rooms for discussion. Perhaps a better plan is for each group, through wisely led informal discussion, to develop its own set.

Sometimes, as a part of an appropriate assembly program, each candidate is given a sort of "quiz-test" or "examination" by the use of such questions as, "What would you do in this situation?" or "What do you believe should be done here?" Perhaps there is some logic in this plan. However, there are good arguments against it: (1) assuming that there are two candidates, it is quite likely that both of them would react in about the same way; (2) the individual who is asked second, if he had about the same general ideas in mind, would be handicapped because about all he could say would be a weak, "I'd do the same thing"; (3) maybe, on the other hand the second speaker would have the advantages, if he were asked the same question, of having more time in which to consider his answer, and also some definite ideas to talk about, ideas which might not necessarily be his own; (4) in all probability the points so considered would have been already covered by the candidates in their campaign addresses.

It follows therefore that, if this plan is used, the possible advantages and disadvantages to each candidate should be averaged by the use of quite a number of questions or problems, each candidate being allowed some "all his own." Varying the order of first and second answerer would also tend to make the examination equally fair. However, on the whole, this competitive type of campaign "address" represents more disadvantages than advantages.

The use of a written examination or demonstration of ability, or both, may be justified in the selection of officers for certain types of positions which require more or less technical knowledge or skill such as, for instance, traffic police, office assistants, or projector or radio operators. Of course the final rating depends also upon an appraisal of the candidates' character and personal qualifications, preferably by teachers who are most competent to make them.[1]

Vacancies.—Where the council elects its own officers, and a vacancy occurs in an office of this group, it is filled immediately by this body. Often vacancies in council membership, and in offices to which the school as a whole elects, are filled by appointment until the time of the next regular election. This is the usual practice where tenure is for one semester only or where the time remaining in the tenure is short. Such appointment is preferable to leaving the vacancy unfilled. In case of terms running the entire year, vacancies should be filled by special election as soon as practicable. This special election should follow the same general procedures as the regular event. Even in case of council membership where the vacancy concerns only the group to be represented, the election should be authorized and supervised by the council or its elections committee.

Recall.—Because a recall is really an election in reverse, it follows about the same procedure as a special election and this procedure will vary according to the organization of the particular plan, whether it is by the entire school or by some particular group of the school. Recall begins with a formal petition, containing the signatures of a rather considerable proportion of the membership of the group—usually one-fourth or one-third—to the council. Although the council recognizes the right of the group desiring the recall to name its own representatives, yet it has a perfect right to investigate the reasons for this petition and, if it appears to be for the best interests of the school, to deny it. If the council approves the petition, it authorizes, organizes, and supervises the election. Very often more than a simple majority of the votes cast, two-thirds or three-fourths, is required to recall a representa-

[1] Note that this appraisal plan concerns only a civil service type of selection. Its use is not justifiable in a popular election.

tive or officer. A recall does not fill a vacancy; it merely removes the individual from office. The resulting vacancy is then filled later by a special election.

Evaluation of an Election.—Because, in all probability, there will be few elections in which everything will have gone off as smoothly as planned, it is a good policy for the central committee to make and file away a written evaluation of each one. This appraisal will answer in detail such questions as, Where was this election weak? Where was it strong? What are the reasons for these weaknesses and strengths? Specifically, in what ways may the next election be made more satisfactory?

Quite naturally, such an evaluation will probably always be made informally through general discussion, but it will be much more valuable if it is prepared in definite form because the personnel of the student body, election units, committees, and groups may have changed considerably by the time of the next event. Further, if this appraisal is not made immediately in permanent form, much of it may be lost by the time it becomes necessary to plan for another election.

Selected References

Dennison, H. A.: Student Government Elections, *School Activities*, 13: 361, May, 1942.

Hansen, T.: Fool Proof Elections, *School Activities*, 13: 342, 359, May, 1942.

Harder, A.: Wise Selection of High School Officers, *School Activities*, 15: 60, October, 1943.

Nesbit, A.: A Better Citizenship Organization, *School Activities*, 7: 8–9, September, 1935.

Student Elections, *High School Journal*, 24: 346–351, December, 1941.

Terry, P. W.: "Supervising Extra-curricular Activities," Chap. VII, McGraw-Hill Book Company, Inc., New York, 1930.

Chapter VIII

Internal Organization of the Council

THE objective of the participation idea is not mere participation—in an unorganized mob there is participation—but a systematized, effective, and wholesome participation, and this involves the discovery, capitalization, and coordination of pertinent interests and abilities. This is true not only in the area of the entire school organization but also in the area of the council, and, in turn, in the smaller areas represented by the elements of this body, its committees, boards, and departments, each of which is a group of leaders organized around leaders. In a council, then, there are leader-individuals, usually called officers, and leader-groups, commonly designated committees.

OFFICERS

The basic officers of a council are president, vice-president, secretary, and treasurer. In certain types of participation plans these officers go under other names or titles, but the duties are easily classifiable as those represented by the officers listed above. Sometimes a plan is used in which there are several vice-presidents, each of whom automatically becomes responsible for some particular department or committee. Such minor officers as sergeant-at-arms, chaplain, reporter, usher, parliamentarian, doorkeeper, cheerleader, and songleader are also found. The responsibilities of these various officers will be discussed later in the chapter.

Election of Officers.—There are two main possibilities in the election of student council officers: (1) election by the student association, and (2) election by the council itself. Sometimes there is a combination of these two plans, the school electing the major, and the council the minor, officers.

The arguments in favor of the first method of election are that (1) this is the customary procedure in municipal, state, and federal elections, hence it will give vital and functional experience to the voters; (2) the school at large will become more interested in the participation plan; and (3) it can capitalize worthy ability which is not in the council. The chief arguments against it are that (1) there is a danger that mere popularity will determine the outcome of an election; (2) it may result in officer-council friction similar to that often found in governor-legislature and president-congress relations; and (3) cheap and riotous campaigns may result. The main arguments in favor of the council electing its own officers are that (1) the council is in position to know and evaluate the various abilities represented in it; (2) there is less possibility of friction; and (3) it should logically have the right to elect those under whom it is to serve. Probably the first plan, election by the school, is preferable; at least it is being used by more schools than the second plan. But both have been, and are being, used successfully.

A few schools use a plan whereby the four main officers progress upward from the bottom, the treasurer only being elected each time. The following term this treasurer automatically becomes secretary, then vice-president, and finally at the beginning of the fourth term, president. This means, of course, that each officer is elected for four terms in a single election. The procedure is based upon an assumption that any individual can be equally efficient in all offices, an assumption that is held nowhere in adult life, and one that is as absurd in school life. In short, this plan has nothing to commend it. It is not based upon a consideration of competency.

Restrictions on Candidacy.—In an earlier section (pages 53–56) it was pointed out that the only justifiable restriction to membership in the council is the requirement that the student be passing in his academic work, and that high marks, sex, taxation, conduct records, and reelection should not be given consideration. This policy is as justifiable in the election of officers of the council as it is in the election of members to the council. In addition to these there are two other commonly imposed restrictions that must be examined.

The first of these restrictions is that certain officers shall be elected from certain groups; for instance, the president and vice-president shall be elected from the one or two upper classes of the school. This restriction is based upon two assumptions. The first is that students from these groups are more experienced in school affairs, more mature in judgment, will command more respect, and hence should make better leaders than those from the lower classes. This assumption may usually be correct, but not necessarily so; mere seniority does not guarantee these qualifications, nor does lack of seniority prohibit them. The second assumption is based upon a fear that because there are more students in the lower classes, these will dominate an election. This is another assumption which may possibly be true, provided the education of the electorate has not been undertaken, but not necessarily so. It is true that the officers will usually be elected from these two upper classes, but the author can see no logic in making such election mandatory. Certainly such limitation is not to be found in the democratic machinery of adulthood.

The second restriction is that not more than one council officer shall be named from any one group, the theory being that if more than one officer is elected such a situation would give that particular group too much attention or prestige, and further, that some of the groups might exert undue influence in order to achieve this distinction. In most plans this restriction is unnecessary because only one representative or officer is elected from each group. Even where it is possible, due to the practice of allowing more than one representative from each group, this restriction is of doubtful value. In actual practice two officers from the same group would rarely be elected. If they were, what difference would it make, provided they represented the best material for the offices? The purpose of an election is to get good officers; where they come from is a minor consideration.

Election Procedures.—The procedures, materials, and mechanics of elections have already been discussed in Chap. VII, and the discussion need not be repeated here. However, there is one undesirable practice which is to be found in some schools which should be mentioned and condemned. This is the practice of totaling the votes for the various candidates and then declaring the individual with the greatest number elected president, the individual with the second greatest number vice-president, etc. Some schools provide this plan for only the two top offices, but some follow it for all major offices. Such a procedure is unwise because it is based upon the false assumption that any individual can fit easily and successfully into any one of the four offices. Certainly the fact that one candidate for the presidency received the third highest total of votes does not qualify him for the position of secretary. Candidates should be considered candidates for particular offices. The student body must be taught to think in terms of specific abilities for all offices and to evaluate, nominate, and elect on the basis of these requirements and qualifications. Otherwise the election will be blind, and the school will be encouraging the development of blind voters.

Time of Election.—In nearly all plans of participation, whether the officers are chosen by the general student association or by the council itself, they are named at or near the beginning of the term or year, though usually not at the very beginning because this does not allow for a serious consideration of officer material. Increasingly, however, officers are being elected at or near the end of the semester or year, the purpose being to ensure an early start the following term or year, and to allow some little time in which the officers can be thinking about and planning their work. There is considerable merit in this second plan.

Term of Office.—The tenure of council officers varies widely from school to school, usually, but not always, depending upon the tenure of the representatives elected. In a few plans the officers are changed as frequently as once a month, and in others as infrequently as once in two or three years. The most commonly established tenures are one semester and two semesters or one year. Either of these is far more justifiable than any of the others to be found.

The advantages of one-semester tenure are that (1) it gives more opportunities for officer-electing and officeholding experience; (2) it adds to interest in the participation idea; and (3) in the case of incompetent officers, it allows for their early removal. The chief disadvantage of one-semester tenure is that it may break into a desirable continuity of policies and activities. If the program is to have balance, many of these policies and activities must be planned far in advance, beyond the limits of the present semester. A change in officers may mean drastic changes in them, and frequent changes of basic plans are usually both wasteful and uncomplimentary. Another possible disadvantage is the necessity for frequent elections. In systems in which the council elects its own officers this may not be a very serious matter because relatively little time is devoted to it.

Often, in cases in which the representatives are elected once a semester, which is probably desirable and may even be necessary where students enter the school at the beginning of each semester, the officers are elected in the fall for the entire year. In such instances these officers together with the reelected council members will tend to provide the continuity necessary.

Probationary Period.—A few schools have an arrangement whereby all officers upon election are considered probationary and are finally approved only after they have successfully demonstrated their ability in this try-out period. Although such a plan may tend to motivate office holding, it is hardly complimentary to either electors or electees. This, together with the difficulties of satisfactorily evaluating short term efforts, makes it impracticable.

Vacancies.—If a vacancy occurs in the roster of officers it should be filled by the same procedure which was originally used, election by the school or by the council. In case of necessity, the president may appoint some student to fill the office temporarily until the proper election can be organized and held. Officers who are elected to fill a vacancy serve out the unexpired term of the officer they succeed.

Insignia of Office.—A very common practice, especially in junior high and elementary schools, is to give each councilor a badge, pin, letter, bow, ribbon or other insigne of office which he wears, either continuously or on the day of council meetings. Perhaps, in general there is nothing wrong with this practice provided the insignia are attractive and appropriate, that is, modest. A large metal police-type badge is not appropriate because of its connotations and its size. However, in the case of officers of the council special insignia are probably impracticable. For instance, what insignia should the president wear? The vice-president? The secretary? The treasurer? How would these insignia differ? And what great difference would it make anyway if they were or were not worn?

Duties of Officers.—Although the duties of officers may justifiably vary according to the plan of participation adopted, the following lists will suggest the usual responsibilities of each official.

President.—The president is the chief executive officer of the council and is responsible for the efficient organization and administration of its policies and programs. Often he is ex officio member of all committees. Among his specific duties are the following:

- Presides at all meetings
- Ascertains presence of quorum
- Calls for minutes and reports
- Recognizes speakers
- States motions made
- Calls for vote
- Votes in case of tie[1]
- Announces result of vote
- Decides points of order
- Appoints officers pro tem
- Preserves order and decorum
- Appoints and discharges committees
- Executes contracts
- Calls special meetings
- Answers parliamentary queries
- Orders audits
- Enforces observation of constitution
- Directs making of the budget
- Executes council's wishes
- Adjourns the meeting

Vice-president.—This officer performs the duties of the president in the event of his absence, disability, or disqualification. He acts as a general assistant to the president in all matters, and accepts responsibilities specifically delegated to him. Usually he is chairman of some important committee, often being so designated by the constitution. The practice of naming a number of vice-presidents, each of whom is chairman of a committee, results in an unnecessarily cumbersome organization and also detracts from the importance of the real vice-president.

[1] In some schools the highest elected official is not allowed to vote on matters before the house. There is no legal or moral justification for this restriction.

Secretary.—In larger organizations there are often a recording secretary, who keeps records, and a corresponding secretary, who attends to the necessary communications. However, in most councils these functions are combined in one officer. The secretary is usually chairman of a committee, often the publicity committee. His duties include the following:

Makes and keeps in permanent form detailed records of all meetings.[1]

Reads minutes of previous meeting. These minutes should include the following items:

Kind of meeting	Name of presiding officer
Name of organization	Action on previous minutes
Date	Record of business transacted
Hour	Record of attendance
Place	Secretary's signature

Organizes and files records for instant use upon call
Receives and preserves correspondence, records, reports, etc.
Attends to necessary correspondence
Keeps record of attendance at meetings
Sends out notices of special meetings
Prepares, with the president, the order of business for meeting
Reads resolutions, motions, communications, or documents demanded
Records the results of all elections
Notifies committee members of their appointment
Delivers to chairman any necessary papers or documents
Authenticates documents requiring his signature
Records motions—makers, seconders (if required), and disposal

[1] In some schools these minutes are mimeographed and a copy sent to each home room. In other schools they are published in the newspaper.

- Acts as president in absence of president and vice-president
- Keeps scrapbook of clippings, programs, pictures, etc.
- Acts as publicity officer of the council
- Authorizes upon approval payment of bills and accounts
- Compiles and maintains a calendar of school events
- Keeps and maintains registration lists
- Sees that amendments are added to the constitution
- Keeps and distributes copies of the constitution
- Receives and files organizations' constitutions and documents

Treasurer.—This officer is responsible for the administration of the council's financial policies and activities. Generally, he is a member of the budget committee and frequently chairman of the thrift or banking committee. His qualifications should include a spotless record of integrity, a knowledge of commercial forms, records, and procedures, good business judgment, neatness of penmanship, and a reputation for carefulness and accuracy. Good business principles demand that he be properly bonded and that careful audits of his records be regularly made by disinterested persons. Among his duties are the following:

- Receives, deposits, and, upon proper authority, disburses funds
- Keeps complete and accurate records of all financial transactions
- Files all necessary statements, bills, receipts, vouchers, checks
- Keeps all records in shape for authorized inspection and examination
- Prepares and submits regular financial statements to the council. These reports should include the following items:

Balance on hand	Disbursements
Receipts	Current balance

Assists in preparing all regular and special budgets
Takes advantage of discounts wherever possible
Makes all records and material available for authorized audits
Keeps and distributes activity and admission tickets
Supervises the selling and taking of tickets
Sends a copy of all audits to the principal

Sergeant-at-arms.—Nearly every business meeting of any size needs a general handy man, and this is the sergeant-at-arms. He may attend the doors, see that visitors are welcomed and seated, maintain order, run errands, and perform such other duties as may be assigned.

Minor Officers.—Occasionally such minor officers as reporter, usher, doorkeeper, chaplain, and parliamentarian are elected or appointed. In general, a minor officer usually represents minor need, or practically no need at all, and hence may represent a bit of useless ornamentation which may prove to be distracting.

COMMITTEES

There are two kinds of committees, standing and special. Standing or permanent committees are usually specified and their work defined in the constitution; special or temporary committees are merely authorized by the constitution, to be created when necessary by the council or its president. The official appointment of a committee comes from the president after a consultation with the council, the individual members of the council, or other competent individuals. It is not necessary for the council to approve the appointment of a committee; such approval is assumed by the presidential appointment. Many constitutions, in describing a committee, place a lower limit to its size, such as, "This committee shall include not fewer than three members." Where a committee faces a rather considerable or complicated task it may organize subcommittees for specialized duties. These subcommittees need not be approved by the council. It is usually a good plan for a faculty member to be appointed (by the council president following a conference with the principal and the teachers) as an adviser for each major committee. Such an arrangement brings judgment and experience to the groups' deliberations and also means an additional faculty-student-association contact.

The following outline of the work of twenty-five committees, with some of which are indicated other possible designations, and the list to be found at the end of this discussion will indicate some of the possibilities in this area of council organization. The list of activities suggested in Chap. IX will doubtless suggest other committee possibilities. Naturally, these lists include committees that are somewhat duplicative. However, this is not detrimental here because no school would ever have all those suggested. Intelligent committee organization would also reduce duplication to a minimum. Committee organization will depend upon actual needs. The job first and then the committee to do it, is a much better procedure than the reverse.

Activity. Charter. Club. Organizations.—The main job of this committee is to recommend the chartering of school organizations. The interested group makes formal application for a charter, submitting such information on the proposed club as name, purposes, membership, organization, meetings, financing, and sponsorship. The committee studies this application, evaluates these details, and considers the contemplated group in relationship to the entire school program and the constitution. If the committee decides favorably, it recommends to the council that the club be chartered. The council then officially charters the organization with the proviso that if at any time the provisions of its charter are violated, this charter will be revoked and the organization abolished. If the committee decides unfavorably it will recommend rejection, stating its reasons, or, where possible and advisable, suggest the changes which will make the aplication more acceptable. In most schools charters are considered to be more or less permanent, being revoked rarely and then only for good cause. In others, all charters must be renewed annually. The former plan is preferable, unless comparatively little time is taken in rechartering. Other responsibilities of this committee are to study and make recommendations concerning the closer articulation of the chartered groups, to investigate school needs, especially in areas which appear to be uncapitalized, and to suggest adjustments in case of intergroup difficulty. It is well to remember that the action of this committee is not final; the council represents final authority.

Assembly. Auditorium.—This group educates the school in the purpose of the assembly; surveys student body, faculty, and community for program material; schedules, advertises, and evaluates programs; promotes the training of participants; provides necessary equipment and material; assists in staging and presenting the programs; promotes and manages program competitions and interschool program exchanges; develops, maintains, and makes available sources of suitable program material such as books, magazines, and programs of other schools; keeps a scrapbook record of all programs presented; develops standards for programs and encourages approximation of these; encourages the development of assembly courtesy; promotes assembly singing and other audience-participation devices; and supervises seating, ushering, welcoming visitors, etc. The adviser of this committee should probably be the teacher of dramatics, public speaking, or music, or someone else who has an interest and an ability in, and a knowledge of, this type of public presentation. In larger schools this committee may well be organized into such subcommittees as stage and settings, music, and standards, each of which is responsible for specialized duties.[1]

Athletics.—This group helps to promote the organization and administration of various kinds of intrascholastic and interscholastic contests and competitions; purchases, maintains, and cares for athletic equipment, materials, and property; enforces eligibility rules; keeps records of participation and provides proper publicity for meritorious work; awards letters and insignia; promotes and organizes pep meetings, assembly programs, and social events. Where the more professional of these are responsibilities of teachers or coaches, the committee can assist, and also take charge of those which are more in the council's area. The physical director or coach is a suitable adviser for this committee.

Bicycle.—This committee provides for the care and protection of the bicycles ridden to school, and maintains a bicycle rack, shed, or house; commissions a guard or "locker and unlocker"; develops interesting programs on such topics as how to ride a bicycle, care and maintenance of the bicycle, bicycling equipment, vocational uses of the bicycle, stunt and trick riding, bicycle racing, the history of bicycling, bicycling in other countries, and multipassenger bicycles. It organizes bicycle games, relays, races, polo, and hikes; promotes the observance of safety first and traffic regulations; and stages exhibits of bicycles and equipment, and demonstrations of riding and maintenance.

Bulletin Board.—This group makes or purchases a neat bulletin board, preferably glass-enclosed and locked; places

[1] A discussion of the numerous details and activities, together with hundreds of suggestive programs, will be found in the author's "Assembly and Auditorium Activities," The Macmillan Company, New York, 1930. A shorter account will be found in his "Extra-curricular Activities," rev. ed., Chap. 5, The Macmillan Company, New York, 1937.

it in a suitable spot and, if necessary, provides artificial light for it; composes and posts a set of rules concerning the size, shape, materials, neatness, dating, etc., of announcements, as well as the place to which they should be taken or sent; posts new notices and removes old ones; displays interesting school, community, and national news; adds to interest by the use of questions, cartoons, pictures, and similar material. Desirable and deserved publicity for the council may be gained through a neat little card or plaque which indicates the origin of this project.[1]

Cafeteria.—The duties of this committee are to promote intelligent choice of foods by means of competitions based on the rating and scoring of students' trays, and educational material on foods, food values, prices, preparation, care, conservation, etc., through assembly and home room programs, posters, bulletin board material, and the school newspaper; discourage candy eating and fruit eating between meals; promote good cafeteria and table manners; provide needed assistance in the cafeteria; help to plan menus, decorations, music, refreshments, etc., for social events, banquets, parties, hikes, and picnics. Probably a good adviser for this group would be the home economics teacher.

Citizenship. Civic Service. Civic Welfare.—This committee develops and explains a set of standards on school citizenship, such as a point system or rating scale, and a plan whereby the records of all members are taken, posted, and kept; promotes intergroup, interroom, and interclass competitions on home room, classroom, and general school citizenship; trains officers to make the necessary ratings; holds contests for citizenship honors, awards, and mentions; gives proper publicity to these causes, events, groups, and individual students; investigates infractions of school rules and regula-

[1] See DeBadts, Uses of School Bulletin Boards, *School Activities*, 6: 14–16, September, 1934.

tions; assumes various kinds of service responsibilities within the school; dramatizes election procedures and meetings of famous bodies; arranges talks by local municipal officers; promotes organized visits to city, county, state, and federal buildings and offices; organizes an imitative political campaign and election; and stages student debates and open forums on important school and community interests and issues.

Competitions. Contests.—This group originates, organizes, promotes, and judges all kinds of contests and competitions between individuals, rooms, groups, classes, and floors within the school, including contests in citizenship, health, lockers, assembly programs, courtesy, athletics, music, housekeeping, etc.; develops standards and rating devices; provides suitable recognition and awards for winners; educates the school in the real purposes and values of these competitions. This group, acting as a specialist, may assist in the handling of other competitions for which it is not directly responsible.

Courtesy. Etiquette. Manners and Courtesy.—The area of this group is in the development of an understanding and appreciation of the importance, place, ideals, values, and habits of courteous behavior in personal and group relationships and settings. It sponsors campaigns on courtesy in the home rooms, classrooms, corridors, auditorium, office, and cafeteria; in correspondence and travel, and at the theater, game, or party. It develops courtesy competitions, and home room and assembly programs; provides books, magazines, and other material on courtesy; collects quotations and examples of polite and impolite behavior; originates slogans, debates, discussions, courtesy-questions, jingles, songs, parodies, cartoons, posters, bulletins, pantomimes, and shadowgraphs. It cooperates closely with such committees as citizenship, social, and competitions.

Current Events.—This group summarizes and presents each week a few of the most interesting and significant school, community, and national events and happenings by means of assembly and home room programs, and newspaper and bulletin board material. Some of this material might be presented in the form of a radio broadcast to the various rooms or in a simulated broadcast in an assembly program.

Elections.—This important nonpartisan committee is responsible for the organization and handling of all general school elections. It supervises registration, designates polling places, supplies ballots, ballot boxes, and election officials, provides the necessary publicity, adjudicates disputes, challenges votes, declares winners, and certifies the results of the election to the council. It promotes a program for the education of all voters.

Eligibility. Credentials.—This group is responsible for the proper certification of eligible students for participation in athletic, music, debate, forensic, and other interscholastic competition, for elections and officeholding, and all other activities and positions which are restricted in any way. It devises and uses official forms. Naturally, it has access to all pertinent office records.

Health. Sanitation. Health and Sanitation.—General good health, correct posture, cleanliness, and sanitation represent the major interests of this group. It provides instruction in first-aid activities; supervises playgrounds and street crossings; develops a program on fire prevention; arranges demonstrations of all kinds; discourages roughhousing; develops home room, assembly, bulletin board, newspaper, and other material; provides and supervises a first-aid, comfort, or emergency room; makes a health survey of the school and its equipment and brings appropriate recommendations to the council. It provides, stocks, and maintains a first-aid or medicine cabinet; sponsors courses leading to Red Cross certificates; encourages health dressing; promotes health drives and campaigns, "Good Health," "Safety First,"

"Better Teeth," "Good Posture," etc.; develops health rules, codes, slogans, mottoes, quotations; holds contests in posters, poetry, songs, scenarios, slogans, and mottoes; promotes and records the results of health competitions and contests; and provides health material of all kinds for the school library. The adviser of this committee may well be the nurse, the teacher of health, or the physical director.

Home Room. Report Room. Session Room.—This committee assists the faculty and administration in promoting the theory and ideals of the home room plan. It suggests methods of internal organization, program planning, scheduling, presentation, and evaluation; provides suggestive material for programs of all types and uniform material for special drives and emphases; supplies suggestions for the rooms' general activities; encourages neat home room housekeeping; sponsors a training course for home room officers; authorizes home room responsibilities for particular school tasks and services. It develops interroom and interfloor competitions on citizenship, health, courtesy, service, assembly program, athletics, thrift, and other activities; and supervises home room voting in general school elections.[1]

Housekeeping. School Property. House and Grounds. Building and Grounds.—This council committee encourages neatness in the use of blackboards, pencil sharpeners, waste baskets, cloakrooms, lockers, seats and desks, bulletin boards, window shades and curtains, book shelves and tables, wash basins, and general order and arrangement of equipment. It organizes and supervises inspections and competitions; reports broken or loose equipment; promotes the acquisition of, and arranges and provides for the proper care of, flowers, plants, statuary, and pictures; discourages carving, writing, and other

[1] A complete discussion of all these details, together with eleven chapters of program materials, will be found in the author's "Home Room Guidance," McGraw-Hill Book Company, Inc., 1934.

mutilation of school property; develops an intelligent interest in art and beautification by means of exhibits, demonstrations, programs, posters, and newspaper articles. It inspects school grounds; provides containers for waste paper and trash and encourages the use of them; and it recommends desirable improvements such as flower beds, hedges, trees, bushes, and landscaping.

Locker.—This group assigns lockers and locks; promotes care of lockers and their contents; discourages slamming locker doors, leaving them open or unlocked, and filling the lockers with useless trash. It organizes and supervises frequent locker inspections; promotes competitions; and reports damaged locks and lockers.

Lost and Found.—This committee is equipped with a locked box, locker, or drawer in which to keep articles. It receives, classifies, and advertises all articles found, returning them upon proper identification; advertises lost articles; and promotes, through assembly, bulletin board, home room, and newspaper material, the care of personal and public property. It organizes drives and campaigns on appropriate topics. It penalizes by publicity, fines, or increased inconvenience or difficulty in obtaining lost articles those students who, as shown by the records, are unusually careless of their property.

Publications.—Although this group does not actually plan, get up, and print the various school publications, such as newspaper, magazine, handbook, yearbook, or bulletins, it authorizes, organizes, and supervises the election or appointment of staffs, defines their particular areas, coordinates their efforts, and assists them in financing, publicizing, and distributing their products. It sets high standards in material and form because all school publications permanently represent the school and its life; and it demands approximation of these standards. It originates and promotes special publications as occasion demands. Where necessary, as in the case of the handbook, the committee, together with the home room committee or other interested group, suggests a program of proper utilization and capitalization of the publication.

Publicity. Press.—This is an advertising committee which keeps the school and public informed of the ideals, policies, activities, and general spirit of the student council. It handles or supervises publicity for all school activities by means of home room, assembly, and P.T.A. programs, bulletin boards, school newspaper, bulletins, posters, etc. Great care should be exercised that good judgment is represented on this committee.

Research. Investigating.—This group is responsible for the investigation and study of such subjects as scholarship, absence, tardiness, safety, participation in extracurricular activities, health, vocational income of part-time students, etc. Its work will be particularly effective if it shows comparisons of the records of students, groups, rooms, classes, schools, ages, weeks, months, or years. For instance, a mere record of tardiness by itself means little; but when compared with the records of other students, schools, or years, it becomes more meaningful. Such comparative studies as participation in activities and scholarship, absence and marks, home study and marks, and seasons and absence will be worth much more than many sermons. The committee should, whenever possible, present its findings concisely, preferably pictorially by means of graphs and illustrated posters.

Scholarship.—This committee encourages the development of intelligent and logical attitudes toward scholarship; gives proper recognition to holders of high marks and especially to improvement in marks; develops and maintains an honor roll. It promotes competitions—intersex, interroom, interclass, intersubject, etc. It organizes a group of students who stand willing and ready to help anyone who is having difficulty with his work; carries assignments and material to absentees, and bring their papers and other work back to their teachers. It presents program, bulletin board, and newspaper material on such topics as, "Is a 'Gentleman's Mark' (C) a Gentleman's Mark?," "The Difference between the Worked and the Copied Problem," and "The Relation of Scholarship to Success in Adult Life." It discourages "cribbing," copying, and other unethical practices, and it gives proper publicity to its work.

Social. Party.—This group authorizes, schedules, sets regulations for, and supervises social events of all kinds, parties, dances, hikes, picnics, banquets, luncheons, etc. It develops and cross-indexes a library of books, magazines, bulletins, and similar material; trains leaders for various kinds of party leadership; organizes classes in social dancing; makes a study of refreshments, menus, decorations, programs, invitations, music, and costs. It develops a program of education in social etiquette for all occasions. Much of this material can be dramatized to good advantage in the assembly, and other parts of it can be presented through home rooms, gymnasium periods, the newspaper, and the bulletin board. The committee schedules special social events such as noon-hour recreation, parties for visiting teams, new students, teachers, and parents, and celebrations for special days.

Suggestion Box. Question Box.—This committee provides and maintains a conveniently located box into which are dropped pertinent suggestions and questions relative to the improvement of the school, its administration, organization, procedures, and activities; even "gripes" represent justifiable question-box material;[1] encourages free use of this opportunity by requiring no names; organizes public discussions, open forums, and debates on this material. Of course care must be taken that these discussions do not degenerate into petty faultfinding or represent misunderstanding or downright ignorance of procedures, reasons, and customs. This means

[1] See footnote reference on p. 53.

that good judgment must be used in the selection and reflection of question-box material. This group develops interesting campaigns on suitable suggestions and topics, and promotes serious council consideration of appropriate material.

Thrift. Banking.—This group assumes charge of student banking or assists with it. It promotes saving of all kinds, material, clothing, health, time, and money; develops campaigns and competitions in all phases of thrift, such as earning, saving, buying, investing, and giving; discourages borrowing of books, paper, pencils, ink, erasers, and similar materials; makes use of appropriate material on home room and assembly programs, on the bulletin board, and in the school publications.

Traffic. Patrol. Corridor.—This committee organizes and supervises corridor traffic; promotes worthy ideals and habits such as moving briskly and using right side of corridor and proper stairs; and discourages congregating at drinking fountains or lockers, running, loitering, arm-in-arm walking, and boisterous conduct. It makes traffic surveys and charts and works to eliminate jams at particular points. It organizes and directs traffic into and from the auditorium, and organizes and conducts fire drills.

Welfare. Cheer-up. Service.—This group investigates absentees; visits sick teachers and students and arranges for others to visit them; telephones and sends flowers, fruit, notes, books, magazines, etc.; carries assignments and reports on school activities; cares for absentees' property. It provides food, clothing, carfare, books, and other necessary assistance; organizes, develops, and administers a student loan fund; welcomes new students and teachers and makes them feel at home immediately; assumes charge of introductions at any time. It conducts an information bureau or desk; receives teachers and students from other schools, parents and patrons, and other visitors; organizes and conducts campaigns of school service; and assists in worthy community drives and campaigns.

OTHER COMMITTEES

Alumni
Art
Attendance
Auditing
Awards
Book exchange
Booster
Candy counter
Clean-up
Constitution interpretation
Court
Debate
Decoration
Devotional
Discipline
Door
Dramatics
Dressing room
Dues
Employment
Entertainment
Executive
Fellowship
Finance
First aid
Flag
Guidance
Honors
Information
Insignia
Inspections
Law and order
Legislative
Library
Literary
Magazine
Messenger
Monitor
Music
Neighborhood relations
Newspaper
Office
Playground
Point system
Poster
Printing
Program
Reception
Registration
Safety
School spirit
Scrapbook
Seating
Service
Stage
Store
Success
Supplies
Ticket
Training
Trip
Trophy
Usher
Vocations
Ways and means
Yearbook

Council Officer and Committee Relationships with the School.—Unless care is used to prevent it, friction may arise between council officers and committee members and the teaching and janitorial staffs. For instance, a housekeeping committee may provoke the janitor by some recommendation or action, the athletics committee may annoy the coach, and the health committee may displease the school nurse. This is especially possible if and when the students "begin to feel their importance." Similarly, friction may arise between council committees and corresponding school organizations, such as the debate committee and the debate club, the music committee and the band, or the publications committee and the newspaper staff. Naturally, any such aggravation will be harmful to the entire plan of participation. Cooperation between the professional employees and council committees and school organizations on the basis of mutual understanding, appreciation, and respect is essential; and such cooperation does not just happen, it must be designed and built. A sensible capitalization of school teachers and authorities as advisers of appropriate committees will help immensely.

Training of Officers and Committeemen.—The majority of newly elected officers are more or less ignorant of the responsibilities of their positions and consequently should receive instruction in their duties and relationships. Presidents and vice-presidents need instruction in parliamentary procedures; secretaries, in how to write and read minutes and reports; and treasurers, in how to keep financial records. Many schools now provide these educational opportunities and require all officers to attend them. This is a logical and beneficial procedure. In a similar manner, committeemen may receive instruction in the various details of their tasks.[1]

An occasional assembly program for the entire school should be valuable. One good type is a "stop-go" program in which the simpler forms of parliamentary procedure are dramatized, correctly and incorrectly, with the action stopping immediately after each item such as calling to order, making a

[1] In his article, Every Pupil a One-semester Monitor, *Clearing House*, 17: 212–214, December, 1942, M. W. Wallace describes the operation of a plan in which every student must voluntarily serve in some capacity for one semester before becoming eligible for officeholding.

motion, seconding a motion, approving the minutes, nominating candidates, or receiving and accepting committee reports. A master of ceremonies or parliamentarian explains the procedure if it is right, and corrects and explains the reasons if it is wrong. Such a program would probably become tedious if it were too long, but a short program will be found interesting as well as educative. It should do much to reduce the number of "I make a move," "I second the nomination," and similar parliamentary blunders.[1]

Selected References

ASHBROOK, B.: Officers' Training Classes, *School Activities*, 8: 168–169, December, 1936.

BAKER, J. C.: Uncliquing the Clique, *School Activities*, 7: 14–16, October, 1935.

DAVIS, T. S.: A Training School for Pupil Leaders, *School Review*, 43: 603–607, October, 1935.

EVANS, J. R.: Leadership Course, *Clearing House*, 16: 480–482, April, 1942.

HILL, G. E.: Leadership in the Student Council, *School Activities*, 9: 107–108, November, 1937.

MCMILLIN, M. P.: Organizing for Leadership, *School Activities*, 8: 164–165, December, 1936.

MESSER, M. R.: Training for Civic Leadership, Training of Squad Officers, and Training of School Officers, *School Activities*, 8: 194–197, 243–245, 291–293, January, February, March, 1937.

NESBIT, A.: A Better Citizenship Organization, *School Activities*, 7: 8–9, September, 1935.

STRANG, R.: "Group Activities in Colleges and Secondary Schools," pp. 217–226, Harper & Brothers, New York, 1941.

WATSON, N. E.: Intra-mural Leadership Training in the Elementary School, *School Activities*, 8: 296–299, March, 1937.

[1] Two good references on pertinent assembly programs are E. M. Barkley, Assembly Drill on Parliamentary Law, *School Activities*, 13: 186–189, January, 1942; and F. M. Gregg, "Parliamentary Law Dramatized," Personality Press, 1940.

WHITE, R., JR., A Class in Leadership, *School Review*, 46: 448–452, June, 1938.

PARLIAMENTARY PROCEDURE

JONES, O. G.: "Junior Manual for Group Leadership," and "Senior Manual for Group Leadership," rev. ed., D. Appleton-Century Company, Inc., New York, 1934.

———: "Parliamentary Procedure at a Glance," D. Appleton-Century Company, Inc., New York, 1933.

LEIGH, R. D.: "Modern Rules of Parliamentary Procedure," W. W. Norton & Company, Inc., New York, 1937.

REEVES, J. W.: "Parliamentary Procedure," D. C. Heath and Company, Boston, 1931.

ROBERTS, J. T.: "Primer of Parliamentary Law," Doubleday Doran & Company, Inc., New York, 1923.

Chapter IX

Council Activities and Projects

A STUDENT council without a schedule of suitable projects is as worthless as a car without gasoline, and a council with a schedule of unsuitable activities is as useless as a car with the wrong kind of fuel. A glance through the following pages should prove that no council need ever suffer a lack of appropriate work opportunities.[1] There are literally scores of varieties and sizes to be found in any school. However, not all the activities listed are equally suitable for all schools. Therefore, an important part of the council's responsibility is a proper selection of these elements of the program. On what basis should these activities be selected? In answering this question, the use of some such standards or criteria as the following should be helpful.[2]

1. Will the activity be interesting to the students?
2. Is it within the comprehension of the group concerned?
3. Is it a desirable activity? A practicable one?
4. Will it encourage initiative and originality?
5. Will it enlarge the student's horizon?
6. Will it develop responsibility?
7. Will it lead to further interests?

[1] It should be emphasized that, in accordance with principle number fifteen on p. 62, the council should not attempt to carry on all activities itself but should encourage allied groups to organize and promote appropriate projects.

[2] These criteria represent an adaptation of a list found in E. Feuërstein and M. R. Martin, The Activities of an Elementary School Council, *Elementary School Journal*, 37: 370–371, January, 1937.

8. Will it help to develop cooperation with schoolmates, teachers?

9. Will it promote a worthy school citizenship?

10. Will it help students to assume adult responsibilities?

Limitations of space prevent a description of all the numerous possibilities of council activities, and consequently here these will be merely listed together with the references where detailed discussions of each item may be found. General references reflecting a number of activities will be found at the end of the chapter. Where believed advisable, only the more recent references have been included. There is no significance to either the classifications or the order used in this listing. Although not all these activities are in line with the standards set forth in the other chapters of this book, all of them are practicable at the present time.[1]

Service

1. Welcome new students, teachers, and visitors
2. Provide coaches and helpers for weaker students
3. Organize and manage assistance bureau—books, car fare, clothing
4. Establish and manage student employment bureau
5. Assume care of property of absentees
6. Provide make-up helpers for absentees
7. Develop and administer student loan funds
8. Manage book exchange, supply store, candy corner
9. Maintain an information desk
10. Visit sick students; send flowers, cards, letters, books
11. Provide milk and food for needy students
12. Establish, equip, and maintain a social room, rest room
13. Make up and distribute Christmas baskets

[1] See Harvey, C. C., Activities and Projects of Student Councils, *School Activities*, 11: 10–12, 38, September, 1939, and 15: 165–168, January, 194 for very complete lists of activities. See also pp. 174–185 of this book.

14. Provide special help for teachers, librarians, administrators
15. Supervise health and sanitation services
16. Promote assistance for crippled and handicapped students
17. Promote safety first, to, at, and from, school
18. Organize and manage a tutoring bureau
19. Meet and welcome visiting teams and groups of students
20. Provide typing and multigraphing service
21. Assist in community drives and campaigns
22. Assume charge of bicycle parking
23. Promote and administer a scholarship fund
24. Develop a picture lending library, toy lending library
25. Collect, recondition, and distribute toys
26. Cooperate with the local U.S. Employment Service
27. Organize and supervise entertainment and speakers bureaus
28. Promote the sale of Christmas and other service seals
29. Organize Big Brother and Big Sister services
30. Assume charge of bulletin boards
31. Provide playground assistance and supervision
32. Organize and supervise noon-hour activities
33. Assign lockers or clothing hooks
34. Promote fellowship services and activities
35. Organize and supervise school bus activities
36. Assume charge of schoolbook or supply room
37. Cooperate with supplementary youth organizations
38. Promote a "school sacrifice day" for service bureaus

References

Bailey, D. D.: Hood School Service Council, *School Activities*, 12: 170–171, December, 1940.

Brazelton, C. M.: Dean's Committee, *Clearing House*, 16: 80–82, October, 1941.

Bretnall, R. J.: Welfare Workers, *Clearing House*, 16: 329–331, January, 1942.

Lindahl, N. R.: A Council Serves, *School Activities*, 12: 326, April, 1941.

MacLeod, E. W.: A Service Squad for the Junior High School, *School Activities*, 12: 156, December, 1940.

McKown, H. C.: "School Clubs," Chap. XVII, The Macmillan Company, New York, 1930.

Special

Abele, L.: The Organization of Student-governed Study Halls, *School Review*, 34: 377–381, June, 1926.

Alpern, H.: Brotherhood Week in the New York City High Schools, *School Review*, 30: 412–422, June, 1922.

Broad, T. H.: A School Supply Store, *School Activities*, 8: 63–64, October, 1936.

Brooke, E.: Schools Aid the Young Cyclist, *Safety Education*, 17: 199–200, 218, April, 1937.

Browning, R. W.: A Bicycle Club, *School Activities*, 10: 66–67, October, 1938.

Bruckner, G.: Our Sharing Christmas, *School Activities*, 14: 141–142, December, 1942.

Ericsson, M. K.: Spade Brigade, *School Activities*, 14: 286, April, 1943.

Fitzgerald, D.: An Eighth Grade Day in the High School, *School Activities*, 9: 319–320, February, 1938.

Force, E.: The Eighth Grade Gives a Party, *School Activities*, 11: 197–198, January, 1940.

Giving Freshmen a Preview of High School, *School Activities*, 15: 216, February, 1944.

Graham, M.: Pupil Librarians, *Clearing House*, 9: 93–96, October, 1934.

Harrod, D.: Have You a Social Room? *School Activities*, 12: 209, January, 1941.

Jenkins, J.: Let Me Do It, *Clearing House*, 16: 97–99, October, 1941

Johnson, W. A.: Seventh Grade Pupils Need a Course in Adjustment to School Life, *Clearing House*, 10: 553–556, May, 1936.

LIVINGSTON, K. H.: Vitalizing Civic Education through the Speakers Bureau, *School Activities*, 10: 266, 269, February, 1939.

MCKOWN, H. C.: "Home Room Guidance," Chap. XIII, McGraw-Hill Book Company, Inc., New York, 1934.

MOOG, A. J.: Bicycling Made Safe, *Nation's Schools*, 28: 55–56, August, 1941.

ONTHANK, K. W.: Who Pays for Administration of Student Loan Funds? *School and Society*, 41: 733–735, June 1, 1935.

Picture Lending Library, *School Activities*, 13: 245, February, 1942.

POLLACK, S.: Civic Education vs. Hippodroming, *Clearing House*, 12: 360–361, February, 1938.

RAHN, A. O.: Student Council Aids in Orienting New Students, *School Activities*, 8: 344, April, 1937.

ROSENBERG, E.: Each Freshman Girl Has a Big Sister, *Clearing House*, 16: 92–96, October, 1941.

School Library number of *Clearing House*, Vol. 9, No. 9, May, 1935.

SKINNER, G.: Our Library: A Cooperative Community Enterprise, *Clearing House*, 16: 429–430, March, 1942.

SMITH, F. L.: A High School Scholarship Fund, *School Activities*, 6: 3–5, 16–17, September, 1934.

TURNER, K. W.: The High School Entertainment Bureau—How To Start One, *School Activities*, 11: 32–33, September, 1939.

WEGENER, F. C.: The Speakers Bureau, *School Activities*, 9: 227–228, January, 1938.

WILLIAMS, D. G.: Visual Aids Club, *Clearing House*, 16: 77–79, October, 1941.

YAGER, S. A.: The Operation of a Used Book Exchange, *School Activities*, 7: 23–24, January, 1936.

PUBLIC FUNCTIONS

1. Organize and supervise general and special assembly programs
2. Promote music productions, concerts, contests, programs
3. Schedule debates and speaking contests

4. Promote dramatics, movies, pageants, lyceum courses, lectures
5. Sponsor exhibitions—art, shopcraft, hobbies, historical
6. Promote gymnastic and swimming contests and exhibitions
7. Schedule and promote a fashion show or review
8. Promote "open house," "school night," and similar events
9. Organize and conduct field day, May Day, play day, flag day, color day
10. Select, train, assign, and supervise ushers and guides
11. Hold pep meetings, contests, parades, and demonstrations
12. Develop stunts for cheering sections and games
13. Award insignia, trophies, honors, and prizes on recognition day
14. Organize and promote fair, circus, bazaar, carnival, jamboree, frolic
15. Promote "School-community Day," picnic, celebration, dinner
16. Hold a "Student Day"—students replace teachers, administrators
17. Promote student discussion groups, open forums, community forums
18. Organize father-son, mother-daughter social, educational events
19. Hold a reception for the graduating class
20. Hold all-school banquet, picnic, party, hike, trip
21. Dedicate building, athletic field, equipment, service flag, memorial
22. Organize a "Visit-school Day" for parents and patrons
23. Plan victory celebration—parade, snake-dance, bonfire
24. Promote a citizenship day—programs, exhibitions, demonstrations

25. Organize patriotic programs and celebrations
26. Provide tournaments of all kinds
27. Hold devotional and other religious programs
28. Organize and arrange faculty-student chats
29. Develop and use ritual and ceremonial forms
30. Schedule clinics—study, school problems, vocational guidance
31. Promote a high school radio hour
32. Schedule freshman initiation ceremony
33. Organize old-time events, spelling bee, barn dance, box supper
34. Cooperate with local organizations on "Luncheon Club Day"
35. Organize and hold an imitative national convention and election
36. Organize and hold an intercouncil convention[1]

REFERENCES

BAILEY, D. D., and J. L. DONALD: Our Pet Parade, *School Activities*, 11: 75–76, October, 1939.

BAVELY, E.: A Ritual as a School Project, *School Activities*, 7: 8–9, 11, January, 1936.

BEYER, B. S.: Student Forums Find Town, *School Activities*, 12: 197–208, December, 1940.

BLACKMAN, R. E.: Student Day, *School Activities*, 8: 120–121, November, 1936.

BOWER, H. E.: A Community Cafeteria Banquet, *School Activities*, 9: 321–322, February, 1938.

BUNCH, D. A.: Possibilities of High School Forum Clubs, *School Activities*, 13: 213–215, 246, February, 1942.

BUSSEWITZ, W. R.: Banquet for All Activities, *School Activities*, 10: 307–308, March, 1939.

[1] A good book for the conference promoter and leader is A. M. Cooper, "How to Conduct Conferences," McGraw-Hill Book Company, Inc., New York, 1942.

CAHILL, E.: Why Not a Circus Day? *School Activities*, 11: 59–61, October, 1939.

CAMPBELL, C.: Parents' Day in a Cumberland School, *School Activities*, 13: 268, March, 1942.

CANAKER, C.: School Exhibits, *School Activities*, 8: 123–124, November, 1936.

———: Citizenship Recognition Day, *School Activities*, 14: 276, March, 1943.

COLLINS, W. W.: Between the Halves, *School Activities*, 11: 65–66, October, 1939.

CRANDALL, H.: Now Is the Time for an All-school Banquet, *School Activities*, 14: 302, April, 1943.

EKSTRAND, C. A.: Our Pep Activities, *School Activities*, 13: 151–152, December, 1941.

Faculty-student Chats, *School Activities*, 7: 26, May, 1936.

FAUNCE, R. C.: Student Day in Big Rapids High School, *School Activities*, 9: 66–68, October, 1937.

FORMAN, W. O.: The Citation Roll, *School Activities*, 10: 381–382, May, 1939.

GILMORE, A. C.: A Fun Frolic, *School Activities*, 11: 249–250, February, 1940.

HALL, C. C.: Peppy Stunts for Pep Assemblies, *School Activities*, 11: 287–288, March, 1940.

HARVEY, C. C.: Discussion Practice for Youth, *School Activities*, 9: 349–350, April, 1938.

HAYNES, F. S.: A Civilian Service Flag, *School Activities*, 15: 194, February, 1944.

HENTZ, K.: Secondary School Social Functions, *School Activities*, 11: 145–146, 156, December, 1939.

HILL, J. M.: Our School Jamboree, *School Activities*, 10: 267–268, February, 1939.

HOFFMAN, G. S.: Students Take Part in Community Hobby Fair, *School Activities*, 10: 341–342, April, 1939.

HOOVER, F. W.: Open House, a Device for Interpreting the Schools, *School Activities*, 13: 225–226, February, 1942.

How to Hold a Model National Convention, *Scholastic*, 36: 34, April, 29, 1940.

HUGGETT, A. J.: Extrinsic Awards for Those Who Participate, *School Activities*, 11: 189–190, January, 1940.

HUTCHENS, M. S.: The Booster Club Tells Them, *School Activities*, 7: 23–24, October, 1935.

JACKSON, R. W.: Mather High School Frolics, *School Activities*, 13: 345–346, May, 1942.

JACKSON, V., and C. WEINBACH: Our Annual Spring Festival, *School Activities*, 8: 103–104, November, 1936.

JAMES, C. A.: An Extra-curricular Tournament, *School Activities*, 7: 22–23, April, 1936.

JOHNSON, J. B.: Open Forum Club Experiments, *School Activities*, 12: 103–104, 121, November, 1940.

KOLBERG, O. W.: A Program Number for a Pep Assembly, *School Activities*, 15: 130, December, 1943.

MCCORMICK, C. F.: A Junior High School All-school Play Day, *School Activities*, 11: 21–22, September, 1939.

MCKOWN, H. C.: "Assembly and Auditorium Activities," The Macmillan Company, New York, 1930.

MCMILLIN, M. P.: Fair Day, *School Activities*, 7: 15–16, 19, December, 1935.

MCMURRAY, J. F.: Open School Night, *School Activities*, 6: 5–7, October, 1934.

MURTON, L.: Citizenship Day, *School Activities*, 13: 338, 348, May, 1942.

NORRIS, W. W.: The Work of a Student Council, *School Activities*, 12: 129–130, November, 1940.

NUESSE, C. J.: Will Student Forums Grow?, *School Activities*, 13: 271–272, 288, March, 1942.

Parents' Day Assembly Program, *School Activities*, 8: 420–421, May, 1937.

PARRY, K.: A Ship Shape Banquet, *School Activities*, 11: 253–254, February, 1940.

PARSON, L.: A Hobby Show, *School Activities*, 8: 219–221, January, 1937.

PASH, B. T.: Fathers' Day in Athletics, *School Activities*, 11: 291, 310–311, March, 1940.

Radio Quiz—What Do You Know?, *School Activities*, 11: 131–134, November, 1939.

RATHMAN, C.: The Activities Festival, *School Activities*, 8: 207–208, January, 1937.

REED, G. G.: A High School Nite Club That Works, *School Activities*, 9: 412–413, 416, May, 1938.

RIGGS, L. A.: Suggestions to the Discussion Leader, *School Activities*, 15: 47–48, October, 1943.

SHUSTER, L.: An Effective Color Ritual, *School Activities*, 6: 18–19, January, 1935.

———: A School Spirit Contest, *School Activities*, 8: 73–74, October, 1936.

SIMMONS, M. P.: A Father-and-son Exhibit, *School Activities*, 11: 95–96, November, 1939.

SMART, D. V.: School and Merchants Day, *School Activities*, 7: 24–25, April, 1936.

SNYDER, T. A.: The School Carnival, *Clearing House*, 13: 160–163, November, 1938.

STAPLES, M. L.: School Morale through the Pep Assembly, *School Activities*, 11: 17–18, September, 1939.

———: Social Aims of the School Rally, *School Activities*, 11: 67–68, October, 1939.

———: Watering the Elephant at the Circus, *School Activities*, 11: 107–108, November, 1939.

———: Building a Desirable School Spirit, *School Activities*, 11: 143–144, December, 1939.

———: The Technique of the Pep Talk, *School Activities*, 11: 195–196, January, 1940.

———: The Victory Celebration as a Social Opportunity, *School Activities*, 11: 245–246, February, 1940.

———: Sportsmanship—an Outgrowth of the School Rally, *School Activities*, 11: 285–286, March, 1940.

———: Does Your School Have a Pep Specialist? *School Activities*, 11: 327–329, 339, April, 1940.

STARR, G. G.: Something to Be Said for School Exhibits, *School Activities*, 10: 377–378, May, 1939.

———: The Pep Meeting—an Educational Opportunity, *School Activities*, 9: 361–362, April, 1938.

Stoval, L. A.: Developing Pep Leaders in a Democratic Way, *School Activities*, 14: 31–32, September, 1942.

Teer, K. W.: Do Not Abolish the Pep Squad—Reorganize It, *School Activities*, 13: 233–234, January, 1942.

Thompson, D.: Our Hobby Fair, *School Activities*, 10: 299–300, March, 1939.

Van Nice, C. R.: "How to Plan and Carry Out a School Carnival," School Activities Publishing Company, Topeka, Kans.

Voxland, M.: High School Students Dedicate New Building, *School Activities*, 8: 412–413, May, 1937.

Weller, G. M.: 75 Visits from Community Leaders, *Clearing House*, 16: 26–28, September, 1941.

Wilbur, H.: Hobby Riding, *School Activities*, 11: 126–127, November, 1939.

Drives and Campaigns

1. Safety first
2. Better health
3. Fire prevention
4. Punctuality
5. Better speech
6. Clean-up
7. Better health
8. Look nice
9. No unnecessary absence
10. Stay in school
11. Better English
12. No smoking
13. Know your school
14. Good sportsmanship
15. Books for library
16. Gardening, tree planting
17. Good posture
18. Finger printing
19. How other schools do it
20. No gum-chewing in school
21. Self-inventory
22. Smile
23. Know your neighbor
24. Better book
25. Courtesy
26. Safe driving and riding
27. Better lessons
28. School beautiful
29. Friendliness
30. Know your community
31. Buy wisely
32. Activity ticket sale
33. Pictures for school
34. How to study

References

BLANKENBAKER, R. F.: A Drive on Tardiness Pays Dividends, *School Activities:* 11: 319, 344, April, 1940.

BONAR, H. S.: High-school Pupils List Their Anxieties, *School Review*, 50: 512–515, September, 1942.

Community Appreciation, *School Activities*, 14: 76, October, 1942.

Finger Printing, *School Activities*, 7: 29, April, 1936.

HAWKER, A.: Parade of Posture, *School Activities*, 13: 341–342, May, 1942.

HUGGETT, A. J.: Guiding Student Buying, *School Activities*, 6: 7–10, January, 1935.

HUSHMAN, E.: A Campaign against Absence and Tardiness, *School Activities*, 14: 194, January, 1943.

LEE, W. E.: Local History Makes a School Project, *School Activities*, 15: 52, October, 1943.

MCKOWN, H. C.: "Home Room Guidance," Chap. XIX (personal relationships) Chap. XX (health), McGraw-Hill Book Company, Inc., New York, 1934.

MANN, N.: Civil Identification Project, *School Activities*, 14: 325–326, May, 1943 (finger printing).

MARTIN, L. C.: Our Pupils Rate Themselves, *Clearing House*, 16: 413–414, March, 1942.

MORRISON, C. A.: Organization of a Thrift Club, *School Activities*, 12: 109–110, November, 1940.

OWEN, V.: We Cleaned Up the Town, *Clearing House*, 16: 212, December, 1941.

PORSCHE, R. W.: Fire Fighting as an Extra Curricular Activity, *School Activities*, 14: 227–228, February, 1943.

SHAFFER, S.: A Local History Club, *School Activities*, 13: 146–149, December, 1941.

SHELDON, J. A.: Community Life Problems, *Clearing House*, 16: 8–11, September, 1941.

SPENCE, L.: Block Beautiful, *Clearing House*, 16: 3–7, September, 1941 (school and city).

VON BERGE, E.: Personality Clinic, *School Activities*, 10: 150, December, 1938.

ZASTROS, L. M. Introducing Safety Education, *School Activities*, 9: 370–371, April, 1938.

CARE OF SCHOOL AND PERSONAL PROPERTY

1. Organize and conduct lost and found department
2. Promote care of desks, walls, school equipment, grounds
3. Promote care of personal property, clothing, materials, equipment
4. Promote respect for neighboring private property
5. Encourage respect for all public property
6. Encourage conservation of school and personal supplies and equipment
7. Assume care of school trophies
8. Inspect school for broken or loose seats, desks, tables, locks, charts
9. Collect and post "fools' names" carved or written
10. Promote instruction in proper use of books
11. Survey library books and materials, estimate damage
12. Promote proper care and use of bicycles[1]
13. Organize and schedule appropriate assembly programs
14. Develop publicity—bulletin board, posters, cartoons, articles

REFERENCES

LORENZ, A. L.: For Bicycle Safety, *School Activities*, 10: 205–206, January, 1939.

MCKOWN, H. C.: "Home Room Guidance," pp. 324, 392–394, 398–402, McGraw-Hill Book Company, Inc., New York, 1934.

SUSTERICH, J.: Bicycling Is Our Hobby, *Student Life*, May, 1931, p. 7.

THALACKER, A.: The Conservation Club, *School Activities*, 12: 253–254, February, 1941.

TREDENNICK, F.: Youth Solve Their Own Bicycle Problems, *School Activities*, 12: 211–213, January, 1941.

[1] In addition to the references below see those of Brooke, Browning, and Moog on pp. 192–193, and Lawson on p. 299.

Education

1. Better radio listening
2. School orientation
3. Summer hobbies
4. Sports—new rules
5. Use of college catalogues
6. History of our school
7. Parliamentary law
8. Classes for school officers
9. How to study effectively
10. What other schools are doing
11. Use of school handbook
12. Participation opportunities
13. School songs and yells
14. Community opportunities
15. Smoking and drinking
16. Consumers' activities
17. Music and art
18. Slot machines
19. School citizenship
20. Trips and tours
21. How to improve school marks
22. New educational movements
23. All about council activities
24. Use of self-rating devices

References

CARLSON, L. L.: Radio Work Serves Two Purposes, *School Activities*, 9: 311, 317, 324, February, 1938.

Commercial Radio Station Broadcasts Directly from the City High Schools, *School Review*, 47: 11, January, 1939.

CORY, E. B.: Curio Club, *Clearing House*, 8: 306–309, January, 1934.

COYTE, F. J.: High School Sports Broadcasting in Pittsburgh, *School Activities*, 8: 404, 407, May, 1937.

DIXON, F. B.: Why Not Develop a Bill of Duties? *School Activities*, 14: 13–14, September, 1942.

Educational Program, *School Activities*, 13: 250, March, 1942.

FISHBACK, E. H.: Summer Hobbies for High School Pupils, *School Activities*, 7: 11–13, 24–25, May, 1936.

GOUDY, E. L.: Radio is Dynamite!, *Clearing House*, 17: 71–75, January, 1938.

HAUSER, L. J.: The Arithmetic in Slot Machines, *School Activities*, 9: 371–372, April, 1938.

HAWLEY, F. T.: Senior Skip Day Becomes Worth While, *School Activities*, 9: 374, April, 1938 (trip).

HERRING, C. E.: Anti-gyp Education, *School Activities*, 9: 221–222, January, 1938.

JESSEN, C. A.: School Tours, *School Life*, 24: 199–200, April, 1939.

KNEECE, E. E.: From a Radio Program to a City-wide Project, *High School Journal*, 22: 177–182, May, 1939.

LANGFORD, P.: Know Your School Day, *School Activities*, 13: 360–361, May, 1942.

MACINTOSH, H. K.: Grand Rapids Schools Develops Children's Hobbies, *Educational Method*, 14: 300–304, March, 1935.

MCKOWN, H. C.: "Extra-curricular Activities," rev. ed., Chap. XII, The Macmillan Company, New York, 1937.

MATTHEWS, C.: A News Idea, *School Activities*, 10: 401–402, May, 1939. (Broadcast.)

MEYER, F.: A Train Trip as a Council Project, *School Activities*, 12: 233–234, February, 1941.

ROSE, H. O.: Coshocton High School Student News Broadcast, *School Activities*, 9: 271, February, 1938.

Students Go on the Air, *School Activities*, 10: 277, February, 1939.

TAYLOR, R. E.: An Education Tour, *School Activities*, 9: 357–358, 390, April, 1938.

———, R. G.: Before the "Mike" in the Providence R. I. Schools, *Clearing House*, 14: 109–112, October, 1939.

TRAVERS, L.: The Voice of Washington Junior, *School Activities*, 10: 385–386, May, 1939.

VAN METER, L. R.: A School for Basketball Fans, *School Activities*, 8: 214–215, January, 1937.

WOODS, W.: High School Seniors Take Educational Tours, *School Activities*, 8: 254–256, February, 1937.

YOUNG, B.: A Radio Program Becomes a School Project, *School Activities*, 7: 22–24, 43, March, 1936.

SCHOOL EQUIPMENT[1]

1. Electric score board
2. Museum equipment and exhibits

[1] See footnote on p. 216.

3. Flag pole, room poles and flags
4. Service flag, plaque, memorial
5. Medicine cabinet and supplies
6. Public address system
7. Voting booths, ballot box, railings
8. Nickelodeon or juke box for social room
9. Motion picture projector and screen
10. Magazines, books, papers, pictures, etc., for library
11. Library shelving, racks, and tables
12. Music, instruments, racks, for music organizations
13. Filing cabinets and supplies for council and court
14. Piano or organ
15. Stage drapes, curtain, and equipment
16. Encyclopedia and other large book sets
17. Electric clock and bell system
18. Athletic equipment and material
19. Fish bowls, tanks, fish, and supplies
20. Bird houses and feeding stations

References

Broderson, G.: Our Museum, *Journal of the National Education Association*, 25: 211–212, October, 1936.

Gay, M. C.: A Classic Museum in a High School, *Classical Journal*, 28: 484–488, April, 1933.

Goldman, L.: Reincarnation through a Museum, *School Activities*, 12: 239–240, February, 1941.

How to Purchase a Hammond Electric Organ, *School Activities*, 12: 328–329, April, 1941.

Kolk, D. V.: An Inexpensive Electric Scoreboard, *School Activities*, 10: 163–164, December, 1938.

Meksin, J.: Experimental Museum-exhibition Work for Children, *Clearing House*, 9: 535–538, May, 1935.

Mosher, O. W.: School and Community Museums, *Journal of the National Education Association*, 24: 63–65, February, 1935.

Shares in Piano, *School Activities*, 8: 410, March, 1937.

SURAK, J., and F. RABEHL, An Electric Score Board as a Club Project, *School Activities*, 8: 257–258, February, 1937.

COURTESY AND CONDUCT

1. Make and enforce general rules and regulations
2. Encourage good behavior about the school
3. Promote proper behavior at assembly and public events
4. Discourage "class scraps" and similar traditional roughhousing
5. Encourage good conduct before and after school
6. Appoint and supervise study-hall and library monitors
7. Commission and supervise playground and street officers
8. Organize and supervise corridor, stairway, and rest room officers
9. Establish and supervise a student court
10. Eliminate cribbing, petty thieving, dishonesty in homework
11. Teach school courtesy—classroom, cafeteria, library, office
12. Promote instruction in social etiquette and courtesy
13. Teach "outside" courtesy—home, theater, street, automobile, bus
14. Encourage the development of good sportsmanship
15. Promote an honor study hall
16. Develop appropriate assembly and home room programs

REFERENCES

CAMP, E. E.: Eliminating the Junior-senior Class Fights, *School Activities*, 8: 272–273, February, 1937.

DEIMER, R. R.: Aberdeen Has a Courtesy League, *High School Journal*, 23: 178–179, April, 1940.

DUNKEL, E. G.: The Social Dance Class—a Laboratory for Acquiring Social Ease, *School Activities*, 10: 105–107, November, 1938.

KASTNER, W. G.: Honor Study Halls Train Pupils for Self-control, *School Activities*, 15: 37, September, 1943.

LAING, H. E.: Pupil Bus Officers, *Clearing House*, 16: 12–14, September, 1941.

MCCUNE, B.: Better Conduct Week, *School Activities*, 8: 390–391, May, 1937.

MCKOWN, H. C.: "Home Room Guidance," Chap. XVI (ethical, moral), and XXI (courtesy), McGraw-Hill Book Company, Inc., New York, 1934.

MACLENNAN, F.: The School Dance, *School Activities*, 7: 8–9, 34, December, 1935.

RAHN, A. O.: Does Courtesy among Students Prevail in Your School? *School Activities*, 8: 394–395, May, 1937.

SCHOOL PUBLICATIONS[1]

1. Newspaper
2. Magazine
3. Handbook
4. Yearbook
5. School directory
6. School history
7. Song and yell sheets
8. School reports
9. Guidebooks, rules, manners, maps
10. "How to study" helps
11. Bulletins and notices
12. Book, motion picture reviews
13. Self-rating cards and forms
14. Advertising posters, handbills
15. Programs—music, dramatic, athletic
16. Council forms and blanks

SPECIAL DAYS AND WEEKS

Illustrative of the special days and weeks that may be reflected in the work of the council through assembly, home room, and community programs, campaigns, exhibits, store window publicity, newspaper and magazine articles, bulletin

[1] Detailed discussions of the newspaper, magazine, handbook, and yearbook, together with references, will be found in H. C. McKown, "Extracurricular Activities," rev. ed., Chaps. XIV–XIX, The Macmillan Company, New York, 1937.

board material, social events, and other devices, are the following some of which vary in date:[1]

1. Arbor Day—April, 2nd Friday
2. Armistice Day—November 11
3. Bird Day—May 5
4. Brotherhood Week
5. Book Week—November, 3rd week
6. College Week
7. Columbus Day—October 12
8. Christmas—December 25
9. Constitution Day—September 17
10. Education Week—November
11. Fire Prevention Week—October
12. Flag Day—June 14
13. Girl Scout Week—October
14. Good Will Day—May 18
15. Hallowe'en—October 31
16. Labor Day—September, 1st Monday
17. Lincoln's Birthday—February 12
18. Memorial Day—May 30
19. Mother's Day—May, 2nd Sunday
20. Navy Day—October 27
21. New Year's Day—January 1
22. Parents' Day
23. Roosevelt Day—October 27
24. St. Patrick's Day—March 17
25. St. Valentine's Day—February 14
26. State Day
27. Thanksgiving—November, last Thursday
28. Washington's Birthday—February 22

[1] Detailed programs and appropriate suggestions for use in the assembly will be found in H. C. McKown, "Assembly and Auditorium Activities," pp. 379–447, The Macmillan Company, New York, 1930. "Anniversaries and Holidays: A Calendar of Days and How to Observe Them," by Mary E. Haseltine, published by the American Library Association, Chicago, is the most comprehensive single volume in this general field. This book is not a collection of programs, but a calendar of "holidays, holydays, and seasonal days of the world," with a brief historical sketch of each, together with sources of material, poems, songs, plays, pageants, and pictures, for their observance. Each fall the *Journal of the National Education Association* provides material suitable for "Education Week."

Finance[1]

1. Organize and adopt a financial system
2. Appoint treasurers, bankers, finance officers
3. Act on budgets of all school activities
4. Develop budget for the entire extracurricular program
5. Develop and supervise money-raising plans
6. Assume charge of and distribute activity funds
7. Promote proper auditing of all accounts
8. Give proper publicity to council finances
9. Issue activity, membership, and admittance tickets

School Gardening and Landscaping

1. Organize and supervise a campus beautification project
2. Plan flower beds, shrubs and tree groups
3. Fill in or level, and plant, unsightly campus spots
4. Provide trash receptacles
5. Plant a school vegetable garden
6. Demonstrate spraying methods and materials
7. Trim trees and shrubs
8. Remove dead trees and shrubs, replace with new
9. Exhibit and demonstrate use of tools and equipment
10. Develop special features, flower designs, arbors, poles, trellises
11. Beautify classrooms with flowers and plants
12. Develop freak vegetables, flowers, and plants
13. Present appropriate assembly and home room programs
14. Hold exhibits of flowers and vegetables
15. Survey neighboring lots and develop plans for their use
16. Plan trips to neighboring estates, woods, hothouses, nurseries
17. Make scrapbooks of photographs "before" and "after"

[1] Appropriate references for these activities will be found at the end of Chapter X.

18. Organize competition in fruit, vegetable, and flower growing
19. Promote building of birdhouses and feeding stations
20. Cooperate with community services and organizations

References

Cultivating a Forest as a School Memorial, *School Activities*, 12: 245, February, 1941.

Gerhardt, A. H.: Swamp Planting, *School Activities*, 13: 160–161, December, 1941.

Kurtz, R. J.: Citizenship and a Watermelon Patch, *School Activities*, 13: 137–138, December, 1941.

McKone, M.: A Landscape Beautification Project, *School Activities*, 12: 304, April, 1941.

McKown, H. C.: "School Clubs," pp. 235–237, 324, 331, The Macmillan Company, New York, 1929.

Sumi, E.: Why Not a School Garden? *School Activities*, 11: 161–162, December, 1939.

Taxon, J.: Central High Beautifies Its Campus, *School Activities*, 11: 262–263, February, 1940.

Welder, C. E.: Our High School Garden Project, *School Activities*, 13: 361–362, May, 1942.

Surveys and Investigations

1. Study habits, time, place, procedures
2. Out-of-school activities of students
3. Student finances, money earned, spent, saved, invested
4. Student interests and hobbies
5. Tardiness and absence—extent, causes, losses
6. Student opinion and viewpoints
7. Participation in extracurricular activities
8. Relationship of scholarship to participation in activities
9. Democratic experiences of students
10. School health—illness, accidents, cost, time loss
11. School and community health hazards

12. Misuse of school library books, equipment, materials
13. Educational backgrounds of students
14. Local history, resources, problems
15. School marks and participation recognitions
16. School equipment, material, and supplies
17. School and community problems, needs, solutions
18. School grounds—shrubs, trees, flowers, grass, walks
19. Misconduct, delinquency, disciplinary problems
20. General school citizenship
21. Street traffic to and from school
22. Evaluation of council activities
23. Alumni and former students

References

ADKINS, E. P.: Student Council Goes to Town, *Clearing House*, 13: 451–453, April, 1939.

CAMPBELL, L. R.: Plan a Consumer Survey, *School Activities*, 15: 152, January, 1944.

CRAWFORD, C. C., and R. W. MAYER: How High School Seniors Spend Their Time, *School Review*, 43: 598–602, October, 1935.

GRIM, P. R.: Housing Study, *Clearing House*, 16: 402–404, March, 1942.

HARNLY, P. W.: Attitudes of High School Seniors Toward Education, *School Review*, 47: 501–509, September, 1939.

HASSE, M.: Extra-curricular Time Survey, *Nation's Schools*, 24: 60, 62, November, 1939.

HIATT, L. R.: Junior High School Citizenship, *School Review*, 35: 756–759, December, 1927.

HOBBS, S. M.: An Eighth Grade Studies Public Opinion, *Clearing House*, 16: 83–86, October, 1941.

Make Community Youth Survey, *School Activities*, 13: 284, March, 1942.

SIMPSON, L. R.: A Student Project in Rating and Improving Citizenship, *School Activities*, 10: 295–296, 302, March, 1939.

Student Evaluation of School, *Clearing House*, 17: 85, October, 1942.

Intraschool Contests and Competitions

1. Athletics
2. School spirit
3. Scholarship
4. Attendance
5. Punctuality
6. Debate, speaking
7. Dramatics
8. Cheer leaders
9. Birdhouse
10. Banking
11. Poster
12. Program
13. Recognitions
14. Music
15. Subjects
16. Cheering
17. Neatness
18. Housekeeping
19. Citizenship
20. School song, code, yells
21. Team names
22. Courtesy
23. Health
24. Locker
25. Service
26. Sportsmanship

References

BELFOUR, C. S.: Non-athletic High School Contests, *Clearing House*, 12: 81–85, October, 1937.

LIVINGSTON, K. E.: Inter-home Room Competition, *School Activities*, 9: 183–184, December, 1937.

McKOWN, H. C.: "Home Room Guidance," pp. 157–162, McGraw-Hill Book Company Inc., New York, 1934.

MILLER, M.: A Song and Yell Contest, *School Activities*, 8: 22–24, February, 1936.

ROBINSON, M.: A Score Card for Home Rooms, *School Activities*, 10: 391, May, 1939.

WELSH, R.: A Team for Everyone and Everyone on a Team, *School Activities*, 15: 153–155, January, 1944.

Interscholastic Activities

1. Assembly program exchanges
2. Goodwill visits and trips
3. Correspondence idea exchange
4. Student council convention

5. Organization of council in another school
6. Exhibits and demonstrations, exchanges and visits
7. Forums, discussion meetings, conferences
8. Social activities—parties, picnics, banquets, hikes, outings
9. Interschool student council
10. Extracurricular tournament
11. Student conferences—guidance, vocations, study, school problems
12. Literary, debating, speaking, and athletic activities

REFERENCES

An Annual Conference of Student Councils, *School Review*, 46: 321–323, May, 1938.

ARNOLD, H. A.: These Students Go Calling, *School Activities*, 7: 8–10, May, 1936.

BEDICHEK, R.: Interschool Contests, *Clearing House*, 6: 83–89, October, 1931.

BOONE, W. R.: The Exchange Program, *School Activities*, 12: 20, 40, September, 1940.

FINLEY, E. D.: Council Convention in Illinois, *School Activities*, 10: 308, March, 1939.

GERNANT, L.: Kalamazoo's All-school Council, *Journal of the National Education Association*, 120: 226–227, May 3, 1937.

GILBERT, C. R.: The One-day Hi-Y Conference, *School Activities*, 5: 12–14, January, 1934.

HANSON, C. C.: The Visiting School Plan, *Nation's Schools*, 26: 53–54, October, 1940.

HELMS, R.: Pupils Visit to Learn of Other Schools, *School Activities*, 10: 160, 182, December, 1938.

JAMES, C. A.: An Extra-curricular Tournament, *School Activities*, 7: 22–23, April, 1936.

KLINGBEIL, M.: To Encourage Inter-school Friendliness, *School Activities*, 14: 27, September, 1942.

McKOWN, H. C.: Recognizing Academic Heroes, *School and Society*, 20: 23–24, July 5, 1924.

Masters, J. G.: Student Conference on the Basic Principles of Democracy, *School Activities*, 9: 299–300, 342, February, 1938.

Murray, J. L.: Youth in Action, *School Activities*, 11: 91–92, 112, October, 1939.

Porter, V. L.: A Federation of Student Councils, *School Activities*, 14: 24–25, September, 1942.

Temple, O. J.: Student Governing Body Sponsors Council Round-up, *School Activities*, 13: 352, 365, May, 1942.

Wilds, E. H.: Improving the Inter-school Contest Program, *School Activities*, 6: 3–5, 11–13, October, November, 1934.

War

1. Letters, boxes, books, papers to service men and women
2. Scrapbook of pictures and items about former students
3. Service memorial, flag, plaque
4. Purchase of war stamps and bonds
5. Panel discussion on war problems
6. Assembly programs relating to war and local students
7. Airplane models for the government
8. Conservation of school and home supplies and materials
9. Air raid drills
10. Cooperation with Red Cross and Junior Red Cross
11. "Buy a Jeep" and "Name a Bomber" campaigns
12. Home and school war gardens
13. Collection and sale of salvage materials
14. Organization of a School Defense Council
15. Red Cross and first aid classes
16. Promotion of relief drives
17. Air-raid wardens' and fire wardens' groups
18. Promotion of USO canteen
19. Assistance for draft and rationing boards
20. Music and entertainment for USO and neighboring camps
21. Appropriate motion pictures, books, magazine articles, maps

22. Student speakers bureau for war drives
23. Preinduction orientation courses
24. High School Victory Corps
25. Collect phonograph records, jewelry, books

REFERENCES

ANDERSON, H. A.: The High School Goes to War, *School Review*, 50: 609–614, November, 1942.

ANNELLO, M. E.: Special Activities, *Junior College Journal*, 12: 471–476, April, 1942.

BROOKS, J. M.: Students Learn How to Canvass, *School Activities*, 14: 124, December, 1942.

FENN, I. M.: Recognition Boosts Sale of U.S. War Stamps and Bonds, *School Activities*, 14: 336, May, 1943.

HALDY, D.: War Effort at Guyton, *School Activities*, 15: 128, 135, December, 1943.

Handbook of War Savings School Assembly Programs, Education Section, War Savings Staff, United States Treasury Department, Washington, D.C.

HARLAN, J. E.: A Carnival with a Patriotic Slant, *School Activities*, 13: 343–344, May, 1942.

HATTER, L.: Gatesville High School Student Defense Council, *School Activities*, 13: 232, 247, February, 1942.

JOHNSON, I. C.: Training for Defense, *School Activities*, 13: 349–350, May, 1942.

LARRICK, N.: Total War Means Schools at War, *Clearing House*, 17: 76–79, October, 1942.

Letters to Service Men, *School Activities*, 14: 198, January, 1943.

MEYER, F.: Defense Stamps Every School Day, *School Activities*, 13: 338, May, 1942.

MOHRUSEN, J. W.: Our Student Government in Wartime, *School Activities*, 15: 17–18, 22, September, 1943.

MORGAN, R. E.: What the School Can Do in the War Program, *School Activities*, 14: 3–9, September, 1942.

———: School Activities for School Morale, *School Activities*, 13: 331–336, May, 1942.

Perhaps These Ideas on Defense Will Work in Your School, *Nation's Schools*, 29: 16–17, March, 1942.

Reavis, W. C.: What the Secondary Schools Are Doing to Help Win the War, *School Review*, 50: 241–255, April, 1942.

Rumble, H. E.: A Junior High School Buys a Jeep, *School Activities*, 14: 342–344, May, 1943.

Schmidt, A. L.: A School Defense Council, *School Activities*, 13: 266, March, 1942.

Scrapbook of War Efforts, *School Activities*, 14: 236–237, February, 1943.

Wagner, G.: The Campus School Program to Help Win the War, *School Activities*, 13: 302–306, 324, April, 1942.

War Efforts in Schools, *School Activities*, 14: 35–36, 273–274, September, 1942, March, 1943.

War-time Projects in the Schools, War-time Consumer Education, and War-time Practices in Secondary Education, Bulletins No. 108, 109, 110, Vol. 26, National Association of Secondary School Principals, October, November, and December, 1942.

Yagjian, C.: A 100 Per Cent Record in the Purchase of War Bonds and Stamps, *School Activities*, 15: 9–10, September, 1943.

Miscellaneous

1. Compile and keep activity scrapbooks or other permanent records
2. Develop and administer a point scale or similar system
3. Organize a school news clipping service
4. Organize and supervise flag raising and lowering
5. Charter and regulate all school activities and organizations
6. Promote interroom exchanges and visits
7. Charter and supervise a school bank
8. Establish and enforce eligibility rules
9. Promote a summer camp or school cabin
10. Assist in developing home room programs and activities
11. Develop and post, or print and distribute school calendars

12. Register school automobiles; keep record of offenses
13. Promote the ideals and practices of good citizenship
14. Adopt insignia and regulations concerning them
15. Give publicity to commendable school work
16. Organize and supervise school elections
17. Promote store window publicity for special causes and events
18. Inspect school grounds, building, lockers
19. Organize and conduct fire drills
20. Maintain and utilize a question box
21. Develop a school seal, emblem, or plaque
22. Promote custom of annual gift to the school[1]
23. Organize annual reunion for former council members
24. Promote and supervise school bus activities
25. Assume charge of school trophies
26. Promote proper school publicity
27. Make a school movie
28. Promote the development of an alumni association
29. Assume charge of study hall
30. Organize and hold a kite tournament
31. Originate and supervise a civil service system
32. Promote school-community projects

References

Adams, M. D.: Lunch Time Activities, *School Activities*, 13: 282–283, March, 1942.

Adkins, E. P.: School Goes to Town, *Clearing House*, 13: 451–453, April, 1939.

[1] For several years the graduating class of the Warren Central High School, Indianapolis, has presented a gift to the school, each gift being recorded on a metal plate which is a part of an attractive plaque located in the main corridor. The gifts now listed (1944) are, score board, cyclorama, banking boards, portable amplifiers, stage sound equipment, multigraph, running track, glass black boards, mimeograph, gift plaque, parallel bars, flag pole, ditto machine, printing press, entrance pillars, moving picture machine, and public address system.

———: A Student Council Takes to the Community, *Clearing House*, 15: 138–140, November, 1940.

BRYAN, R. C., and G. A. SPAETH: Pupil-managed Study Halls at Western State High School, *School Review*, 50: 196–203, March, 1942.

BUNCLARK, H. M.: Bulletin Boards That Attract and Teach, *School Activities*, 8: 74–75, October, 1936.

BUEHLER, J. B.: Noon-hour Intramural Organization, *Education*, 3: 34–36, October, 1932.

CALVERT, M. M.: For the Alumni, *Clearing House*, 17: 327–330, February, 1943.

COLEMAN, D.: Recess—an Opportunity for Ideal Democratic Living, *School Activities*, 12: 229–230, 255, February, 1941.

DE BADTS, M.: Use of School Bulletin Boards, *School Activities*, 6: 14–16, September, 1934.

ECKELMANN, D.: A Kite Karnival for Windy March Days, *School Activities*, 10: 303–304, March, 1939.

FEINGOLD, G. A.: Pupil Protectors in Study Halls, *School and Society*, 35: 159–161, January, 30, 1932.

HADSELL, R. R.: A National Election Project, *Journal of the National Education Association*, 25: 79–80, March, 1936.

HARDING, A. A.: Alumni Survey, *School Activities*, 13: 139, 156, December, 1941.

Honor Study Halls, *School Activities*, 10: 274–275, February, 1939.

JAMES, C. A.: Noon Hour Leisure, *School Activities*, 6: 17–18, March, 1935.

LAING, H. E.: Pupil Bus Officers Work for Safety in Transportation, *Clearing House*, 16: 12–14, September, 1941.

LINDSEY, R. V.: History of the Pekin Community High School Emblem, *School Activities*, 8: 62–63, October, 1936.

LORENZ, E. R.: Bedlam Used to Begin at 12.15, *School Activities*, 8: 108–109, November, 1936.

MCKOWN, H. C.: "Extra-curricular Activities," rev. ed., Chap. XXV (point system), pp. 622–623 (kite competitions), The Macmillan Company, New York, 1937.

MEYER, F.: Exhibiting Student Government to Parents, *School Activities*, 12: 99–100, November, 1940.

MILLER, C. M.: "Kitecraft and Kite Tournaments," Manual Arts Press, Peoria, Ill., 1914.

MOON, D.: Directed Noon Hour Activities, *School Activities*, 12: 26, 29, September, 1940.

MOOT, E. N.: A Functioning Alumni Association, *School Activities*, 8: 27, 30, September, 1935.

PEDERSON, K. L.: Student Council Launches Noon-hour Recreation Plan, *Clearing House*, 14: 100–102, October, 1939.

PETTY, H.: Interpreting the Student Council, *School Activities*, 11: 323, 351. April, 1940.

SANGSTER, F.: Pupil Participation in Study Hall Supervision, *School Management*, 4: 134, March, 1935.

SCHEER, R. A.: A Noon Hour League, *School Activities*, 7: 16–17, November, 1935.

SCOTT, R. F.: Movie-making Moves In—to Stay, *School Activities*, 10: 197–199, January, 1939.

SHRODE, C.: Student Responsibility in Evansville, *Journal of the National Education Association*, 113: 274–275, March, 1931.

SNOW, C. B., and L. NOTHSTINE: Noon Hour at the Consolidated School, *School Activities*, 13: 196, 206, January, 1942.

STENIUS, A.: The Newsreel—a New Student Activity, *School Activities*, 9: 156–157, December, 1937.

WELSH, R.: A Noon-hour League, *School Activities*, 7: 15–17, November, 1935.

WILLEY, W. M.: The "How" and "Why" in Forming High School Alumni Associations, *School Activities*, 11: 150, December, 1939.

———: What of High School Alumni Associations? *School Activities*, 9: 405–406, May, 1938.

YARNELL, D. A.: Teaching Citizenship by Living It in Honor Study Halls, *Clearing House*, 5: 565–567, May, 1931.

ZIEGLER, L. E., and T. G. THEILMAN: Are High School Codes Worth While? *High School Teacher*, 10: 139–140, 160, May, 1934.

SUPPLEMENTARY ORGANIZATIONS

There are many organizations for young people, initiated and directed by outside groups, which may be developed inside the school or articulated with it. In general, the main objective of all these organizations is the same, the development of character and good citizenship. A letter of inquiry to their headquarters will bring information concerning purposes, membership, programs, and activities. Among the best known of these organizations are the following:[1]

American School Citizenship League, 295 Commonwealth Avenue, Boston, Mass.

American Society for the Prevention of Cruelty to Animals, 50 Madison Avenue, New York, N. Y.

Big Brother and Big Sister Federation, 425 Fourth Ave., New York, N. Y.

Boy Rangers of America, 186 Fifth Ave., New York, N. Y.

Boy Scouts of America, 2 Park Ave., New York, N. Y.

Boys' Brotherhood Republic, 1530–1536 South Hamlin Ave., Chicago, Ill.

Boys Clubs of America, Inc., 381 Fourth Ave., New York, N. Y.

Camp Fire Girls, Inc., 41 Union Square, New York, N. Y.

Four-H Clubs, U.S. Department of Agriculture, Washington, D. C.

Girl Reserves, 600 Lexington Ave., New York, N. Y.

Girl Scouts, Inc., 14 West 49th St., New York, N. Y.

Hi-Y, National Council, 347 Madison Ave., New York, N. Y.

Junior Achievement, Inc., 33 Pearl St., Springfield, Mass.

Junior Red Cross, Washington, D. C.

Kiwanis "Brothers" and "Dads," 520 North Michigan Ave., Chicago, Ill.

Knighthood of Youth, 70 Fifth Ave., New York, N. Y.

Knights of King Arthur, Lock box 776, Boston, Mass.

National Association of Audubon Societies, 1775 Broadway, New York, N. Y.

National Association of Secondary School Principals, 1201 Sixteenth St. N. W., Washington, D. C.

[1] Descriptions of these and others will be found in E. R. Pendry, and H. Hartshorne, "Organizations for Youth," McGraw-Hill Book Company, Inc., 1935.

National Association of Sponsors of Student Participation in School Administration, 1201 Sixteenth St., N. W., Washington, D. C.
National Association of Student Councils, 1201 Sixteenth St. N. W., Washington, D. C.
National Athletic Scholarship Society, J. L. Roberts, 710 Poplar Boulevard, Jackson, Miss.
National Conference of Christians and Jews, 381 Fourth Ave., New York, N. Y.
National Honor Society, 1201 Sixteenth St. N. W., Washington, D. C.
National Junior Honor Society, 1201 Sixteenth St. N. W., Washington, D. C.
National Recreation Association, 315 Fourth Ave., New York, N. Y.
National Safety Council, Educational Division, 1 Park Ave., New York, N. Y.
National Self Government Committee, Inc., 80 Broadway, New York, N. Y.
Pathfinders of America, 968 Hancock Ave., West, Detroit, Mich.
Parent-Teachers Association, Congress of Parents and Teachers, Washington, D. C.
Pioneer Youth of America, 219 West 29th St., New York, N. Y.
Queens of Avalon, Lock box 776, Boston, Mass.
Rotary Boys' Club Work, 35 East Wacker Drive, Chicago, Ill.
Scholastic Magazine Awards, 220 East 42nd St., New York, N. Y.
School Garden Association of America, 121 East 51st St., New York, N. Y.
School Republic, 501 West Mt. Pleasant Ave., Philadelphia, Pa.
Sportsmanship Brotherhood, Hotel McAlpin, New York, N. Y.
U. S. Junior Citizens Service Corps, Washington, D. C.
U. S. Victory Corps, U. S. Office of Education, Washington, D. C
Woodcraft League of America, Seaton Village, Santa Fe, New Mexico
Young Men's Christian Association
Young Women's Christian Association

Selected General References

Cady, H. K.: Hands Off the Student Council, *Clearing House*, 16 15–18, September, 1941.

Council Activities and Projects

BARNES, M. C.: The Value of the Student Council at East High, Waterloo, Iowa, *School Activities*, 10: 400–401, May, 1939.

BARTHOLD, L.: Some Student Council Projects in the Larger School, *School Activities*, 10: 335–336, April, 1939.

BEATTY, J. R.: How Our Student Council Does It, *School Activities*, 7: 5–6, 32, October, 1935.

CELLA, D. H.: Student Participation in School Government, *School Activities*, 7: 5–6, 32, October, 1935.

DIXON, F. B.: The Council at Work Building Morale, *School Activities*, 11: 3–4, September, 1939.

HAGENY, W. J.: 24 Projects of Our Student Council, *Clearing House*, 16: 236–238, December, 1941.

HAND, H. C.: "Campus Activities," McGraw-Hill Book Company, Inc., New York, 1938.

HARVEY, C. C.: Activities and Projects of Student Councils, *School Activities*, 15: 165–168, January, 1944.

———: Seed Corn for Ideas: 60 Group Projects for High Schools, *Clearing House*, 18: 396–401, March, 1944.

HAYES, A. G.: The Student Council, *Education*, 56: 101–103, October, 1935.

HOLPER, S. D.: The Student Council at Work, *School Activities*, 11: 200–201, January, 1940.

JARVIE, L. L.: Students Take Part in Policy Making, *Clearing House*, 13: 223–225, December, 1935.

JORDAN, F.: The Secretary Speaks of a Student Council, *School Activities*, 11: 111–112, November, 1939.

KELLEY, E. C.: Utilizing Student Power, *Journal of the National Education Association*, 25: 217–218, October, 1936.

KITTELL, R.: How One School Does It: Elberle Learns by Doing, *Survey Graphic*, 26: 350–351, June, 1937.

MEYER, F.: Pupils Share in Control of Our Small Junior High School, *Clearing House*, 16: 87–91, October, 1941.

PINTO, D.: Citizenship Activities of Lakewood High School, *Clearing House*, 17: 97–98, October, 1942.

Practical Experiences in Democracy (two series of six articles each), *Clearing House*, 16: 3–23, 77–99, September, October, 1941.

SPRAGUE, J. B.: How Student Participation Functions at Bernards, *School Activities*, 11: 202–203, January, 1940.

The Student Council

STRANG, R.: "Group Activities in College and Secondary School," Harper & Brothers, New York, 1941.

VAN TIL, W. A.: Student Council: An Adventure in *Real* Education, *Clearing House*, 13: 524–526, May, 1939.

WATSON, N. E.: A Program for the Elementary School Advisory Council, *School Activities*, 8: 349–350, April, 1937.

WILKINS, W. L., and W. D. WILKINS: Student Activities in the Junior College, *Educational Administration and Supervision*, 25: 425–434 September, 1939.

Chapter X

Financial Administration of School Activities

MOST of the extracurricular activities of the high school and college "just grew up," uninitiated, unencouraged, unguided, unsupervised, and often even uncontrolled, by educational authorities, each developing out of a need felt by the students themselves. In like manner the methods of financial administration, if these could be dignified by such a designation, "just grew up" with the activities. The result was that each organization raised, handled, and spent its money in any way it pleased. As could be expected, the result was, and still is in some schools,[1] financial chaos, slipshod methods of raising funds; numerous and scattered accounts; careless and unbusinesslike methods of bookkeeping and banking, or none at all; squandered and lost, and sometimes stolen, funds;[2] unauthorized and unsupervised purchases; unpaid bills and unaccountable deficits; orgies of "spending what's left"; duplications of functions and activities; and senseless jealousies and conflicts between organizations. The inevitable final result was an unbalanced program, the over-development of some activities and the underdevelopment of others. Naturally, such loose and unbusinesslike financial administration brought the program into disrepute and handicapped its healthy and wholesome growth.

[1] "We are still in the hoop-skirt, horse-and-buggy era in financing our school activities" is the opening sentence of H. J. Becker's article, Financing Activities the Modern Way (see references).

[2] An interesting discussion of student graft in connection with college activities is G. S. Smith, Student Racketeering, *Scholastic Editor*, 10: 8–9, 28, March, 1931.

However, a few years ago when authorities began to appreciate the educational opportunities of the activity program and took steps to capitalize these, they immediately sensed the necessity for extending supervisory control to its financial administration. This recognition and acceptance of responsibility brought improvement, but even today extracurricular finances are still far from satisfactory.[1] As a matter of fact, this phase is the weakest part of the extracurricular program. Naturally, any schedule of work designed to improve the activity program must, of necessity, include provisions for the proper handling of its finances. If, as has been indicated throughout this book, the student council should assume a considerable share of the responsibility for this program, it should also assume a considerable share of the responsibility for its financial administration. How to do this satisfactorily is the theme of the present chapter.

PURPOSES OF FINANCIAL ADMINISTRATION

The objectives of financial administration of the activity program are implied in the above paragraphs, but a short discussion will clarify them and emphasize their importance.

1. To Ensure the Development of a Wholesome and Well-balanced Program.—Financial control represents the

[1] It is interesting to note that the phase of extracurricular activities most investigated by graduate students and others is financial administration. The following earlier surveys are illustrative: P. E. Belting, "The Community and Its High School," pp. 264–266, D. C. Heath and Company, Boston, 1923; H. C. McKown, and M. B. Horner, "Financial Administration of Extra-Curricular Activities," Twenty-fifth Yearbook, National Society for the Study of Education, Part II, pp. 111–126, 1926; and A. G. Starr, A Study of the Methods of Handling Student Finances in the Public Secondary Schools of California (unpublished master's thesis), Stanford University, 1927, reproduced in E. K. Fretwell, "Extra-curricular Activities in Secondary Schools," pp. 449–454, Houghton Mifflin Company, Boston, 1931. The most recent comprehensive published survey is E. B. Brogue, and P. B. Jacobson, "Student Council Handbook," Chap. X, National Association of Secondary School Principals, March, 1940.

most effective means of guiding the development of school activities. An inflated organization can be quickly deflated by a tightening of the purse strings, and a deserving undeveloped activity can be encouraged by a loosening of them. Wise financial regulation promotes a natural, steady, and healthy growth of activities, proper correlation and constructive supervision, and helps to guarantee a permanency of ideals, policies, and practices which are little affected by changes in membership or sponsorship.

Further, by being in the hands of a competent central committee or council which is interested in the school as a whole rather than in specific activities only, overemphasis and too generous support on the one hand and underemphasis and lack of support on the other will be avoided. To repeat, the healthy growth of the extracurricular program depends more upon the use of sound methods of financial organization and administration than upon anything else.

2. To Educate Participants, Both Direct and Indirect.— A quotation from Fretwell is pertinent.

"The school that provides a favorable situation for loose practices in handling money is little short of criminal. The crime is not so much that some pupils, teachers, or board members have an easy chance to be dishonest. It is rather that, as a result of the school's muddling along, pupils come to think that public business should be handled in this way."[1]

Ultimately all students will handle funds of their own, and some of them will hold positions of trust and confidence in which they will handle the money of employers, employees, and the general public. Wisely designed and closely supervised, the numerous and varied responsibilities involved in the financial administration of activities will set the proper ideals and give some little actual practice in approved business methods. For instance, a student who learns how to keep an

[1] FRETWELL, *op. cit.*, p. 446.

organization's financial account, or to make out a statement or report in proper form; who helps to audit the books of some organization or watches the auditing of his own; who feels responsibility for every single penny entrusted to him; and who learns to use care in making purchases or paying bills, receives a practical education which he can use as long as he lives. So also does the student who is not directly charged with these responsibilities but who learns about them in his group meetings, from his school newspaper, and from casual contacts and conversations. Whether participating directly or just witnessing, the students can profit from these educational settings. Hence, only the best methods of business organization and procedure should be used.

SOURCES OF ACTIVITY FUNDS

Extracurricular finances really represent "big business." A program of activities costs a very considerable amount of money; perhaps, in the average school, five dollars or more per student. In nearly all schools all or most of this money must be raised, because it is not provided by the board of education. Because the methods of raising funds are inextricably bound up with the purposes, ideals, policies, and practices of these activities, a critical examination of these methods is an essential part of the council's responsibilities and program. As might be expected in the case of an educational program and its financial system, both of which "just grew up," the methods of raising money also "just grew up." Although these methods are more or less thoroughly established in American schools, this fact in itself is not sufficient justification for their continued use.

1. Admission-fee Events.[1]—With the possible exception of seeking collections, donations, and subscriptions, charging

[1] Discussions of the troublesome admission-fee tax will be found in The Public School Pays the Tax on Admissions, *Bulletin of the National Associatio*

admission fees is the oldest method of financing activities. Such fees were charged to dramatic, music, speaking, and social events long before organized athletics appeared, and today this method is the main standby of financial support. Therefore it will be considered in detail. For our purposes here these events will be divided into two main groups, "inside shows" staged by students and teachers, and "outside shows" staged by outside individuals or groups.

Inside Events.—The most common inside admission-fee events are:

Athletics	Social activities
Dramatics	Assembly programs
Music	Motion pictures
Fairs, carnivals, circuses, and bazaars	

Because its income is relatively large while its expense is relatively small, this type of public show is the activity program's best revenue producer. What are the arguments for and against admission fees to inside shows? To what extent are these arguments valid? Why? A detailed discussion should help to answer these all-important questions.

Arguments in Favor of Admission Fees.—1. The practice is well established in adult and school life and hence students expect to pay admission fees to public events. In other words, "The money is there for the taking, so why not take it?"

The main objective of the school is educational development, and any school practice or procedure must be justified on the basis of its direct or indirect contribution to this objective. Because the above argument does not include a consideration of whether the practice is right or wrong, beneficial or detrimental, it is not sound.

---

of Secondary School Principals, 26: 77–90, January, 1942; and Federal Tax on Admissions, *School Activities*, 14: 191–193, January, 1943.

2. Children and their parents spend money for other shows, entertainments, and spectacles, why should they not spend a part of it at school events where the quality of production is higher than elsewhere?

One of the wonders of the age is that school people will use such an argument, but they do. What the child and his parent do with their money is, directly, none of the school's business. Certainly the school is in no way charged with the supervision of the family's expenditures. True, it should have some responsibility in providing training in thrift, but it would surely have a great deal of trouble in trying to prove that a performance staged by a group of juvenile amateurs would represent more thriftiness than spending it for an event produced by a group of professional adults.

3. Charging an admission fee ensures a show of higher quality than if no such fee were charged.

In the first place, this argument is based upon the theory that the more a thing costs the more it is worth, and the less it costs the less it is worth. Hence, something which costs little or nothing is worth little or nothing. This belief is well established in the public mind. For instance, it is well known that manufacturers often sell practically the same article for two different prices, and also that many individuals buy the higher priced item believing that they are getting more for their money. The above argument is only conjectural. Perhaps fewer parents would attend an event if no fee were charged, perhaps more would attend. Judging by the extent to which parents attend concerts, games, exhibitions, and motion pictures in public parks, and visit museums, zoos, exhibits, public libraries, swimming pools, bathing beaches, and other free shows, entertainments, and diversions, this argument will not hold. Anyway the main concern is not whether or not the parents attend, but rather whether or not the production is educationally profitable, directly and indirectly, to the students.

It may not be encouraging to promoters of school events to say this, but nevertheless it is true that parents attend these affairs largely only because their children or their children's friends are in them. If such events were staged by a group of students from a distant school, there would hardly be a "corporal's guard" in attendance.

In the second place it is argued that because admission fees are charged the production must be good "in order to give the public its money's worth," and hence the event will be well motivated. To some extent this may be true, but it does not take into consideration the important fact that there is a point of diminishing returns in the expenditure of time and effort on such polishing. Doubtless, in many instances, the extra time spent in polishing a public show would be much better expended if it were invested in some other, or in several other, events or activities. Another pertinent discussion of this audience-pleasing policy will be found on page 233.

4. Activities must be supported by admission fees and other methods because the board of education does not pay for them.

This is a tacit admission that there is probably little or no justification in charging admission fees, but under the circumstances, if the program of activities is to be continued, there is no alternative to following this practice. From an immediate point of view there may be some strength in this position; but from an ultimate point of view it is unsound. If the policy is illogical and detrimental educationally, as will be shown later, then it is wrong irrespective of the objective in view. Further, there is ample reason to believe that if the community were properly enlightened it would demand adequate support for the program from the board of education. This topic will be discussed more in detail in the following section.

Arguments against Admission Fees.—1. An admission-fee policy overemphasizes the raising of money. The educational potentialities of an activity cannot be completely capitalized so long as there is also an emphasis upon developing it for some other purpose. So long as an activity is considered as a means of raising money the efforts are no longer unified in an attempt to achieve one purpose but are divided in an attempt to achieve two purposes. If one purpose must be relatively neglected it is sure to be the educational, never the financial. Hence, when the success of a public event is determined by the extent to which it pleases the spectators, its educational possibilities are forgotten.[1] Despite teachers,' coaches,' and administrators' voluble assertions to the contrary, the average school show is staged mostly for the benefit of the public with an eye to the box office receipts.

Consider athletics for a moment. More money is involved in this program than in all other school activities combined. Expenses of equipment, travel, officials, and guarantees are heavy and these must be met. Herein lies the greatest weakness of our modern athletic program, the necessity for a "winning" team; patrons do not crowd into the gymnasium or stadium when a "losing" team plays. Hence, the emphasis must be upon "winning" games, not necessarily boys.

An excellent example of this sad state of affairs recently came to light. A large American university, known in the 1920's for its winning football teams, promoted a bond issue and built an enormous stadium. Sometime thereafter the administration in a campaign of "purification" fired the famous coach and most of his staff, including a high-salaried and high-powered publicity agent, abolished lush scholarships—

[1] A very sensible attitude toward activity financial profits is reflected in this statement from "Rules for Conducting Student or School Funds and Certain Activities in All Day and Evening, Elementary, Junior, and Senior High Schools, and Junior College," a bulletin published by the Los Angeles City School District, Sept. 21, 1930: "It must be clearly understood that student body activities should not be carried on primarily for the purpose of making profit."

footballships is more accurate[1]—and deemphasized football to such an extent that within two or three years this university had great difficulty in breaking even in games with small colleges of the immediate vicinity, and of course it fell regularly before opponents in its own class. Three results were inevitable: (1) an empty stadium on game days; (2) inability to pay interest on stadium bonds, let alone retire them; and (3) a loud wail from the bondholders who had financed the great white elephant. The final result was the appointment of another famous coach, a great fanfare of publicity, and the start of a brand-new program designed to turn out winning football teams, all in order to pay interest and retire the bonds on the stadium. Football in such a setting is not an educational, but a financial, institution. Many other similar examples could be offered.[2]

[1] During a ten-year period at one university the author had eight All-American football stars in his classes. Only one of the eight was even an average scholar.

Following their investigation, High-school Letter Men—Their Intelligence and Scholarship, *School Review, 42:* 534–539, September, 1939, W. H. Reals and R. G. Reess conclude, "In summary, this study would indicate that (1) athletes have slightly lower intelligence than non-athletes, (2) track athletes are significantly higher in intelligence than other athletic groups, and (3) baseball athletes as a group rank intellectually below all other groups. Even more pronounced, it would seem, is the evidence that, with intelligence held constant, the scholarship of athletes is below the scholarship of non-athletes when an objective measure is the criterion."

[2] Said a college coach recently, "We play football to make money. What's more, nearly every one of our players is recruited. . . . Every one of them is getting tuition, room, board, and books. We don't go for that hypocritical stuff of giving them money for phony jobs like winding clocks and tearing pages off calendars at fifty cents an hour. That makes liars out of the players and fakers out of the school. . . . I am a firm believer in giving a football player what he is worth. Most of them are badly underpaid." It is refreshing to hear a college coach tell it straight from the shoulder instead of prattling about "educating for character," "developing good citizens," etc.

In his article, Test Case at Pitt, *The Saturday Evening Post*, Oct. 4, 1939, Francis Wallace states that the salaries of Pitt football players varied, during

Another proof of the influence of the "gate" is to be found in the fact that since 1933 a smaller ball, newer rules, and trickier plays (often greatly publicized) have found their way into intercollegiate football in order to provide more thrills for the spectator and so attract larger crowds. The "lively" ball was introduced into professional baseball for exactly this same purpose. During the present basketball season two proposed changes received wide publicity: the "penalty box"—players who foul out would be sent to this "box" for a short period instead of being removed from the game permanently—and "shooting at either hoop." The coach who proposed the second innovation stated frankly, "This plan will do away with the unpopular zone defense completely and give basketball back to the fans where it belongs."[1]

Note how this demand for a winning team affects the other activities of the program. If the team is successful and draws huge crowds, the resulting "gate" will help to buy instruments for the band, books for the library, a projector for the auditorium, music for the orchestra, or equipment for the dramatic

---

the period 1924–1936, "from $400, plus tuition and books (some $350 additional), to $650, plus tuition and books," and these salaries did not include "gifts by alumni and business men."

Football's Civil War, is the title of an article in *Look*, Oct. 22, 1940. "Dixie pays athletes and accuses the North of rank hypocrisy for not doing the same," runs a subhead.

Formerly many coaches "got a slice of the gate" in addition to their salary. As late as 1939 one famous coach resigned because his athletic board decided to discontinue this practice.

A pertinent article is McCarthy, J., Win—Or Else, *The Commentator*, November, 1937.

However, the present picture is not all bad. Johns Hopkins abolished athletics scholarships in 1935, and admission fees in 1937. Chicago University and other institutions have acted to rationalize their athletic programs. It appears that a new day is arriving.

[1] From the newspapers of Feb. 18, 1944. An excellent book to read in this connection is J. B. Nash, "Spectatoritis," Dodd, Mead & Company, Inc., New York, 1932.

club. The greater the gate the greater the benefits for all activities, and, vice versa, the smaller the gate the fewer the benefits. This is a vicious relationship.

Naturally, the arguments advanced by the athletic or dramatic coach and the music director are that (1) such participation is educationally valuable to the participants; (2) a crowd adds to motivation and improves competency in the activity; and (3) being on a winning team is more educative than being on a losing team.

The first argument is belied by the facts. If the coach was so deeply interested in education he would use players who were relatively incompetent instead of those who are already "good." In other words, those students who most need the benefits claimed do not receive them, and those who do receive them do not, relatively speaking, need them. The second argument is met on page 228. The third argument fails to recognize that, as any teacher and coach knows, being a member of a winning team often has a bad instead of a good effect on the player. A team that loses all its games would hardly represent a good educational vehicle; and no more would one that won all its games. The responsibility for a fair balance of wins and losses should be placed upon the individual who schedules the games with the other schools.

What has been said about athletics is also true of dramatics, and, to a lesser extent, of music programs.[1] It accounts for the fact that the average high school play is a low-grade farce, staged to tickle students and parents, produce belly-laughs, and bring fee-paying crowds. In general, the music program is better, except in those instances in which, owing to important interscholastic competitions, winners are demanded.

2. Admission fees are probably illegal. Perhaps no one knows for certain, at least the author has never been able to locate a test case, but it is quite likely that admission fees to

[1] See Klein, M., Music or Show, *Etude*, 61: 716, 756, November, 1943.

school events are unlawful.[1] Certainly they are most illogical. The school belongs to the patron, the teachers and coaches are his employees, and the players, actors, and musicians are his own children. Theoretically, at least, he has as much right to walk into a school event without paying an admission fee as he does to walk into the school office or classroom at any time he wishes.[2] Some parent could perform a real service by refusing to pay an admission fee, being thrown out, and then bringing suit against the school. Such a case would set a precedent which would help to define the legality of all such fees.

More than twenty years ago Cubberley wrote,

> A very good case can be made out against entertainments to raise money for school needs. . . . It can be argued that it is not the business of the principal or teachers to raise money for school purposes . . . that any form of entertainment for school purposes in a public schoolhouse ought to be free for all, and that the school, being a state institution, should have its legitimate needs met by general taxation instead of trying to extract small sums of money from parents and children who often can hardly afford to pay. . . . Once begun, the board of education is likely to use their success as an excuse for not appropriating funds another year, and the abuse persists.[3]

Outside Shows.—In an earlier day it was a common practice for the school to contract for lectures, plays, lyceum courses, exhibits, moving pictures, etc., to be given or shown

[1] In the San Francisco schools such fees are illegal, as the following quotation from *School Executive*, January, 1941, indicates: "On the basis that education for children of school age should be free, the legal representatives for the San Francisco board of education have ruled that student fees are illegal. This affects the practices with reference to laboratory materials, locker keys, band instruments and many areas of extracurricular service."

[2] About the most completely illogical practice is that of charging an admission fee to the baccalaureate sermon or the graduation exercise.

[3] Cubberley, E. P., "The Principal and His School," p. 540, Houghton Mifflin Company, Boston, 1923.

at the school building. Perhaps before the development of radio, motion picture theaters, and easy transportation this policy was somewhat justifiable because it did bring high class talent into the school and the community. Today, however, there is comparatively little of this done. Even now, as then, there are several weaknesses and dangers: contracting for such a program is rather speculative due to the expense, uncertainty of the weather, a lack of definite knowledge as to how the event will attract, etc.; a split responsibility between the school and the two contracting parties; probable unpleasantness due to children sandbagging their parents and friends and others into buying tickets; and the relatively small share of the profits which go to the school. The present-day practice in some communities of the students' selling tickets, on a commission basis, to the local theaters represents another example of misguided effort.

Other Admission-fee Events.—In addition to athletics, dramatics, and music, there are other admission-fee activities. Although nearly all the possible criticisms of these plans have been suggested in the previous pages, a very brief discussion of these additional activities will help to complete the picture of this type of financial support.

Assembly Programs.—There is no more legality or justification for charging the student an admission fee to an assembly program held during school hours than there is for charging him an admission fee to his classes. The assembly program is recognized as a school essential, and as such it should be paid for by the educational authorities. The argument, "this is a special program and costs extra" does not change the picture in any way. There is a little more to be said for an "assembly program" or a motion picture show held in out of school hours for the distinct purpose of raising money, but not much. Usually, too, in the case of the motion picture, the theater owners will protest, charging unfair competition.

Fairs, Circuses, Carnivals, and Bazaars.—Concerning these events one educational authority recently stated, "At least these activities are honest in that they make no bones about being largely educational; they are designed as money raisers, pure and simple—and they are usually simple." This statement appraises them quite fairly. In spite of the fact that they are financially profitable, such activities are cheap, undignified, and generally disorganizing to the school. The gambling games and lotteries and the sales of vulgar novelties, which are banned in any other school setting but often approved for the carnival, reflect credit on no one connected with the school.

Social Events.—Scheduling parties, dances, banquets, teas, light entertainments, and other social events for the purpose of raising money represents another form of misdirected effort. While it may be perfectly proper for those attending these affairs to pay for the music, refreshments, decorations, and other legitimate expenses of the occasion, any effort to make money from them represents a commercialization that is unjustifiable for the reasons suggested before.[1] Further, the argument sometimes heard, that by charging an admission fee the school can exclude undesirable guests, is stupid; it means that all students are charged an admission fee so that the school can exclude an undesirable guest by refusing to accept his money, a procedure hardly fair to desirable guests. Nor is such an argument complimentary to those responsible for handling properly any unpleasantness that may arise at the event.

Sales of Articles and Services.—In another commonly used method of financing the activity program various kinds of articles and services such as those indicated below are sold

[1] Sometimes, in order to discourage expensive events, a school will "tax" heavily an admission fee over a certain amount, say fifty cents. A much better plan would be to prohibit such excessive fees.

by the students. Sales of articles may be classified into "store," "special event," and "auction" sales.

The School Store.—In many schools a "G.O." or General Organization store or counter is maintained at which books, paper, pencils, ink, candy, ice cream, soft drinks, pennants, jewelry, gym clothes, and other articles commonly used by students are sold, all profits being turned into the activity fund. From a strictly service point of view, this project is quite praiseworthy and, too, it probably does provide some educational opportunities for the few students who are directly and indirectly in charge of it. However, from a financial standpoint, this plan has less to commend it. The volume of business as well as the percentage of profit is usually relatively small, and the final return is rarely large enough to represent any considerable contribution to the activity fund. The fact that a stock of goods must be kept on hand, a part of which will move slowly, if at all, means that there is always some capital tied up in it, capital which someone must provide. Frequent changes of personnel with a consequent wide range of responsibility, plus the often bothersome and confusing details of store-sales procedure, also tend to make for looseness. In general, this activity can be justified on the service basis much more easily than on the financial-profit basis.

Special Sale.—This is an occasional event at which student-produced articles (baked goods, candy, toys, games, art and craft work of a number of different kinds, etc.) and purchased articles (autograph books, pennants, pictures, magazines, photographs, cards, etc.) are offered for sale. Often ice cream, soft drinks, candy, peanuts, popcorn, hotdogs, and similar items are sold at games, programs, and other school events. This method of supporting the activity program is weak and inadequate. Purchasing and selling articles is always speculative and in this setting rarely returns a profit commensurate with the efforts and risks involved; and further, although the students may get a thrill from seeing their work sold, these items and articles probably do not generally represent real values because they cannot compare favorably with similar goods made by professionals which can be bought in nearby stores. What is more, the income from such irregular sales is usually relatively small.

A slightly different form of this device is the selling of activity bonds. Under this plan an organization or activity prepares and sells a short-term (usually from three to five years) interest-bearing bond, generally in small denominations of from one to five dollars, payable out of the profits of the activity. However, such difficulties and uncertainties as lack of substantial security, unassurance of profit, frequent changes in personnel, and possible changes in basic organization and function during the period, combine to make this an unattractive investment. Of course, limited student bank accounts also militate against it. This plan is no more logical than those discussed previously because it emphasizes the financial instead of the educational motive.

Another type of special sale centers around the collection and disposal of junk, scrap iron, paper, and rags. Often this event is a part of a special "clean-up" or similar campaign, but sometimes it is planned, organized, and promoted for the support of a particular event, cause, or activity.[1] Such a campaign may result in some little financial contribution but it should not be tolerated in any self-respecting school because it is so cheap and undignified; and a cheap and undignified method of financing an activity always depreciates that activity. Often classes are dismissed in order that the students may collect junk. The author once visited a school in which two classes were abolished for an entire week in order that their rooms might be used for storage space for the junk

[1] Here we are not considering the use of such an event as a part of a patriotic program.

collected in the annual drive. Incidentally, nearly all the money raised during this particular campaign was used in the necessary repairing and redecorating of these two rooms. Very likely the reader, as well as the author, has seen more than one school corridor or front yard piled high with stacks of old papers and magazines, sacks and bundles of rags, and heaps of scrap metal. What a capitalization of a community's educational plant!

Selling magazines, greeting cards, garden seeds, and similar articles to the patrons of the community represents another form of sale. Several companies have worked out a rather plausible sounding "educational program," organized and supervised by company representatives, for these campaigns, utilizing the art, English, commercial, and other school departments. The advantages claimed for this plan by these companies are greatly outweighed by the disadvantages. The high-pressuring of parents and patrons, the disorganization of regular school work, the relatively small amount of income, and the inevitable conflict in authority between the school and the company are more detrimental than they are beneficial to the school. Of course, such a plan is usually beneficial to the company.

Auction Sales.—This event, often staged in the regular assembly, or in a special assembly, is a sale of unclaimed found articles, items donated by students, such as toys, handcraft, baked goods, etc., "white elephants" from homes, left-overs from carnivals and shows, and general rummage. The arguments in favor of it are that it provides (1) amusement, (2) financial support, and (3) needed articles. Obviously, all of these arguments are very lame. This is another cheap and undignified financial method. And inevitably parts of it are downright "gyps" because some of the sales do not represent full and needed value for money paid.

Sales of Services.—In some schools such services as raking lawns, mowing yards, cleaning up rubbish, running errands, distributing circulars, advertisements, and papers, and doing other odd jobs are organized and sold through a special committee, sometimes in a "Give a Day's Work" plan. Very often this method is used by some particular group, club, or activity for the purchase of equipment, materials, and supplies. Although such a practice may represent a practical capitalization of the best of student ideals, it is only a makeshift plan of financing because of the uncertainty of employment and the small amount of money earned. Further, if these sales are effected through any sort of high-pressuring, and they often are, the practice will certainly cause the school to lose friends instead of gain them. There is very little to be said in favor of this device.

Miscellaneous Methods of Raising Money.—In addition to the more or less commonly used method suggested above, the following practices are to be found in some schools.

Subscriptions, Collections, and Donations.—These are the oldest methods of supporting a school activity, even of supporting the school itself, but at best they are only makeshifts. Their income is not only usually inadequate but also irregular, due to the varying influence of the season, weather, zeal of the workers, and the financial condition of the school and community. Naturally, such irregularity and indefiniteness bring very difficult budgetary problems. Further, by placing the program on a charity basis, such methods cheapen it.

Membership Fees, Dues, and Assessments.—Although it has been long used and is imitative of adult practice, supporting a school organization or activity through membership fees, dues, and assessments is an unwise practice. Obviously, if these fees are so small that all students can pay them they will usually provide little material assistance; if they are large enough to be of any material assistance they are almost certain to prevent some students from belonging or participating. In case these fees provided insufficient funds, use would have to be made of other forms of financing. The usual method of making an organization "exclusive" is to set a high initiation or membership fee. Needless to state, such a procedure should never be permitted in the school. Because the school is an institution supported by public funds, all the students should have free and equal rights to join any organization irrespective of color, race, creed, or financial standing. Even the use of such a well-established custom as levying class dues is very questionable.

Locker fees are charged in some schools, generally for maintenance purposes, but occasionally for the support of the activity program. Either of these purposes is entirely illogical and unjustifiable. The school has no more right to charge the student a rental fee for a locker than it has to charge him a rental fee for his seat or desk. This, of course, does not apply to a key or lock deposit.

Student Tax.—Quite a number of secondary schools levy a regular tax on all students, usually limiting either or both voting and participation privileges to those who pay this tax. The arguments used in support of this plan are that (1) it corresponds to that used in an adult system of self-government; and (2) it helps to finance the extracurricular program. There is no soundness in these arguments. Such a plan is unjustifiable because (1) it is illegal in a public school—not a court in the land would uphold it; (2) it confuses "self-government" with "participation in control"; and (3) the amount received is relatively insignificant—the usual tax is only a few cents, while the price of the average activity ticket is around four or five dollars.

Admission Fee Tax.—Occasionally, in decentralized systems where each organization or activity raises and handles its own funds, a certain tax, say 10 per cent, is imposed by the council on these receipts, especially those of large revenue-producing activities like athletics, dramatics, and music. These tax moneys are placed in the council's general treasury and are used for the support of non-revenue-producing activities. In itself, this plan is commendable. However, because the decentralized system is weak and the use of this tax plan will tend to perpetuate it, an admission fee tax is really a hindrance to progressive financial administration.

Tag Days.—This is about the cheapest method of supporting anything. Recognizing that such glorified begging, the twin sister of "pan-handling" or "mooching," is a disgrace to a civilized society, many progressive communities have abolished it in favor of dignified drives or direct taxation for chest purposes. This device is cheap because it represents sand-bagging; the individual buys a protective tag against further molestation with "the smallest coin that will make the biggest racket when it is dropped into the can" and cannot tell in half of the instances the name or the purpose of the organization he helped. Further, this practice brings in but small income, makes the organization or activity a recipient of charity, and adds few or no intelligent friends to the cause supported. About the only value is publicity, but publicity will not pay bills.

Popularity Contest.—In this plan votes are sold, and the girl receiving the greatest number is declared "School Queen," "Miss Blank High School," or "Our Pin-up Girl." Obviously, this is not a "popularity" contest at all; it is a "pocketbook" contest. No school which values community respect would stage such a "medicine-show" device, and no self-respecting girl would permit herself to be commercialized in such a manner.

Interest on Funds.—A few years ago a rather substantial movement began in this country for the development of "interest-bearing funds" for the support of activities. However, it was short lived because its promoters soon recognized its inadequacies: (1) it would require an enormous amount to return an appreciable help; and (2) the emphasis is upon saving, rather than upon wise investing in immediately improved activities. A bank balance is not an interest-bearing fund. It is, of course, desirable for good business reasons, provided it is not too large.

Profits.—Planning the newspaper or yearbook or other activity with a view to making a profit with which to increase the general activity fund is no more reasonable than planning athletics, dramatics, or music programs for a similar purpose. Where the finances of all activities are not handled through one central fund, any such apparent profits should be returned in the form of more or better publications or pertinent activities.[1] About the stupidest form of such a plan is that in which the profits from the cafeteria or other essential and recognized school service are used to support activities.

Fines.—The practice of turning library fines into the activity fund is not justifiable because these fines are designed to repair and replace library materials. Student court and similar fines for violations of rules, regulations, or traditions are questionable, and anyway, they are so irregular and small that they are of no financial consequence. The same objections can be made to the small fees some Lost and Found committees assess for their work.

Home Room or Class "Guarantees."—Under this plan, used by a few schools, each home room, class, or other general organized group in the school guarantees a certain amount, say one dollar, for each of its members. All activities are free and no tickets are issued or used. This money is raised by all

[1] Charging for advertisements in the school newspaper, yearbook, or other legitimate publication, provided these displays represent bona fide advertising of items which the students buy, is justifiable. Advertisements of the "Compliments of" and "Best Wishes" type represent charity, not advertising, and should not be used.

sorts of devices, sales, playlets, movies, collections, etc. Obviously, while this plan eliminates all admission-fee routines, it is based upon the unsound procedures discussed previously, and really multiplies their use by the number of home rooms or groups participating. Further, it is easy to see the possibilities of the conflicts and confusions which would probably arise.

Activity Ticket.—For quite a while most colleges have had the practice of assessing a registering student a certain amount and giving him a ticket entitling him to the various extracurricular privileges. A few years ago this plan began to find its way into the secondary schools and during the past decade this practice has extended widely. Originally, in the high school, the ticket concerned only a few of the activities, mainly admission-fee events; but now in many schools it covers any and all participation. The price depends, of course, upon the total amount represented by the items covered, generally running from about one-third to one-half of this sum.

The usual plan is to sell the student a numbered card, book of coupons, stamp book, or strip of tickets which admits him to the games, programs, and other events of the year, entitles him to the newspaper or other publication, and affords him all the general privileges and opportunities for which fees are charged.[1] Generally, these tickets are sold in the fall during a special drive or campaign. Usually provisions are made for them to be paid for in installments, at a slightly higher price

[1] Descriptions of these devices will be found in the following articles: H. M. Brier, Stamps Finance Publications! *Scholastic Editor*, 15: 2–3, March, 1936; Activity Ticket, *School Review*, 44: 326–327, May, 1936; F. L. Jewel, A Coupon Finance Plan, *School Activities*, 6: 12–14, September, 1934; E. C. May, One Fee for All Pupil Activities, *School Review*, 37: 304–306, April, 1929; and W. H. Green, The Activities Budget, *Clearing House*, 4: 284–290, January, 1930. A considerable part of this last article is reproduced in Fretwell, *op. cit.*, pp. 456–461.

The purchase of tickets is voluntary, but those who do not purchase them pay regular full prices for the activities.

This plan of financing activities has four main advantages: (1) it eliminates all or nearly all of the cheaper methods; (2) the amount paid for the ticket is considerably less than the total amount if each item were paid for individually; (3) because the approximate amount of money from the sale of these tickets is known early in the fall, a more accurate activity budget can be made; and (4) it makes possible activities which are valuable but have no income or insufficient income. The main disadvantage is that the price of the ticket is rather high and may discourage buying. However, as suggested above, provision for partial payments obviates this difficulty. Such a provision does, of course, entail some work in keeping records, collecting payments, and stopping tickets if payments cease, but the additional amount charged for partial payments may compensate for this work. In general, this is the most sensible and businesslike method of financing activities that has been discussed so far in this chapter, but it, too, is illogical, as will be shown in the following section.

Board of Education Subsidies.—Every one of the methods of supporting activities so far discussed in this book is illogical, unjustifiable, inadequate, and detrimental. There is only one logical, justifiable, adequate, and beneficial method of supporting these activities, and this is by means of subsidies, grants, or allotments by the board of education. It is entirely reasonable that if extracurricular activities are educative they should be supported in exactly the same way that all other educative opportunities are supported; and, if they are not educative, they should be eliminated from the schools. However, they have been accepted as sound educational devices and consequently they should be financed by the board.

Such financing by the board of education would (1) make these activities more dignified and important; (2) ensure adequate support for all of them; and (3) improve them because of the resultant demand that they represent profitable educational investments.

It is only fair to point out that school boards increasingly are recognizing and accepting their responsibilities in this connection. For instance, nearly all boards have done one or more of the following, and a few boards have done all of them: (1) allowed school time for these activities; (2) allowed teacher time for them; (3) provided equipment, supplies, and materials; (4) abolished admission fees to public events; and (5) completely financed certain non-self-supporting activities. All of these represent desirable progress. The next and final step, which will ultimately come, is a complete subsidizing of all activities by the board of education and the abolishment of all the uncertain, illogical, and unbusinesslike methods by which they are at present supported. Hasten the day!

THE ORGANIZATION OF FINANCIAL ADMINISTRATION

Types of Financial Organization.—There are two main types of financial organization of school activities, the decentralized and the centralized. In addition there are, sometimes, variations and combinations of these.

Decentralized Type.—This type of financial policy and organization, frequently found in smaller schools, is quite similar to that which was common several years ago when each organization or activity raised, handled, and spent its funds in any way it pleased. Today, however, there are more regulations and limitations concerning bookkeeping, accounts, reports, audits, use of surplus, etc., than there were in an earlier day. However, despite some improvement in procedure, this plan still has many of the disadvantages and weaknesses suggested at the beginning of the chapter, and has so few of the advantages and strengths of the centralized plan that it will not be discussed further.

Centralized.—In this type of financial organization all funds from whatever source are placed in one central account which is handled by a central treasurer acting under a board of control, council, or committee. The money is disbursed upon the requisitions, properly authorized by the central administrative group, of the officers of the various organizations. Sometimes the procedure is routed through the commercial department or through the school bank.

Although the central treasurer is responsible for all activity funds, he does not supplant the treasurers of the various organizations. These still function in the collection of fees, dues, assessments, and other moneys, as well as, in certain instances, receiving funds from the central treasurer and disbursing these. Generally, though, all disbursements are made by the central treasurer.

Methods of Handling Council Finances.—There are several methods of handling the financial matters of the council, some of which are better than others. A brief evaluative discussion of these will show their appropriateness.

The Principal.—In many schools, especially the smaller, the principal makes all or nearly all the decisions involving money, and he handles the funds. This plan is unwise because it attempts to separate financial matters from all other council interests and projects—something very difficult, if not impossible, to do because nearly all of the council's program will be very closely tied up with finance. Activities may be developed, controlled, and, if necessary, even abolished through the financial policies of the council, and if these policies are decided upon and established by the principal, the council, for all practical purposes, might just as well quit. The wisdom of having the principal serve as central treasurer is discussed on page 251.

The Council as a Whole.—Perhaps in a small school, or in one where the council does not have a very large program of activities, it might well handle all financial matters. This plan is logical because the council has final responsibility for financing irrespective of the plan used. However, because in almost any school the council will have a rather large job, a better plan is for it to delegate these financial responsibilities to a specialized group.

The Financial Committee.—A very sensible method of handling the financial affairs of the council is through a permanent financial committee. At least the chairman and perhaps other members of this group should be members of the council, but key individuals about the school who are competent in financial administration may be appointed to it by the council. This group prepares and recommends the school budget, on the basis of organization and activity budgets, receives applications for funds, suggests forms, blanks, and bookkeeping methods and financial organization and procedures; recommends general financial policies in raising and disbursing funds; provides for careful audits of all records and reports; submits regular reports to the council, principal, and newspaper; and trains and supervises group finance officers. In short, this committee is the council's clearinghouse on all financial matters. It may, or may not, depending upon the details of the plan adopted, do the actual bookwork, correspondence, and other detailed operations.

It must be noted that this committee, like all other council committees, is an advisory, not a legislative, group. The council constitutes final authority on all financial matters just as it does on all other matters concerning activities within the area of its jurisdiction.

The Commercial Department.—The main difference between this plan and that suggested immediately above is that here the actual clerical, bookkeeping, and financial work is done by the students of the regular commercial classes under the direction of the finance committee.[1] The necessary forms and procedures may not differ in any way from those used in the committee form of administration. If desired, because of the competency of these students, more complicated forms of financial records and practices may be incorporated. In this plan the commercial department really becomes the council's banking headquarters. In some schools a special room or space is set aside in this department for the use of this committee and its helpers. The plan is especially good if the commercial teacher acts as central treasurer. In such an instance all the work is done under his close supervision.

In addition to receiving, handling, and disbursing funds, this type of arrangement may also provide competent help for other important duties, such as the dictating, typing, and mailing of all necessary correspondence, the promotion and supervision of ticket selling and other campaigns and drives, and the securing of competitive bids for important equipment, articles, materials, and services.[2] All these activities represent very practical education for the students concerned. This plan also represents a very tight centralized control. It should be emphasized that this arrangement does not eliminate the council committee; rather, it provides competent, closely supervised help in the handling of the detailed operations.

The School Bank.—The most highly developed form of student-council administration is that in which all business matters are handled directly through a regularly organized school bank. This is imitative of actual adult practice. In general the procedures of this plan do not differ greatly from those of the plan suggested above, and, in schools in which

[1] An article describing such a plan is F. L. Bacon's The Correlation of Extracurricular Activities with the Department of Business Education, *School Review*, 30: 671–678, November, 1922.

[2] For a pertinent article see A. J. Huggett, Guiding Student Buying, *School Activities*, 6P7–10, January, 1935.

commercial students fill the positions in the bank, it is practically the same. Here again, the bank does not displace the council or its finance committee, it merely acts as a clearing house for the actual handling of the details of the committee's business, and as custodian of the council's funds. The central treasurer may be the bank's adviser. In this plan the treasvrer does not have any more authority than he has in the committee arrangement. He is still an employee of the council and is responsible to it irrespective of the type of financial procedures used.[1]

THE CENTRAL TREASURER

Student or Adult?—Should the central treasurer be a student or an adult? The arguments in favor of the student treasurer are that (1) such a plan is logical—if all other council and organization officers are students, so should the treasurer be a student; (2) a student can gain valuable experience through his work as treasurer; (3) the simplicity of the forms and procedures used means that the average student could successfully discharge the duties of this office; (4) the term of office is only for a semester or two and therefore if inefficient administration should appear it would be of short duration; and (5) an adult treasurer might carry too much weight—he might be too officious and not recognize his proper place as an employee of the council.

The main arguments against a student treasurer are that (1) because student officer terms are short such a plan does not provide for a desirable continuity and permanence in service; (2) students are too immature to be held responsible for considerable sums of money; (3) the school may lack complete confidence in a student treasurer; and (4) it will be

[1] A recent description of a school bank will be found in H. E. Collins, Student Savings Bank Activities in Commercial Education, *School Activities*, 12: 8–10, 33–34, September, 1940.

difficult legally to bond a student treasurer because he is not of age.

It appears, in general, that the practice of having an adult for central treasurer is the more desirable plan. There is much more to be said in favor of student treasurers for individual organizations and activities because they are not custodians of any great amounts of money for any considerable length of time. What school officer should be the central treasurer? A consideration of those available should help to answer this very practical question.

School Board Member.—In some schools a member of the school board, often the secretary or treasurer, is appointed central treasurer for all activity funds. This plan is impracticable because such an individual is too far away from the activity program, he lacks sufficient technical and professional knowledge of it, and his position carries too much weight.

The Principal.—In smaller schools the principal usually handles all activity funds and, if he respects his responsibility to the council and does not vitiate the council's program through his own arbitrary decisions and influence, this plan may be reasonable. In schools of any size this plan is hardly desirable. It adds greatly to the principal's load, and is much more likely than in a small school with a limited and closely articulated program to result in a domination of the council's work. In short, the principal of a larger school is too busy to be thoroughly acquainted with the many details of the entire activity program and to handle the burden of the numerous operations which compose the treasurer's job.

The Council Sponsor.—This teacher already has a very heavy responsibility in sponsoring the council and consequently should not be loaded with additional burdens. In addition, his position as treasurer might lead to conflict if his opinions differed seriously with those of the finance committee or council.

The Principal's Secretary.—This individual often acts as central treasurer. Such an arrangement is not particularly bad because this secretary is always available, knows financial methods, and is a responsible and more or less permanent school officer. However, she, too, already has a wide variety of duties to perform. It would probably be better to have some individual who specializes in this area of council relationships and activities, and who is assigned this responsibility as a part of her regular load, not in addition to it.

A Commercial Teacher.—This teacher is more suitable for central treasurer than any other individual in the school. He knows financial methods, materials, and equipment, is respected as a competent technician, and is in better position than anyone else to give definite and professional assistance. If needed, he is in position to provide the necessary help in handling financial correspondence, checking records and invoices, and in the other specialized duties of this office. He should be the sponsor or adviser of the finance committee. It is worth emphasizing again that the council only delegates its authority to the treasurer and he must follow its policies, procedures, and orders.

Bonds and Insurance.—Good business practice demands that the central treasurer be suitably bonded. The expense of such a bond will be small and this money will be well invested because it will not only protect the funds but also it will bring deserved credit to the system, especially from business and professional men.[1] If any considerable amount of money is kept in the school building it should be protected by burglary insurance. Here again the expense will be small, especially if a good safe or vault is used.

[1] The Oklahoma legislature recently enacted a law which requires bonded custodians of student funds, annual audits, and direct supervision of withdrawals of all moneys.

FINANCIAL FORMS AND PROCEDURES

A number of different types of forms and procedures may be used in the administration of activity funds, and a description of all of these would be both confusing and unnecessary. Consequently, only one set of simple and direct forms and the corresponding procedures will be described. These will indicate basie principles, materials, and operations. All forms should be printed rather than typed or mimeographed. Provision should be made for dating all papers and, in the case of receipts, pay orders, checks, requisitions, and similar documents, for serially numbering them. Good business demands that bills be paid promptly and that careful records be kept of all transactions.

Other blanks, forms, and records may be originated and prepared according to the needs of the individual school, and these will, of course, depend upon the size, number of elements, and general organization of the local program. It cannot be overemphasized that, irrespective of the number and type of forms and procedures used, the financial system should be "tight"; it should allow no loopholes through which funds might disappear, duplication of payments be made, errors be unaccounted for, responsibility be unplaced, or officers be unprotected.

In developing forms and procedures, the knowledge and experience of the school's commercial department or teachers and the bank in which the funds are to be deposited should be capitalized. Expert advice will help to devise a plan which is both businesslike and appropriate. The use of such a plan will not only ensure competent handling of funds but also bring desired respect from the firms with which the student council deals. Standard forms ordered from the catalogues of publishers will usually not be as appropriate to the local situation as forms specially designed and printed, and the latter will cost little more.

Activity Report.—Financial reports should be required of all admission-fee events, athletics, music, dramatics, and similar activities. Such reports should show gross receipts, expenditures, and net income. One copy should be filed with the organization staging the event, and the other with the central treasurer.

Ticket Report.—Unless carefully safeguarded, the sale of tickets of any kind may easily bring trouble because of the number of tickets handled and the number of individuals handling them. Hence, a very close and accurate record should be kept. All tickets should be receipted for and a properly balanced final report should always be required. The sale of periodicals, stamps, and other similar items is charged and reported in the same way.

Central Treasurer's Receipt.—This numbered receipt in duplicate, is made out by the central treasurer whenever he receives money from organizations, activities, or individuals. If an organization is being credited, the receipt should indicate it and the name of the officer making the deposit One copy is given to the depositor to become a part of the records of the activity or organization and the other copy is retained by the treasurer for use in making the proper book entries after which it is filed away. This simple and businesslike procedure protects all individuals and organizations concerned

Pay Order.—This form is used whenever the treasurer or other authorized officer of an organization desires to pay a bill or have it paid. It includes the name and address of the payee the amount, the items being paid for, and the account to be charged. It is made out in duplicate, often of different colors the original being clipped to the invoice or bill to be paid and delivered to the central treasurer. The duplicate order remains with the records of the organization. When he receives the order the treasurer checks its authenticity, and in case the organization is operating on a separate account or on a budgeted account, checks the record to see whether there are sufficient funds to pay it, and then issues a check for the amount, retaining a duplicate record on the check stub. Depending on the system used, either he or the treasurer of the organization sends the invoice and check to the payee. If all statements come directly to the central treasurer he sends them to the proper organizations for proper checking and authorization.

Requisition.—There should be a closely observed rule that no purchases may be made and no services engaged without an authorized requisition. Such a form is made out to an individual or firm ordering certain merchandise or service delivered to a specified student. It usually includes items, quantity, and price. "Ordered by" and "charge to" blanks are necessary. This numbered form is filled out by the officer or officers of an organization. Usually the central treasurer must sign it before it can be used. Such a procedure ensures that the organization has sufficient funds either in account or in budget to pay for the purchase. The form is made out in triplicate, one copy for the organization's files, one for the vendor, and one for the central treasurer. Thus it is easy to check the purchased goods against the original order.

Treasurer's Check.—Although the ordinary form of check is satisfactory, provided it is accompanied by some form of remittance advice—invoice, bill, or statement—so that the vendor may know the items being paid for, wide use is now being made of a remittance check or voucher check on which this information appears. The use of such a form does away with the necessity of using a separate remittance advice and when the check is returned through the bank it provides a perfect and permanent receipt for the paid bill. Further, this plan allows the original bill or invoice to be retained for future reference. If an ordinary check is used, the stub should show the account charged and the requisition or order number, in addition to the usual check stub items.

BOOKKEEPING

Accuracy, completeness, and simplicity are the basic requirements of a good system of activity bookkeeping. Complicated systems are inappropriate because of the extra work required and the probability that the frequent change of officers will increase errors. The usual standard columnar book which can be purchased at any bookstore will be found quite satisfactory. In general, a looseleaf type is preferable to the bound book because of the ease of removing and filing old records, the replacement of incorrect, torn, or messed pages, and, in the case of special accounts, the alphabetizing of added accounts. The requirements of the activity program will determine the size of page most desirable. This book may serve as a cashbook, journal, ledger, distribution ledger, or for any other incorporated accounting service. It may be used to good advantage in the general and special account forms discussed below. The book should be of good quality; no "dime store" account or record books should be used. A good book will encourage the keeping of careful records and will also help to guarantee their permanency. Outdated records and accounts should be filed in similar covers where they can be easily referred to as occasion demands.

General Account.—In the simple general-special accounts form of bookkeeping, all transactions, irrespective of type, organization, or purpose, are entered in a separate book, or in set-aside first pages, if a single book is used for all records. In the latter instance, if a bound book is used, it is essential that sufficient pages be reserved to operate the general account for the entire year. If a looseleaf form is used, additional pages may be inserted as needed. In such a case the pages should be numbered in order as they are inserted. Each item in this account is later checked off as it is entered in the proper special account.

The items and corresponding columns in such a book will depend upon the details of the system used, but in general the following are essential: date, item, receipts, total receipts, account, requisition number, check number, amount disbursed, total disbursements, and balance. In some systems, receipts, total receipts, date, and item are placed in this order in the first four columns, but usually the first two columns are used for date and item and the third and fourth for receipts and total receipts. This plan is less confusing and facilitates operations.

Special Accounts.—These are detailed accounts for each organization of the school. They are alphabetized and, in case a single book is used, follow the general accounts. An index helps in locating desired accounts. Usually the same data and columnar arrangement used in the general account are also used in the special account. The "balance" at the beginning of the account is the amount allowed by the council. The practice of carrying a balance in the final column after each entry provides a record which can be immediately located by the central treasurer when he receives a requisition or pay order from the organization. By referring to it he can quickly determine whether or not the organization has sufficient funds with which to pay for the material or services desired.

In this plan trial balances are easily struck. The total receipts of all special accounts can be checked against the total of the receipt column in the general account. The total disbursements of all special accounts can be similarly compared with the total disbursements in the general account. The balance as shown by the bank statement can be easily and quickly compared with the balance as shown in the general account. Of course, unless all checks issued have been banked these balances will not be the same. However, the subtraction of the unreturned checks from the bank's balance will give the real balance as indicated in this general account. This system facilitates auditing and also the preparation of regular reports to the principal or other school officer, and the council.

Auditing.—Irrespective of the type of financial plan used, all accounts should be audited frequently by a competent, disinterested individual or committee. This procedure ensures an adequate system of accounting and accuracy of records, shows trends in development, and assists in preparing the budgets. Many city school systems have adopted rules requiring these audits, some of them specifying that the audits shall be made by the regular accounting officers of the system. This is good practice. Reports of all audits should be made to school authorities and to the student body.

THE ACTIVITIES BUDGET

The activities budget is a sort of financial blueprint of the program for the coming year. It is very important because of the close and direct relationships between finances and activities. Through budget allowances the council can encourage or discourage the development of an activity, and even, if necessary, eliminate it entirely. Consequently, in the interest of a properly developed and well-balanced program, budget making should be given the most serious and intelligent consideration.[1]

A budget represents an adjustment of two elements, income and disbursements, each of which in turn represents a totaling of estimated incomes from all sources, and a totaling of estimated expenditures by all participating organizations. Hence,

[1] Two pertinent articles are W. H. Green, The Activities Budget, *Clearing House*, 4: 284–290, January, 1930; and R. E. Mason, Budgeting the Funds of Pupil Organizations, *School Review* 42: 111–117, February, 1934.

the first step in the preparation of a budget is to obtain these smaller elements.

Disbursements to organizations may be made on the basis of (1) income provided by the various activities, each source receiving all or a proportionate amount of the funds it supplies; (2) need, all income from whatever source going into one treasury; and (3) "millage," each organization being allotted a certain percentage of the available funds, usually on a per capita formula. The first plan is so obviously unsuited that it will not be discussed. The third plan is based upon the assumption that the larger the organization and the more important it is, the more financial support it requires. This assumption is false; the number of participants is not necessarily an index of either the significance of an activity or its financial needs. This plan, too, is inappropriate for the school activity program. The use of the second plan is justifiable.

The central finance committee requests the officers of each organization or activity to prepare and turn in by a designated date an estimated list of expenditures for the coming year. Of course, this is only a guess, but if it is based upon the expenditures of previous years, and careful consideration is given to the possibilities of the present year, it can be a pretty close guess. The committee now carefully studies these proposed budgets, especially if they differ somewhat from former budgets. The committee does not pretend to know the requirements of each group; rather, it assumes that the officers are in better position to know these needs and are therefore more competent to prepare a proposed budget than the committee itself. Consequently, the committee will respect the proposed budgets. However, because this committee must make the necessary recommendations to the council and must support them, it has a perfect right to raise pertinent questions and in case of unusual amounts or items to ask for explanation or justification or request additional information before making a final decision. Some finance committees hold a more or less formal hearing at which the officers appear, pass out copies of their proposed budgets, explain the items, and answer questions. It is a good policy for the officers to include on these sheets the corresponding budgets of one or two years previous. This hearing requires time, but it is a good procedure.

Income begins with the balance, if there was one, carried over from the previous period or year. To this is added estimated receipts from admissions, fees, sales, gifts, activity tickets, and all other probable sources of income. If these sources of income are about the same as those of last year, and the present year appears to represent about the same general prospects, this probable income can be estimated rather accurately.

Disbursements begin with this year's income; no deficits are allowed. When all budgets have been studied and their amounts totaled, this sum is compared with the estimates of the funds available. If these funds appear to be ample the budgets may be approved and sent to the council with a recommendation for adoption. If the funds appear to be too small to allow for this total amount, and no additional money may normally be expected, revisions will have to be made. It is quite likely that in studying these budgets some of the members of the committee may have questioned certain amounts and items and these can be again discussed, if necessary in another hearing before the entire finance committee, and the required adjustments be made. It is important that the reasons for any necessary curtailment should be explained in order to obviate the impression that the committee or council is acting in an arbitrary manner. If such explanations are made probably no organization or officers would complain. In short, mutual respect and confidence between officers and finance committee are essential.

Incidentally, in this connection two suggestions are in order. Because it is a somewhat general policy for all budget-making central groups to pare the budgets of the smaller units, it is usually wise for the latter to request slightly greater funds than they really need. Then when the committee pares the requisitions, these organizations will still have about what they originally had in mind. Another pertinent idea is for the requesting body to make its suggested budget items out in uneven, instead of round, numbers. For instance, an item of $100.00 looks like a pure guess, while an item of $103.68 looks as if it had been "scientifically arrived at."

After the budget has been adopted by the council—it need not be adopted by the school—it is published in the school paper or posted on the bulletin board, because the school has a perfect right to have this information. Its various items need not be justified by written-in explanations. In adopting the budget the council thereby authorizes the central treasurer to allocate the funds as budgeted, and this he does by placing the proper balance to the credit of each organization or activity. It is then the treasurer's business to ensure that these balances are not overdrawn. Any credits which an organization may have at the end of the year are not carried over; they are merely canceled. Each year's business, as far as individual organizations are concerned, should be a unit by itself.

"Little surplus and no deficit" is a good rule for the budget-maker to follow. The council should not allocate all of its funds but retain a reserve, not too large and not too small, in order to meet unforeseen demands. This is provided through a contingency fund, account, or item regularly included in the final budget. On the other hand, good budgeting, at least in normal times, does not allow for deficits.

Selected References

Ash, F. H.: Budgetary Procedures and Accounting Methods for Student Activities in Teachers' Colleges, *Teacher Education Journal*, 2: 165–169, March, 1941.

Auction Sale, *School Activities*, 15: 219, February, 1944.

BABSON, H. C.: The Financial Support of Clubs, *Clearing House*, 5: 407–412, March, 1931.

BEAVER, B. P.: Organizing a High School Co-op, *School Activities*, 14: 331–332, May, 1943.

BECKER, H. J.: Financing Activities the Modern Way, *School Activities*, 9: 414, 416, May, 1938.

BELL, L. W.: Handling the Extra-curricular Finances in a Small High School, *School Activities*, 7: 20–21, December, 1935.

CLELAND, G. L.: A Centralized System of Accounting for Student Activity Funds, "Student Activities in the Secondary School," pp. 29–46, National Association of Secondary School Principals, January, 1944.

EBER, W. J.: An Accounting System for Student Activity Funds, *School Activities*, 11: 389–390, May, 1940.

DIEFENDORF, J. W.: Extra-curricular Activities and Related Business Training, *School Activities*, 12: 339–341, May, 1941.

ELLIOTT, W. H.: A Financial Plan for Small High Schools, *School Activities*, 10: 23–24, September, 1938.

ENGLEHART, N. L., and G. W. GRILL: Internal Accounting for Extra-curricular Activities in Public Schools, *Teachers College Record*, 26: 753–754, May, 1925.

FRETWELL, E. K.: "Extra-curricular Activities in Secondary Schools," Chap. XVII, Houghton Mifflin Company, Boston, 1931.

FRIER, E. A., Jr.: Control of Student Finances, *School Activities*, 7: 20–22, April, 1936.

HARLAN, J. E.: A Carnival with a Patriotic Slant, *School Activities*, 13: 343–344, May, 1942.

HARMEYER, C.: A Dime a Week Did It, *School Activities*, 12: 10, September, 1940.

HARVEY, C. C.: Our Annual High School Carnival, *School Activities*, 14: 57, October, 1942.

HICKS, E. B.: Systematic Banking of Activity Funds, *School Activities*, 14: 107–108, November, 1942.

HOLMES, H. M.: A Simple Plan of Accounting for Pupil Activity Funds in the Small High School, *School Activities*, 14: 21, 39, September, 1942.

HOSTETLER, O. C.: Magazine Sales as a Source of Revenue, *School Activities*, 14: 185, January, 1943.

HUGGETT, A. J.: Burglary Insurance, *School Activities*, 8: 171–172, December, 1936.

LANGFORD, A. G.: Student Activities Financing, *School Activities*, 10: 113–114, 137, September, 1938.

LEWIS, G. T.: Centralizing Student Activities in the High School, *School Review*, 31: 612–626, October, 1926.

MASON, H. V.: The Accounting of Extra-curricular Activity Funds, *School Activities*, 11: 7, 9, 45, September, 1939.

———, R. E.: Budgeting the Funds of Pupil Organizations, *School Review*, 42: 111–117, February, 1934.

MEYER, H. D., and S. M. EDDLEMAN: "Financing Extra-curricular Activities," A. S. Barnes & Company, New York, 1929.

MORNEWECK, C. D.: Evaluation of Current Practices in Financing Extra-curricular Activities, *School Activities*, 10: 3–4, 45, September, 1938.

OGDEN, W.: A School Co-operative, *School Activities*, 9: 159–160, 185, December, 1937.

OLSON, M. W.: Activity Manager in a System of Financing, *School Activities*, 7: 20–21, March, 1936.

PARRY, K.: Maquon's All-school Carnival, *School Activities*, 13: 267–268, March, 1942.

REAVIS, W. C., and G. E. VAN DYKE: "Nonathletic Extracurriculum Activities," pp. 113–117, National Survey of Secondary Education, 1932.

RICHARDSON, H. G.: High School Contests Should be Free to the Public, *School Activities*, 10: 383–384, May, 1939.

SETTLE, M. L.: An Activity Ticket, *School Activities*, 13: 16–17, September, 1941.

SIMPSON, J. L.: Does Your School Have an Albert Conley? *School Activities*, 14: 65–66, October, 1942.

SLOBETZ, F.: An Internal Accounting System, *School Activities*, 11: 113–114, November, 1939.

SMITH, E. C.: Financing Extra-curricular Activities, *School Activities*, 14: 15–16, 34, September, 1942.

Stensaas, W. M.: Who Should Finance Extra-curricular Activities? *School Activities*, 13: 7–8, September, 1941.

Strang, R.: "Group Activities in College and Secondary School," pp. 43–48, Harper & Brothers, New York, 1941.

Terry, P. W.: "Supervising Extra-curricular Activities," Chap. XIX, McGraw-Hill Book Company, Inc., New York, 1930.

Welday, R. A.: A Practical Book Exchange, *School Activities*, 9: 323, February, 1938.

Zeliff, L. A.: Simplified Accounting for Extra-curricular Funds, *American School Board Journal*, 99: 50–52, November, 1939.

Chapter XI

The Student Court

THE one phase of student participation about which there is greatest disagreement is that of student-administered discipline, encompassed by the conception of the student court. The council idea has been generally recognized and accepted by school administrators and teachers, but this recognition and acceptance has not extended to the student court despite the fact that there have been successful courts since the days of Cronson, Gill, and George. A few years ago there was quite a student court movement in America but, probably because of unhappy experience, this movement soon slowed down considerably. However, at the present time there is an increased interest in this form of participation and a new movement is already under way.[1] Whether this interest will continue depends upon the sagacity of court organizers and supporters.

Definition of the Student Court.—A student court, as represented in the discussions of this chapter, is a formally organized and officially authorized group of students charged with the responsibility of assisting in maintaining discipline, especially in out-of-class settings and activities. This court may vary in size and complexity from a simple form built around a single individual or a small committee to a large and highly complicated plan involving a whole system of interrelated bodies. The council itself or one of its committees may be the student court; or this group may be specially

[1] In his study of 1431 councils, Kelley discovered that about one-fifth had student courts; and that 78.9 per cent of these would recommend the court idea, 5.4 per cent would not recommend it, and 16 per cent did not reply to this question. See footnote reference on p. 15.

appointed or elected for this specific purpose. In short, irrespective of the plan used, if the student group is authorized to handle infractions of rules and regulations, the body is a student court.

ARGUMENTS FOR THE STUDENT COURT

The educational purposes or values of a plan of student participation in the handling of discipline are as follows:

1. Wholesome democratic living demands not only that standards of conduct be set, but that actions be judged on the basis of these criteria. Obviously, there is little logic in setting such standards and not making a serious attempt to achieve them. The student court is one device which may be used in this accomplishment. Judicial activities are as important as legislative and executive functions.

2. Through actual participation in helping to develop and uphold desirable standards of conduct, the student will better understand the necessity for these, have a greater interest in them, and more fully appreciate his own responsibilities as a school citizen. Without such personally felt sentiments of law and order there can be no real and true democracy.

3. The student court, through the procedures of complaining, arresting, prosecuting, defending, adjudicating, and punishing, gives realistic training in the duties of citizenship. The student applies what he has learned about such procedures, therefore his education becomes functional.

4. The student-court idea emphasizes constructive education rather than punishment. Defendants are considered as fellow students who need counsel and assistance rather than as school outcasts who should be stigmatized and persecuted. The main purpose is to change a student's attitude, not to punish him.[1]

[1] A good article, which shows the differences between the older and the newer conceptions of discipline, is H. C. Kramer's, Is Punishment a Method of Education?, *Educational Method*, 21: 188–191, January, 1942.

5. The court idea is psychologically sound because it represents discipline from within. As suggested in Chap. II, the average student would much rather face the disapproval of his teacher than the disapproval of his fellow students. Therefore the court can be very effective as a restraining influence.

6. Ultimately the training received through a well conceived and administered school court plan should be of immense value in bringing about a much needed reform in adult court procedure. Endless bickerings over legal technicalities, lengthy delays, the undue influence of precedent and tradition, an emphasis upon law instead of justice, all too common in adult courts, tend to decrease public confidence in this important element of our democratic organization. These undesirable features are not present in a good school court. Hence, it is not unreasonable to expect that a student's experience with his school's judiciary body should be beneficial when, as an adult, he is in a position to cry out against a clumsy and outmoded legal system.

ARGUMENTS AGAINST THE STUDENT COURT

Although some educational administrators have accepted the student court idea, and a few have made vigorous attempts to develop it, the majority of them have been very conservative in their thinking about this device. A critical examination of the arguments raised against it will show the validity of these objections, help to give a proper conception of the plan, and suggest desirable safeguards.

1. Students are not experienced and mature enough to handle cases of discipline. They are likely to be influenced too much by emotional reactions and too little by intellectual considerations.

This was, and to some extent still is, an argument against the general participation plan. However, as shown on pages 14–16, this position is not justified by the facts; there are literally hundreds and hundreds of successful student councils. Similarly, the best proof that this objection to student courts is unsound is the fact that there are a great many of these organizations which do work successfully and bring well deserved credit to those who recognized, appreciated, and capitalized pertinent student interests and abilities.

2. Parents will object to having their children disciplined by other children.

This argument overemphasizes the probability of discipline; it implies that all children of all parents will be so disciplined and that all parents will object. As a matter of fact, relatively few students will ever be disciplined, and even in such cases it cannot be properly assumed that all parents would make such an objection. Of course, some parents would object to discipline at the hands of anyone, school authorities or civil authorities. The average parent who understood the purpose, psychology, and the effectiveness of the plan would in all likelihood credit the school authorities with being very intelligent disciplinarians. Surely the school official who is criticized by some parents for just about everything he does or says should not hesitate to face a little additional criticism by these habitual objectors. In any case, this argument represents a fear much more than it represents a fact.

3. Students are not authorized to discipline their fellow students.

This objection is closely related to that above, but it is enough different to warrant a separate discussion. School officials, administrators, and teachers, only, may legally handle discipline. They are responsible for everything that goes on in the school. However, in any school there are many activities and responsibilities which are delegated to students, such as, for instance, running errands, working in the office or library, selling and taking tickets, opening the classroom doors, raising and lowering the flag, and copying problems and outlines on the blackboard. All these represent teachers', not students', duties, and handling cases of discipline is not a bit different from these. Here too, authority is merely delegated. Further, there is no school statute provision which specifically states that students shall not participate in discipline.

4. A student court will stir up personal animosities between students. Officials, suddenly invested with authority, will probably become arrogant, dictatorial, and overbearing.

This is entirely possible, not only in school life but also in adult community life. However, the fact that a few officers develop in undesirable ways does not mean that the entire plan is worthless. Most student officials, like most adult officials, will be fair and conscientious, especially if they are properly instructed, because they have intelligence enough to recognize that bad attitudes are detrimental to the system and to the school as a whole. Further, it is not reasonable to believe that all those who violate rules and regulations will be entirely sympathetic with these laws or with those who are empowered to enforce them. Why should more be expected of this school situation than is expected of the corresponding life setting?

5. Students are more likely to challenge court authority than they are to challenge faculty authority.

As suggested on pages 34–39, this is not unqualifiedly true. The best discipline is that which comes from within; the poorest discipline is that which comes from without. The court is within the student body; the faculty is without.

6. Because it is imitative of adult forms, school court machinery is apt to become complicated and cumbersome. The main emphasis may be upon the development of pretty, instead of upon effective, machinery.

This possibility exists, but whose fault is it if it does? The students'? The court idea's? The administrator's? There is no necessity for such undesirable development. The court possibilities are definite, simple, and traditionless, and consequently the school can develop any kind of a plan it wishes. This is an argument not against the idea but against a possible weak capitalization of the plan.

7. The student court will tend to promote petty politics because of student friendships and obligations.

Character education specialists agree that the average student is less susceptible to this type of influence than the average adult; that he takes his responsibilities at least as seriously as the adult. Those who work with student courts do not agree with the above objection; almost every published article reflecting actual experience either expresses or implies surprise at the almost complete absence of petty politics. If desired, it could even be argued with considerable logic that temptations to show partiality represent a good educational setting.

8. Courts will deal too severely with offenders.

This argument is weak because in any good court plan all penalties must be approved directly or indirectly by the principal or designated school official. The court sponsor or adviser is also in a position to exercise judgment and prevent punishments from being too harsh.

9. Penalties may be unwise or downright stupid.

This is entirely possible, and undoubtedly some punishments, such as memorizing a poem, reading an article, writing a theme, or working some additional mathematics problems, are stupid. However, this is not the fault of the student discipline idea; it is the fault of those who supervise it.

10. Trials give the school undesirable publicity.

They may, especially if the reports of cases are widely published in the school and community newspapers. However, if the court's ideal is constructive education instead of vengeance, little publicity need be given to most trials. In fact, some courts meet secretly in order to avoid this possibility. Here again, this is not an argument against the court idea, but against incompetent handling of the court.

11. Trials tend to overemphasize petty violations. Overzealous officials make serious cases out of relatively trivial violations.

This is another objection to the method of handling cases, not to the basic idea represented. Many courts do not penalize a student for a first violation, especially a smaller one. Rather they try to get him to understand his error and appreciate his own responsibility. Admonishing him, admitting him to probation, and suspending sentence are three types of punishment commonly used to minimize the danger implied in the above objection.

12. Formal court procedure represents a slow and cumbersome method of handling discipline. It may be several days before a case comes to trial. A teacher's or principal's handling of a case would be more effective because it would come immediately.

Sometimes "a crack on the side of the head" represents immediately effective punishment. However, it does not necessarily follow that this is always true. Such a punishment may be least profitable because (1) it is made in anger; (2) it may not be, and probably is not, based upon a knowledge of the reasons why the individual acted as he did, and there are reasons for all actions, even those of the "I don't know why I did it" type; (3) it certainly allows no time for a careful consideration of the case; and (4) it rarely represents thinking in terms of student first, the aim of all justifiable student court plans. On the other hand, a short period of time between the commission of the act and the trial will not only provide for an unhurried consideration of all the facts and insure against an immediate outburst, but it will undoubtedly represent punishment in itself because the student cannot help wondering just what is going to happen to him.

13. The court idea tends to sidetrack the council's attention from other important constructive services.

It may, as was pointed out in Chap. III, and no one would disagree that if discipline receives an undue share of attention the plan or its supervision should be changed. This objection is probably more justifiable in smaller schools where the entire council sits as a court. In larger schools where a separate court is organized this objection is less valid.

To summarize, most of these objections are not based upon facts and successful experience but upon fears, prejudices, inexperience, biased opinions, misunderstandings, conservatism, or downright ignorance of the ideals and practices of a good court plan. Further, nearly all of them represent faults of organization and supervision, not faults of the court idea itself. Finally, proof that these arguments are not sound is to be found in the fact that there are a great many very successful courts in American schools, and American schools are conspicuously similar.

TYPES OF STUDENT COURTS

A considerable number of different types of student courts are to be found but in general most of these can be classified into the types discussed below. Although the classifications used are not entirely exclusive—for instance, a council court and a supreme court are really multijudge courts—they will be helpful in showing the general bases upon which the various forms are organized. Here we are concerned only with general organization and lines of responsibility. Later sections will deal with court personnel and duties, and court procedures.

1. Council Court.—The simplest form of court, from an organizational point of view, is that in which the entire council participates as a unit. In some schools the council includes disciplinary cases in its regular schedule of business, and in others it sets aside special days or sessions for this purpose.

In one way this arrangement appears to be logical because the council is empowered by the constitution to discipline bodies or organizations. It can, for instance, revoke the charters of organizations that have violated the provisions of their charters; forbid athletic and social events which do not meet certain requirements; prevent the participation of unauthorized groups in intergroup competitions; and abolish unauthorized publications. It is just as logical that it should and can have similar authority over individuals.

However, such a court faces a very serious handicap, a lack of sufficient time. The council is responsible for a great number and variety of activities about the school and must not allow any one phase of its work to receive a disproportionate share of time and attention. Disciplinary activities are always interesting and there is a real danger that such interest will lead to overemphasis. If cases are hurried through in order to give a proper distribution of time and efforts to all divisions of the program, there is a likelihood that the council's consideration and disposal of disciplinary cases may not always be the most wise. A further handicap is that because the council represents all types of activities, it cannot give competent attention equally to all specialized fields, and discipline is a field in which specialized competency is most essential.

Hence, in general, unless the school is small or violations are very few, it appears that a much better plan is the creation of a division which specializes in this form of activity. Such an arrangement will also ensure that trials are unhurried, thus guaranteeing fair consideration.

2. Discipline Committee.—In this form of student court the constitution or council authorizes a regular standing committee to handle cases of discipline. Usually, as in the case of other council committees, this group is responsible to the council and all of its activities must be approved by this central organization. This plan provides specialized attention and lessens the burden of the council, but it has serious weaknesses.

A committee is a rather informal organization and this lack of formality may mean a lack of necessary standing, importance, and dignity in the eyes of the students of the school. Further, because the council, not the committee, is the real authority, there is certain to be a considerable looseness in attitude and function. Such a committee would not feel responsibility nearly so much as it would if it alone were finally responsible. In short, a more formally organized and more definitely empowered court appears to be preferable to this council-committee type of organization.

3. Magistrate.—This is a one-judge plan imitative of adult police and magistrate's courts and justice of the peace courts. In some schools there are several magistrates, one for each class, floor, or section of the school. Where used, this plan is rarely complete by itself; almost always it involves a higher court to which appeals may be taken from the magistrate's decisions. The necessity for an additional court, plus the practical difficulty of securing a student competent enough to handle a single-judge court's business, with the almost inevitable general school distrust, have combined to make this a little-used type of judicial machinery. Examples are to be found, but they are few in number.

4. Multijudge Court.—In this plan the "bench" is composed of a group of judges, from three to fifteen but usually three or five. The main advantages of this type of court are; (1) several heads are usually better than one; (2) it is formal and dignified; (3) some types of judicial work can be apportioned, thus preventing court duties from becoming burdensome; (4) it provides for a variety of specialized judges, some of whom may be more interested and competent in "civil" cases, and others more interested and competent in "criminal" cases; and (5) it very easily wins school respect and confidence. It may have the possible disadvantage of not including as many students as some of the other plans, such as, for instance, the judge-jury court, but even at best this is not a strong argument against it. It represents a good form of court organization, provided relatively few judges are used.

5. Judge and Jury Court.—This very commonly found type of student court closely resembles in organization and procedure the usual adult judge and jury court. The judge, a sort of court chairman, the clerk or recorder, and the bailiff or handy man are the only "professionals" in it, the jury being drawn by lot from the entire school or from the upper classes. Jury terms are short. Unanimous agreement by the jurors is rarely required, a majority vote or a slightly higher proportion being sufficient to decide a case. Sometimes the judge is allowed to set aside a jury's decision, but most of the plans which specify this possibility also add that the jury may overrule the judge by a two-thirds or three-fourths vote.

This plan is deservedly popular because it (1) offers fair opportunity for everyone concerned; (2) prevents legal fiascoes and time-consuming and confusing retrials and delays by not requiring a unanimous vote; and (3) provides opportunity for wide student participation.

6. Supreme Court.—In a few schools there is a supreme court to which, upon proper representation and authorization, cases may be appealed from the lower court. Sometimes this all-judge court is composed of students only, sometimes of students and teachers, and occasionally of teachers only. In the latter two cases it is not, of course, a student court. Usually the right of appeal to this court is somewhat limited and so only the most serious cases are heard. In procedure, this court may refuse to hear a case, concur in the decision of the lower court, reverse this decision, or remand the case to the lower court for retrial.

Perhaps, in general, there is little need for such a court. In the first place it represents a complicated system of adjudication, and, in the second place, the principal is really the supreme court in any school. In cases which are serious enough to warrant such punishments as suspension or expulsion, which were indicated in several accounts of these supreme courts, he, not a group of students, should make the final decision.

COURT OFFICIALS

A trial involves a number of activities such as making a complaint, summoning the defendant and witnesses, hearing, adjudicating, and recording the case, and, in certain types of courts, selecting the jury; hence even the simplest form of court organization requires quite an array of officials. The following discussion includes the most important of these and indicates their several responsibilities.

1. Plaintiff or Complainant.—This is the individual who makes a complaint or files a charge with the court. He may be an officer who arrests a violator of traffic laws, a council member who seeks to revoke the charter of some organization, or an ordinary school citizen or teacher who witnesses some nonobservance of the council's regulations. In short, anyone with a grievance can file a written complaint provided he is willing to appear against the person or organization at the trial. In a way this individual is not exactly an "officer" of the court in the sense that the judge or clerk is, but in another way he is, because there can be no session without him.

2. Defendant.—The person against whom a complaint is filed is called a defendant because he is required to make answer to or defend himself against the charges filed. He has certain rights and privileges. He need not incriminate himself, the theory being that he is innocent until he is proved guilty. Naturally, if he is innocent he will welcome any opportunity to prove his innocence. But even if he is guilty he does not have to admit it. He may plead "guilty," in which case there is no further trial, the judge immediately sentencing him or setting a date at which time he will sentence him. In such an instance it is assumed that he "has learned his lesson" and is honest about admitting it, and hence his punishment should be a little lighter than it would be if he pleaded "not guilty" and was proved guilty.

3. **Judge.**—The judge is the presiding officer or chairman of the court and is in direct charge of all personnel and proceedings. In the case of multijudge courts there is a chief justice who is chairman of the board of judges. His vote is, of course, worth no more than the vote of any other judge. The judge supervises the selection of the jury, in case a jury trial is held, calls the defendant, states the case against him, advises him of his rights, and asks him how he pleads, decides protests and points of law, advises and charges the jury before it retires, calls for or decides the verdict, and dismisses the charge in case the defendant is acquitted or sentences him in case he is found guilty. In some schools the judge wears an official robe, although there is probably no real reason for such formality.

4. **Clerk.**—A record of each case is kept by the clerk. This record includes such items as date, plaintiff, defendant, nature of the case, witnesses, testimony, jurors, prosecuting and defending attorneys, verdict, and punishment. In school courts there is little necessity for complete stenographic records of all that is said and done, but the main points of each case should be recorded. When a case is disposed of the record is placed in a file for later possible use. Many courts place a brief record of each case on a card and file all cards

alphabetically. Later cases involving the same defendants are recorded on their cards. These records assist the judge in determining the severity of the penalty in case of later trouble. Other duties of the clerk are preparing and posting the docket or schedule of cases, issuing summonses, and recording orders.

5. Bailiff.—The "leg-work" of the court is done by the bailiff. He delivers summonses (orders to appear before the court at a specified date, time, and place) to prospective jurors, defendants, witnesses, plaintiffs, and other individuals concerned. Often he is the disciplinary officer or sergeant-at-arms of the court.

6. Jury.—In a jury trial the jury decides whether or not the defendant is guilty and, if he is found guilty and the plan includes this provision, may recommend punishment. If he so desires, a juror can ask questions of the witnesses or defendant. The standard adult jury is composed of twelve members, but school juries are smaller, usually of from five to nine members. The foreman of the jury is the chairman. He may automatically become foreman by being the first (or last) juror named, be appointed by the judge, or be elected by the jury itself. Only rarely is the last procedure used. Jurors are presumed to be personally unacquainted with the cases before them, to have no direct connection with them or with the individuals involved, and to have formed no opinions concerning them. Jurors are selected by lot from a "panel" or list of bona fide school citizens. Because of their official connection with one side of all cases, council members rarely serve on school juries. Jurors are usually sworn in by the judge or clerk. Different juries are not provided for each case, one jury being selected to serve for a certain period, say a month or so. Opportunity is given by the court for any member who feels himself disqualified, by reason of personal friendship or other cause, to be excused from any particular case.

7. Prosecutor.—In formal procedure a prosecutor handles all cases against the defendants. He calls and examines the plaintiff, defendant, and witnesses and summarizes his case in a final "plea" to the court. In simpler court forms there is no prosecutor (or defending attorney); the judge listens to the testimony, asks pertinent questions, and in other ways attempts to get all the facts in the case before making a decision.

8. Attorney for the Defense.—As suggested above, this official is found only in formal court procedure. Being a "professional" it is assumed that he is familiar with the law and with court procedure; hence he is better able to present the defendant's case than is the defendant himself. He, like the prosecuting attorney, examines the plaintiff, defendant, and witnesses, attempts to discredit the other side of the case, and makes a "plea" to the court or jury. He, too, is allowed to object to remarks, procedures, questions, and testimony which he believes do not concern the case or which are unduly prejudicial to his client. The judge "sustains" or "overrules" each objection.

9. Witnesses.—Those who saw the action about which the trial is concerned, or who have knowledge which is pertinent to the case, are called witnesses. Each side is allowed to offer witnesses. In formal trials these witnesses take an oath "to tell the truth, the whole truth, and nothing but the truth, so help me God." They are called and "examined" by the attorney for their side, but may be "cross-examined" by the attorney for the other side. In the case of simpler procedure they are called and examined by the judge. Their testimony as to the facts in the case helps to determine the guilt or innocence of the defendant.

10. Sponsor.—Because in the best of student courts there are possibilities of mistakes, friction, and unwise decisions, it is desirable for this organization to have a regularly appointed or elected sponsor or adviser. Such an individual can bring experience, judgment, and maturity to the court's deliberations, give the court more substantial standing in the school, and represent the point of view of the faculty and administration. A sponsor does not assume any of the duties or prerogatives of the regular court officials. In no way, directly or indirectly, is he the judge or the jury. He helps the group to arrive at wise decisions and proper penalties but he does not dominate policies and practices. Once the court is thoroughly established, the sponsor's duties, though still important, are more of the watching and less of the participating type.

Selection of Court Officials.—The members of student courts are selected by a number of methods, such as appointment by the principal, council, or faculty, election by the upper classes or other groups, and general election, as well as by various combinations of these methods. There is considerable disagreement between the proponents of the two most commonly used plans, popular election and appointment by the council. Those who favor general election point out that (1) this is a common adult procedure in many forms of court organization, and (2) the students have a right to elect the officers under whom they are to serve and live. Those who support the other point of view hold that (1) appointment is the plan followed in the selection of federal judges; (2) court responsibilities are executive, not policy-making in nature, and the court should be a rule-enforcing, not a rule-making, body, a special committee designed to carry out the council's plans and wishes; and (3) a council-appointed court is more efficient than a student-elected body because it can include the most competent ability in the school, and it is uninfluenced and unbiased because it is not obligated to particular individuals or groups. As yet there is no final answer to the question of which plan is the better. Both are used in school organizations and both are successful and unsuccessful. Similarly, both are used in adult life, and both are often found wanting. In general, though, it appears that the supporters of the council-appointment plan have much the better arguments. However, it is true that any election or appointment that violates the basic principles of democratic representation is hardly consistent with the avowed purpose of such a plan. The term of office of court officials should probably be the same as that of the officers of the other divisions of the student organization.

COURT PROCEDURES

Although it may vary in details according to the plan used, general procedure is about the same in all types of school courts. The main elements of this procedure are those discussed below.

Arrest or Citation.—In a student court plan provision is made for the formal arrest of any violator of the school's "criminal" code, and for the formal citation of any group or organization which violates constitutional or charter regulations, the "civil" code. An arrest or a citation is merely an order to appear before the court and face the charges filed; in itself it does not indicate guilt. The arresting officer gives the violator a formal ticket or slip, retaining the stub or a duplicate, which indicates the date, time, place, name, and class of the violator, nature of the violation, usually the date, place, and time of the court session, and the name of the arresting officer. Often it also includes the names of the witnesses. The duplicate of the ticket is turned over to the clerk of the court who numbers it to indicate its place in the docket and files it. If the date, time, and place of the court session at which the case will be called is not yet known, this information is later sent to the defendant by the clerk. If the violator is an organization, its officers are not arrested but are given a citation or order to appear and answer the charges filed against their group.

In some plans any teacher or student may file charges against any student, even against an officer. The complainant must write out and sign such a charge and be willing to appear in court to support it when the case is called. This system has the advantages of allowing everyone to help enforce the regulations, and of detecting violations which may escape the notice of the officers. However, it is more likely to degenerate into a cheap tale-bearing procedure than where all arrests are made by regularly commissioned and trained officers. There is also more opportunity for personal grudges and dislikes to enter and cause disturbance. Further, it will in all probability not be too effective because of the average student's attitude toward talebearing and "snitching."

If the defendant does not appear at the time of the trial he is sent for and unless he is absent for good reason he is held in contempt of court for failing to obey the summons. He must then face two charges instead of one, the original violation and the contempt of court charge. Similarly, an individual who makes a complaint against another person or group and who then fails to appear at the trial is held in contempt unless he can satisfactorily explain his absence. Naturally, in order to win and keep school respect the court must consider a contempt charge a very serious matter.

All arresting and citation orders should be written so that there is a definite and permanent record of them. Because the court is not in continuous session it is impracticable for the arresting officer to take the violator immediately to court and "locking him up" or detaining him until court meets is impossible. If the date, time, and place of the session are not specified at once it is only fair to the defendant that he be notified at least one day in advance of the trial.

Trial.—Before a case is called the clerk issues summonses to all those concerned, arresting officer, defendant, and witnesses. Upon calling the case the judge or clerk immediately ascertains whether all who were summoned are present, and if they are, calls the defendant, reads the charge against him, and asks him how he pleads. If he pleads "guilty" he is immediately sentenced and the trial is over. If he pleads "not guilty" or "innocent" the trial begins.

The arresting officer tells about the violation and if possible offers witnesses to prove the charge. The defendant is then allowed to tell his story and, if he has witnesses, to place them on the stand. In a simple plan all these individuals are questioned by the court. In a more complex plan where attorneys are used, all of them may be examined and cross-examined by the attorneys. When all evidence is in the court or jury decides the case and either acquits or frees and dismisses the defendant or finds him guilty and states the sentence.

One purpose of the trial is to determine, in case the defendant is found guilty, the seriousness of his guilt, so that this may be taken into consideration when sentence is passed. For instance, even though the defendant is guilty there may have been mitigating circumstances. The regulation might have been violated unintentionally or through carelessness; or it may have been violated intentionally and deliberately. In the latter case, of course, the penalty is more severe. Incidentally, ignorance of the law does not excuse misconduct. Also, the violator may have submitted to his arrest quietly or he may have made a scene, torn up the arresting ticket, been insolent, resisted the officer, and in other ways flouted authority. The latter type of conduct deserves more serious punishment than the former. The court attempts to make the penalty fit the case and the degree of guilt. Second offenders are treated more severely than first offenders.

In a jury trial, after the testimony has been heard, the judge charges the jury, stating the law in the case, indicates testimony which is irrelevant or incompetent and should not be considered, describes the verdicts which the jury may return, and urges it to perform its duty fairly, fearlessly, and conscientiously. The jury now retires from the room, or the room is cleared of everyone except the jurors, and, under the chairmanship of the foreman, the jury holds a secret session in which it deliberates on the case, and finally votes. If it votes "guilty" it usually has the right to recommend punishment according to the instructions of the judge. Upon reaching a decision the jury returns to the room and after being asked by the judge if it has reached a decision, the foreman reads the verdict.

If the verdict is "not guilty" the judge dismisses the case. If the verdict is "guilty" the judge orders the defendant to rise and asks him if he has anything to say before sentence is passed. He then sentences him. Often in school trials after sentencing the defendant the judge asks him if he considers his trial fair and his punishment just. It is interesting to note that only rarely does a defendant consider his trial unfair or his punishment unjust. Of course, even if he does or does not, his opinion does not change the sentence in any manner whatever. In plans where the jury is allowed to recommend the sentence the judge usually follows this recommendation, but he need not necessarily do so. In fact, he may even overrule the jury. As suggested before, if the defendant has a previous record, this will be considered in setting the punishment. The clerk keeps a record of all cases, not merely those in which the defendants were found guilty. As will be explained in the following section, after a sentence has been served the appropriate record is entered on the permanent file card.

It cannot be overemphasized that there is a real danger in a prosecutor-defender procedure—the possibility that winning a conviction or winning an acquittal may become the main objective of a trial. Obscuring the main facts in the case, confusing the witnesses, playing on emotions, and resorting to legal trickery are not at all uncommon in adult courts where the emphasis is upon winning the case. As a result, the "good" prosecutor or defender is the one who wins most of his cases, irrespective of their general merit. Needless to state, such a policy should not be allowed to develop in the student court. This court should be recognized and appreciated as an impartial fact-finding body.

PUNISHMENTS

One of the most troublesome problems of the student court is the matter of punishments. It can be easily appreciated that if these penalties are unfair, sadistic, unreasonable, or freakish they will cause resentment, not only from those sentenced and their friends, but also from the average student of the school. Such school resentment will hinder the work of the court by destroying confidence and giving unfavorable publicity, and, in an extreme case, might even force the abandonment of the plan. It is well known that more student courts have been abolished because of difficulties over punishments than for all other causes combined. Consequently, the utmost in care and common sense should be used in solving this problem. An examination of the commonly used punishments and penalties will suggest their suitability or unsuitability and assist in the derivation of the pertinent logical principles.

1. Lowering Marks.—The proponents of this practice of lowering the student's mark in some subject, or in all subjects, because he has been found guilty of a misdemeanor point out that this is exactly what happens in real life. In adult life the individual works for money, and the most frequently used punishment is taking some of this money in the form of a fine; in school the student works for marks and fining him in terms of marks is as reasonable as fining his father in terms of money. This form of penalty is most common where the teacher is allowed to reduce a student's mark for misbehavior.

The author can see no justification whatever for this plan of punishment because he can see no justification whatever for reducing a student's mark, after he has actually earned it, for misconduct. A mark should be an index only to what the student knows about or is able to do in the subject, and should not include irrelevant matters or material. The teacher is not allowed to raise the student's mark because he lends her his umbrella, picks up her handkerchief, or greets her courteously, so why should she be allowed to reduce his mark for the opposite kind of behavior?

2. Demerits.—In schools which record and report "deportment" a very common plan of penalty is the use of demerits. This device is much more justifiable than allowing such demerits to lower subject marks, but it is ineffective in those instances in which students and parents are not a bit interested in high marks in conduct or citizenship. And it may be that such students are more likely to get into trouble than those who desire high marks in deportment. Where a citizenship mark is required for participation in activities or for graduation, this plan may be much more effective. It has the advantages of being definite and easily administered. However, its use will not affect all students alike.

3. Detention.—The practice of requiring a student to remain after school or come to school early is an age-old method of punishment. Perhaps, in an immediate and limited way, it has been somewhat effective, but ultimately and broadly conceived, it has been very harmful. Such a plan is fundamentally wrong because of the inevitable implication that all school work is a type of punishment. The student should be led to consider school a great and vital personal opportunity and to welcome a chance to participate in all of its activities, both curricular and extracurricular. But he will never be so led as long as authorities encourage the development of the idea that the school is a house of correction. This attitude is not common in college or in professional and technical schools where the student pays for his training, appreciates its importance, and wants to get as much for his time and money as possible. This more favorable type of attitude should also prevail in the lower schools, but it can never be developed so long as the school is considered a sort of prison. Sentencing a violator to a few more of the "prison activities" is not only an admission that the school is a penal institution, but in essence, because of the advertising such a plan receives, it is a public announcement of the fact.[1] Further, this type of procedure violates a basic tenet of educative punishment, appropriateness, that is, a close and felt relationship between offense and penalty.

4. "Pest Room."—This is a study hall, supervised by a strict teacher, to which offenders are sentenced. This plan is different from detention because it involves no additional study periods and no out-of-school periods. There is much more to be said in favor of this plan than of detention. It represents a denial of the privilege of studying in a pleasant atmosphere and among friends. The pest room is a commonly recognized dishonorable setting, somewhat jail-like, a place which a self-respecting student will try to avoid. Being assigned to it would hardly be considered complimentary by anyone in the school, including the student so sentenced.

5. Extra School Work.—Another long-used method of school discipline is the requiring of extra tasks such as working a set of problems, memorizing a poem or section of the constitution, writing a theme, or reading and outlining an article or book. All such penalties are absolutely illogical and unjustifiable, irrespective of whether they are set by the teacher or court, because, as suggested above, they make all school work a punishment. What is more, they are not appropriate

[1] So also is the practice of awarding honor students a holiday—a "reduce your sentence by good behavior" plan.

because they do not reflect the regulations violated. Moreover, these activities are the professional responsibilities of the teachers, not the students. From a practical point of view, just imagine how much inspiration a student would receive, or how his love of poetry would be enhanced, from such a required memorization of some beautiful poem!

6. Disbarment from Activities.—This is a type of punishment which is logical and fair, provided it is administered appropriately, because it represents the removal of highly prized privileges, and it can reflect the activities concerned in the violation. For instance, if the student has been convicted of causing trouble during assembly, a logical punishment is to exclude him from these programs for a certain period; similarly, he may justifiably be excluded from honor rooms, social events, or athletics for unbecoming conduct in these settings or activities. For running in the halls or other boisterous conduct he may be required to leave the room only after all other students have left; or for a violation in the cafeteria he may be required to wait until all other students have been served, or to eat by himself or in a special "pest room," or even excluded entirely from the lunchroom. Although limiting such privileges in one activity or setting because of conduct in some other may be very effective, it has less justification. For example, excluding the individual from assembly programs because he violated some rule in athletics is not as appropriate as limiting his privileges in the original setting. To repeat, this form of punishment, if appropriately used, is justifiable and usually brings desired results.

7. Demotion, Suspension, or Removal from Office.—In cases where a student holds a rank or post of honor, a demotion or removal from this position represents a very real punishment. It is a justifiable penalty because conviction proves that the student has not lived up to the high standards of good school citizenship. There is a possibility that such a penalty may be too severe. For instance, removal from a semester or year position for an infraction which deserves a shorter term, say a month, is too harsh a penalty. This weakness may be avoided by carefully considering the seriousness of the violation and assigning a suitable penalty. Suspension, instead of permanent removal from office, may be designated for less serious infractions.

8. Suspension from School.—This type of penalty should probably be imposed only by the principal himself. It may be logical that the individual who will not adjust himself to accepted school customs and usages should be deprived of school privileges, but the decision in such a serious case as this should be left to the administrative head of the school. Possible complications, due to school age requirements, may make such suspension, even by the principal, rather questionable from a strictly legal point of view.

9. Assignment of Menial Tasks.—Sentencing the individual to such a task as washing dishes in the cafeteria, raking the lawn, painting a wall, sweeping the walks, or emptying the wastebaskets, unless it is appropriate, hardly represents justifiable punishment. In cases where it is appropriate it is entirely justifiable. For example, the student who littered up the corridor might very logically be required to clean it; or the one who marred a wall, to repaint it; or the one who mutilated a desk, to refinish it. In such instances the culprit pays for the damage he caused.

10. Physical Punishment.—This form of punishment should not be found in the court's list of penalties. It is generally condemned even if administered by teachers, and certainly it would be more strongly condemned if administered by students.

11. Humiliation.—Requiring the student to stand at the school entrance or in the hall with a dunce cap on his head, or a sign suspended from his neck, or clothed in the dress of the opposite sex, or requiring him to submit to other similarly humiliating penalties represents a thoroughly inappropriate and unjustifiable form of punishment.

12. Consultation with Parents.—Some schools have a plan whereby the convicted student must bring one or both of his parents to school for a consultation with the court. This is unwise. The average parent would quickly resent a requirement that he talk over his youngster's conduct with a group of students. Undoubtedly, if he did come he would immediately storm to the principal with the embarrassing demand, "Say, who's running this school, anyway?" A parent in this frame of mind could hardly be expected to listen patiently to a description of the ideals and procedures of the court idea. What would be done if the parent refused to come to such a consultation? The parent's general reaction would surely bring undesirable publicity to the plan and to the school.

13. Admonition.—A common practice in the case of first offenders or not too serious violations is for the court to rebuke and warn the individual and release him. Probably in a great many cases this will have the desired effect of improving conduct. The facts that the student has been put to some little inconvenience, has had to stand trial, and has been found guilty, are mortifying and may frequently represent very effective punishment. In case the offender is an organization, a letter of admonition to its officers may similarly be effective. If it is not, then more serious penalties such as a suspension or revocation of its charter or a failure to provide it with needed or budgeted funds may be inflicted.

14. Probation.—A little more severe punishment than admonition is releasing the guilty student with the proviso that he must report to the court or probation officer at stated intervals until his time is up, and with the understanding that if for any reason he is brought to court again within this period the case will be considered serious. This, too, represents a good form of punishment, especially in fairly serious first offenses. It is unsuitable for repeaters. Incidentally, it is to be regretted that so little use has been made of this device. Only rarely is it to be found in schools and it is one of the most sensible of punishments, especially if the objective of the court plan is reconstruction, not vengeance.

15. Suspended Sentence.—For more serious violations by first offenders a suspension of sentence represents a good method of punishment. After having been found guilty the defendant is actually sentenced, but the judge, after making a suitable explanation and voicing confidence in the individual's desire and ability to go straight, suspends the sentence. The student will clearly appreciate the fact that this suspension amounts to "another chance" and as a result will in all probability be very careful not to be again brought to court.

16. Apology.—Being required to make a suitable apology often represents another very adequate type of punishment. The individual who sincerely makes such an apology thereby admits his error and either by direct statement or indirect implication resolves not to repeat his misconduct. Further, such an individual will generally make very serious efforts to avoid trouble later because he knows that everyone is watching him. In such instances the penalty is constructive. Apologizing to another individual or to a group requires considerable courage, which is all the more reason for believing in the sincerity of the individual making the apology. On the other hand, a forced apology may really be detrimental rather than helpful, because the individual may make an outward expression of something which he does not inwardly feel.

In some cases, such as the destruction of school property, mutilation of another's book, thievery, or a similar offense involving loss or damage, an apology is not sufficient; the individual should also be required to pay for any loss or damage caused.

Principles Underlying Effective Punishment.—From the foregoing critical examination of forms of punishment it should be clear that a good penalty is one which (1) is based upon educational reconstruction, not vengeance; (2) is logically appropriate to the case; (3) is felt by the individual; (4) is reasonable in severity; and (5) is more or less immediate. The first two principles are those which are most commonly violated by student courts.

Allowing a Choice of Punishments.—In this plan the judge or jury, after convicting a defendant, indicates two punishments and allows the individual to choose one of them. Such a procedure is unwise because (1) punishment is not "swift and sure"; (2) it brings a disorganizing element of looseness and indecision which will never command respect; and (3) it is impracticable, if not impossible, to provide two penalties which are equally constructive, appropriate, and reasonable. The decision as to the penalty should be entirely in the hands of the court.

Allowing the Defendant to Set His Own Punishment.—Very often in cases in which the defendant pleads guilty, and less frequently when he is convicted after having pleaded not guilty, the judge will ask him what he believes would be a reasonable punishment for his misconduct. Undoubtedly, sometimes the student will suggest a most logical and fair penalty. Of course the court is under no obligation to accept and pass this sentence, but if it is suitable there is no good reason why it should not, and there is a good reason why it should. The fact that the individual suggests such a penalty is ample proof that he is truly penitent and willing to make proper amends for his act. The possible weakness of the plan is the fact that the student may not have had enough experience to suggest a suitable punishment. Consequently, if this plan is used, it should be used only in cases where very definite and reparable damage has been done.

Enforcement of Sentences.—A penalty which is not enforced is worse than useless because it brings discredit upon the court. Hence, the plan should include provision for the enforcement of all sentences. In most cases such enforcement will involve no serious difficulty because the average student will do what he is told in order to clear his record. But if a student refuses to accept his penalty or serve out his term of punishment, the court should meet the situation immediately, squarely, and vigorously. Depending upon the nature and seriousness of the case, this may be done by resentencing with a more severe penalty and, in case this order too is flouted, by appealing directly to the principal. This administrator will appreciate the necessity of maintaining the court's prestige and will, undoubtedly, at once enforce the order. Only rarely will it be necessary to call upon the principal, but the court should not hesitate to do so if the case justifies it.

Relatively few court plans have special enforcement machinery, nearly all of them depending upon the cooperation of the regular officers, council members, home room presidents, and even teachers. Often the clerk makes out a penalty slip and either hands it to the student or sends it to an appropriate school official. When the sentence is served this slip is returned to the clerk, who completes the case by making the necessary notation on the proper card.

Penal Code.—In very few court plans is there to be found a penal code which specifically lists all rules and regulations, and in practically none of these is to be found a schedule of corresponding penalties for violations. Nearly all this information, where it is included at all, is stated in very general terms. The most commonly found information of this type is that which concerns the chartering of organizations and the possible revoking of such charters. In most cases the penalties for infractions of these generally stated council or court rules and regulations are set by the court itself at the time of the trial.

Probably this is a desirable practice. In the first place, the development of such a code would represent an enormous job, and similarly devising suitable penalties for all these violations would mean another prodigious task. In the second place, such a definitely organized schedule of penalties would be too rigid. If the main purpose of the student court is to reconstruct student attitudes and behavior instead of merely to discipline, then the court should have great leeway in setting penalties because no two violations are of exactly the same degree of seriousness, nor are they caused by exactly the same set of reasons. Naturally, the court will have a rather complete schedule of possible punishments but it will assign these according to the circumstances of the cases, rather than on the basis of an inflexible code.

OTHER STUDENT COURT RELATIONSHIPS

Jurisdiction of the Court.—Although in some instances it is rather difficult to draw a definite line, the jurisdiction of the student court should, in general, be limited to fields and activities which represent nonclassroom responsibilities. For instance, if a student cheats in an examination, this is the teacher's fault and the teacher, not the court, should be charged with the responsibility of settling the difficulty. The argument that the teacher was not in a position to see the cheating and the students were, does not absolve the teacher. It is his job to be in a position to see what is going on in his classroom. Similarly, tardiness, absence, marks, classroom conduct, etc., are the teacher's professional responsibilities. The practice of referring cases of insolence to a teacher or the disobeyal of a teacher's orders to the student court has no justification whatever. The area of jurisdiction should be pretty definitely established in the constitutional plan of the court so that no later misunderstanding and duplication will result. This area should be no longer than the court can easily and effectively handle.

The Court Room.—It was pointed out in Chap. III that if at all possible the student council should have a special permanently assigned room in which to hold its meetings and committee meetings, and keep its records, materials, and equipment. In the case of the student court, such provision is probably even more desirable because a court session involves more students than a council meeting, and most of these students do not attend court as regularly as members of the council attend council meetings. If the court has to hunt up and use any room that for the period happens to be vacant, the result is sure to be confusion. And in such cases scheduling sessions very far ahead will be difficult if not impossible.

If the council has a room of its own, this may be used for court purposes provided the sessions do not conflict with the meetings of the council. Here, too, court committee meetings and conferences may be held, and records, materials, and equipment be kept. The chairs, tables, and other equipment should be so arranged that a court room atmosphere is provided. A mailbox in the central office into which arresting slips and other pertinent material may be placed will also help to make for efficient court procedure.

Frequency of Court Sessions.—The frequency with which the court sessions are scheduled will depend upon the local setting. A few courts meet daily and a few monthly, but nearly all of them schedule weekly meetings; others schedule sessions once every two weeks. Probably in most schools a regular weekly session will be found most practicable and useful. The disadvantage of a daily meeting is that the court may tend to become routinized and formal and if it has little or no business it will soon become unimportant in the eyes of the school. A monthly meeting means that some cases will have to be carried over too long a period before they are given consideration, and, too, will probably mean a congested docket. A weekly session avoids these difficulties. If at all possible, all court sessions should be held during regular school periods.

Open vs. Secret Trials.—Should the student court trial be held publicly or secretly? The arguments in favor of an open trial are that it (1) follows established adult procedure; (2) provides an educational opportunity for those who witness it by showing how trials are conducted and what happens to offenders; (3) makes a trial an important event in the life of the school, thus adding to interest in the plan and to the dignity of the court; (4) provides well-deserved honor for court officials; (5) helps to establish school confidence in the plan because there are no suspicious secret sessions which may be easily labeled, and may in reality degenerate into, "star chamber" proceedings; and (6) recognizes the right of the school citizen to visit an activity for which he is indirectly responsible.

The main arguments against the open trial procedure are that it may (1) give undue and undesirable publicity to disciplinary cases, especially those which are most sensational; (2) unwholesomely and unnecessarily embarrass the defendants; (3) tend to encourage the development of an exciting "public show" with a view to impressing spectators instead of a careful adjudication of the matter at hand; and (4) permit interruptions of various kinds. In general, the arguments in favor of secret trials are the reverse of those against open trials, and these need not be respected.

At the present time there is no final answer to the question concerning the relative desirability of these two procedures. Both plans have been and are being used successfully. However, the majority of schools favor the open trial, and to the author this plan appears to be the more desirable. Doubtless, though, there are cases in which a secret trial is more desirable than a public one.

Newspaper Publicity.—Should the reports of trials be carried in the school newspaper? The arguments in favor of such a practice are that (1) it is imitative of adult practice; (2) trials center around school people and school happenings and therefore represent proper material for the newspaper; (3) such publicity will help to establish respect for law and order in the school; and (4) this news is always interesting to the readers.

The arguments against reflecting trials in the newspaper are that (1) it gives inordinate publicity to school disciplinary problems; (2) it may unduly and detrimentally embarrass convicted students and thus defeat the purpose of the student court; and (3) such reports are likely to overemphasize all violations, both trivial and serious.

In nearly all schools the activities of the court are reported in more or less general terms and only rarely are detailed accounts of trials presented. Often, too, the accounts that are specific in details omit the names of the defendants. It is the opinion of the author that this policy is far better than that which allows the publication of complete and detailed reports. Further, it is his opinion that all such reports should be kept out of the local community papers.

Final Authority.—It has been repeatedly emphasized in this book that the principal represents the final authority in the school, and in connection with the student court, the question naturally arises, Just how should this final authority be properly recognized?

Obviously, running to the principal for his official approval on every decision made or punishment set would be impracticable, unwise, and unnecessary. In delegating authority the principal either consciously or unconsciously sets general boundaries within which the court is empowered to act. In cases which appear to go beyond these boundaries it is perfectly proper for the court to request official confirmation of its work, or counsel. Inside these boundaries such a policy would be a nuisance to all concerned. Anyway, the fact that an interested faculty member sponsors or advises the court means that the principal's point of view is represented and that his authority is respected. Only in the most serious or unusual cases taken under advisement should the court confer with the principal before final decisions are made.

Should the defendant who is found guilty by the court be allowed to appeal to the principal? In a few schools this procedure is incorporated in the court plan. Perhaps in an occasional case where there is a very evident miscarriage of justice, such a practice might be justified, but making it a definite part or organized procedure is probably unwise. It would bring needless work to the principal, and would weaken school confidence in the court. It would represent too easy an "out" for the defendant irrespective of whether or not the principal approved the court's ruling; it is improbable that in such a setting, with only one side of the case being represented, the principal could arrive at a better decision than the court which heard both sides.

Incidentally, it is a wise administrative policy for the principal occasionally to visit the court while it is in session. Of course he does not stop the trial or participate in it. He, like any student or teacher, is merely a spectator. Such visits will be helpful to the principal in keeping him informed of court activities, and they will be beneficial to the court because they evidence the principal's interest.

Selected References

Althouse, M. G.: Our "Circuit Court," *School Activities*, 15: 202, February, 1944.

The Student Court

BRYAN, R. C.: Should Pupils Take Part in Maintaining Good Discipline? *School Review*, 43: 451–455, June, 1935.

Department of Justice, *School Activities*, 8: 418, May, 1937.

FEELHAVER, C. T.: Student Court, *School Review*, 40: 357–363, May, 1932.

FOOTE, M.: The Student Honor Committee, *School Activities*, 10: 25–26, September, 1938.

GREENE, E. R.: The Student Court at Manley High School, *School Activities*, 11: 386–387, May, 1940.

GRUHN, C. V.: Aberdeen Has a Student's Court, *Journal of the National Education Association*, 119: 462–464, Nov. 2, 1936.

GRUNER, R.: Students Go to Court and Jail, *School Activities*, 9: 114–115, 121, November, 1937.

JUERGENSMEYER, L. K.: Students Run This School, *School Executives' Magazine*, 54: 314–315, June, 1935.

LAWSON, M. T.: A Bicycle Court, *School Activities*, 14: 86, 90, November, 1942.

McCAIN, W. J.: Developing a Student Tribunal, *School Activities*, 12: 151–152, December, 1940.

MESSER, M. R.: The Student Court in the Junior High School, *School Activities*, 6: 3–5, February, 1936.

MEYER, F.: A Functioning Student Court, *School Activities*, 11: 277–278, 288, March, 1940.

———: A Student Court Passes, *School Activities*, 13: 227–228, February, 1942.

NOLTE, R. W.: Student Property Protection Council, *School Activities*, 11: 174, December, 1939.

SMITH, E.: A Club Attack on Stealing, *Journal of Education*, May, 1938.

SPEAR, J. S.: Student Court at the Abraham Lincoln High School, *High Points*, 17: 31–39, January, 1935.

SPESSARD, O. T.: School Court, *Clearing House*, 18: 347–349, February, 1944.

TERRY, P. W.: "Supervising Extra-curricular Activities," Chap. VIII, McGraw-Hill Book Company, Inc., New York, 1930.

Chapter XII

The Student-council Sponsor

PROBABLY nothing will wreck a council more quickly than student recognition that the sponsor is not sufficiently interested, prepared, or personally equipped to lead it. The faculty representative is the most important single member of the council, not only because he is older, more mature, and experienced, and has better judgment than have the students, but because he, more than they, must accept responsibility for developing suitable policies and procedures, also for coordinating student and teacher relationships. Obviously, then, much of the success of a plan of participation depends upon this specialized guidance officer.

How should the sponsor be selected? What qualifications should he have? What should he do? How should he do it? These are basic questions which this chapter will answer.[1] Undoubtedly some of the principles suggested are self-evident, but they are included for purposes of emphasis and completeness.

The sponsor may be an ex officio member of the council because of his position as dean, director of activities, guidance director, assistant principal, or sponsor of some particular school group, such as the senior class; he may be appointed by the principal or other administrative officer; or he may be elected by the faculty, by the students, or even by the council itself. Election by the faculty has more to commend it as a democratic procedure than has any other method, while election by the students or by the council is the least justi-

[1] See also pp. 51–52.

fiable of these methods, only a shade lower than the ex officio plan suggested first. At the present time about one-half of all sponsors are appointed by some administrative officer. However, the proportion of schools in which sponsors are elected by the faculty is considerably larger than it was a decade or two ago, and this fact is encouraging.

A number of expressions are used to designate the teacher-member of the council, such as "sponsor," "dean," "guide," "supervisor," and "counselor." With the possible exception of the first, none of these is appropriate, either because it has some other well established meaning, or because its connotation is unattractive. The term "sponsor" is not exactly accurate if the teacher is elected as a regular member of the council, but because it is widely accepted and understood, and also because it is fairly accurate in those instances in which this officer is appointed by the principal, it will be used in the following discussion as a synonym for teacher-member or faculty-representative of the council. The principles discussed refer to any such teacher-representative irrespective of whether there is only one or several.

1. The Faculty Should Recognize and Accept Its Responsibility in Electing Sponsors.—Because the council represents the entire school and all of its activities, it must represent every teacher and student in it. Therefore the faculty, as well as the student body, must appreciate and accept its obligation in the selection and support of its representative or representatives. It cannot select carelessly or in a purely routine manner on the basis of tradition or custom and then promptly turn its attention to something else assuming that its responsibility in the matter has been fully discharged. The faculty must set a good example for the student body to follow in its elections.

The bases of selection of faculty representatives are exactly the same as those of student members: a careful consideration of personality, judgment, tact, sympathetic understanding, initiative, originality, leadership, cooperativeness, interest and enthusiasm, experience, training, administrative, executive, and business ability, and general social competency. This is truly a high set of standards, and it cannot be assumed that all teachers can meet them; not all teachers would make good sponsors any more than all of them would make good teachers of agriculture, music, science, athletics, or dramatics, each of which requires peculiar knowledges and capabilities. To emphasize this point, the election of faculty representatives cannot be left to chance.

Naturally, the teacher's own interest in the matter should be given serious consideration. Forcing him into a job which he does not want would handicap the plan from the very beginning. Respecting his wishes will increase the possibility of the plan's success, and add to the sponsor's feeling of importance and self-respect because of the compliment paid him by his colleagues' recognition of his interests and abilities.

How many faculty members should be elected? In smaller schools perhaps one faculty member may be sufficient, but in large schools probably two or maybe even three or four might justifiably be named to the council. The election of one faculty member tends to give the impression of the club-adviser idea, while the election of more than one tends to give the impression of the faculty-representation idea. Further, usually two or three teachers together have better ideas than any one of them would have by himself.

Should faculty members be reelected? The answer to this question will depend upon a number of considerations, particularly those which relate to the individual's interest in the plan and his success with it. Reelection usually does mean a proper capitalization of knowledge, experience, and skill, and this is important, considering the number of members who will be new each year. It also tends to make for a desirable continuity and growth in policies. On the other hand, reelection should not be allowed to become a rigidly established policy. It must be justified upon the basis of something far more substantial than precedent or tradition.

Should the older or the newer teachers be elected to the council? The older teacher knows the school's organization, traditions, personnel, procedures, and possibilities of council work, but even this knowledge by itself does not necessarily constitute sponsoring competency. The new teacher, especially the younger, may be much more recently educated than the older, have a better understanding of young people and therefore be more acceptable, be more free from local bias, have had more courses and training especially designed for effective student leadership, and quite probably have had considerable firsthand experience as a council member in high school and college. But even these by themselves do not necessarily constitute sponsoring competency. In short, no general and complete answer, suitable to all settings, can be given. The question must be answered by the local school on the basis of a study of all the elements of the situation. Incidentally, any traditional practice of having a certain teacher, say the sponsor of the senior class, automatically become sponsor of the council does not reflect the ideals and practices of representative government.

In the majority of instances the director of activities is in a most favorable position to do a good job of council sponsoring, and the practice of automatically making him a member of the group can be justified. However, in such instances it is probably a good policy for the faculty to elect another teacher or two to represent it and assist him.

2. The Sponsor Must Really Represent the Faculty.—It was pointed out in Chap. III that the faculty as well as the student body should feel its representation in the council. The faculty can never have such a feeling unless the sponsor assumes the proper attitude. If he considers himself a "sponsor" with full authority instead of a "faculty-representative" with obligations to his constituency, there will be no felt representation. Nor is it likely that such a feeling will be encouraged where the sponsor is officially appointed by the principal, because he will feel his accountability to the principal alone.

It is difficult to draw the line clearly between what the faculty has a right to expect from its representative and what he has a right to expect in the way of support from the faculty. It is assumed that because he is a professional specialist he will be "ahead" of the faculty and consequently be more competent than it to guide the council. However, in cases in which the faculty is decidedly for or against some policy or procedure the sponsor as the duly elected representative of this group must reflect its opinion. In such cases he should, of course, continuously educate the faculty to his point of view.

3. The Sponsor Must Understand and Appreciate the Participation Idea.—It is trite to say that the faculty member who does not understand and appreciate the objectives and values of the participation idea has no business attempting to work with the council, but this statement is well worth emphasizing because many a group has been handicapped by such a sponsor. The faculty member should know why the participation idea developed, how it fits in with modern educational philosophy, its purposes and values, its methods of organization, procedures, activities, and projects, and how it may be evaluated. A few council members will have some knowledge and some experience, and the faculty representative will have to keep well ahead of these to command their respect. He will also have to be a sort of council missionary to the council itself, to the school, and to the faculty. It is not to be assumed that he will know everything about participation—no one knows that much—but it can be assumed that he has a good basis and is continuously strengthening it. He is, of course, in a much better position than any student to get books, magazine articles, conference reports, and similar materials, and to initiate, plan, and conduct trips to other schools and councils.

4. The Sponsor Must Be Sympathetic with the Participation Idea.—It is not enough for the sponsor to know about the council idea, he must also be sympathetic with and deeply interested in it because (1) a lack of interest will hinder or destroy the organization, and (2) he cannot help showing his attitude. If he is unfavorably disposed because of former experience, rumors, stories, preconceived notions, or an arbitrary unwanted assignment, he need never expect council members to reflect satisfactorily the opposite attitude. But if he is sympathetic, appreciative, and interested, youthful enthusiasm for the cause will be engendered.

5. The Sponsor Must Be Discriminatingly Loyal to the Council.—In a way this principle is but an extension of that preceding, but it is important enough to be separated and stressed. The faculty member of the council is in a peculiar position in which he must maintain several loyalties, some of which may often be more or less conflicting; he must be loyal to locally accepted educational principles, loyal to his colleagues and superiors, loyal to the school of which he is an integral part, and loyal to the council of which he is a member; at the same time he must be loyal to his own educational ideals and beliefs some of which may be at variance with local policies and practices.

In this situation the sponsor must recognize that an important part of his job is the educating of teachers and students to his council point of view. As a specialist in this field he should demand proper rights and recognitions, be prepared for differences of opinion, expect criticism, and, where necessary, criticize, and meet difficult problems courageously, recognizing that no missionary has an easy time of it. He will recognize that voiced criticisms of and objections to the participation idea really represent most valuable educational settings which he cannot allow to go uncapitalized. He need not continually have a chip on his shoulder but he should not hesitate to stand up for what he believes to be a proper conception of the sphere of the council. He will cooperate with others, but at the same time he will demand that this cooperation be mutual. Only in this way will he ever be able to command the respect of the school for himself, his position, and his council.

6. The Sponsor Should Be an Enthusiastic Member but Not a "Teacher."—In a typical class the center of authority is the teacher; he assigns, requires, orders, questions, comments, and criticizes. In the council there is no such center of authority; it is a setting in which free expression of thoughts and opinions is encouraged unhampered by fear of teacher retaliation. In this setting the teacher has the same rights as any other member, but no more. He can express his ideas freely but he cannot force his opinion on the members. Often he will be disagreed with and maybe, occasionally, even voted down, the same as any other member. Any attempt to dictate, coerce, preach, or even teach in the commonly accepted sense of the word, will be met by a very proper student resentment.

Although the teacher should submerge his individuality in favor of student members, he will recognize his position as a regular full-fledged member, the most important single member of the group. He will be an active, not a passive, member. He will lead but not drive. He will respect the student's right to express himself even if his opinions are quite obviously wrong, but he will disagree tactfully so that no impression of interference is given. Nor will he take an antagonizing "I told you so but you wouldn't listen" attitude if later the students' ideas were proved wrong. He will remember that students are less experienced and mature than he and that they may be a bit slower in comprehending all the varied implications of an idea, so he will be patient even in the face of a conflict of opinions. Through such an attitude he will not only prevent serious cleavages but will ultimately win student respect and admiration.

7. The Sponsor Should Not Make Himself Too Conspicuous in Council Meetings.—It is admittedly difficult for a teacher whose whole experience has been in the most conspicuous place in a group of students to settle down and become only a member of a somewhat similar group. However this is exactly what he must do. The faculty representative who monopolizes discussion, who violates accepted parliamentary procedure by speaking without asking for proper recognition, and who in other ways attempts to "hog the spotlight" will discourage student initiative and mark the council for early disintegration.[1] As suggested above, the sponsor should participate in discussion only as a regular member of the council and not as a self-appointed savior. He provides guidance, especially if things appear to be getting beyond control, but even here there is good-natured and inconspicuous guidance, not domination.

8. The Sponsor Must Win and Hold Student Respect and Confidence.—Where there is no mutual respect and confidence among the members of an organized body there is no solidarity, no unity of spirit, and no feeling of morale.

[1] A few months ago the author saw a sponsor of this type—a dictatorial lady who marched up and down the aisle during the assembly program "keeping order"; who presided at her desk during council meeting while the president "presided" beside it; and who discouraged student discussion and participation by her remarks and general attitude. A recent letter from the principal of this school states, "Our council is now defunct." Little wonder!

Every member of the student council must "win his spurs" before he can be fully accepted and respected by the other members, and this holds equally true in the case of the teacher members. In a way it is even more essential in the case of the latter because there are so few of them, and also because of the importance of their positions. This student confidence grows naturally only out of a recognition by the students of the sponsor's (1) interest and skill in council activities, and (2) sympathetic understanding of the student point of view. Congenial student-teacher relationships are desirable, but mere personal popularity must not be accepted as complete evidence of sincere respect.

9. The Importance of the Sponsor's Personality Should Be Neither Underrated nor Overrated.—Much has been written and said about the importance of the teacher's personality and surely no one doubts the stimulating value of a personable instructor. On the other hand, in student council work where acceptance, participation, and agreements are not required by external authority, too much personality may be as detrimental as too little. For example, if the students' wholehearted acceptance of the sponsor is based only upon personal friendship, there is a very real danger that these students will too completely and easily agree with him and too closely and unquestioningly follow his wishes, which may prevent them from thinking clearly in terms of ideas, arguments, and points of the issues at hand. In such an instance not only are the real ends obscured but also there is no true representative government.

10. The Sponsor Should Have a Wholesome Sense of Humor.—In a dictatorship differences of opinion are discouraged on the theory that the autocrat is always right; in a democracy differences of opinions are encouraged on the theory that any individual is occasionally wrong and hence several heads are better than one because they will tend to reduce the number and seriousness of these mistakes. Because the council is a democratic setting, and the sponsor is a regularly recognized member of the group, he can expect to be disagreed with, to hear his views criticized, distorted, and misrepresented, and maybe even ridiculed, and sometimes to see his plans voted down, in exactly the same way that the opinions of the student members are reacted to.

If, thinking only in terms of himself and considering these reactions as personal affronts, he is resentful, his unsocial attitude will cause friction and mar the harmony of the group. If, thinking in terms of something far bigger than mere personalities, and considering these reactions as honest, even if occasionally illogical and discourteous behavior, he accepts them goodnaturedly, he will not only set an excellent example for the students to follow but will also win added esteem. Even "kidding" by his colleagues should be accepted good-naturedly. In other words, the sponsor should enjoy, in a broad way, his student council associations.

11. The Sponsor Should Have a Good Sense of Relative Values.—A glance through the lists of activities shown in Chap. IX will show not only that these opportunities are numerous but also that they differ widely in size, complexity, and value. The council cannot do all of them and in order to invest its time and efforts to the best advantage, it must carefully evaluate all possibilities. This is especially important in the case of a new and inexperienced council which may be tempted to work on the more or less spectacular projects, some of which may be, relatively, of little ultimate value. Just here, in a quiet but substantial way, the sponsor must be a real leader. He should not consider himself the sole critic of the council's program of activities, but should encourage the group to take a discriminating attitude toward the various possibilities of action. In short, he should set a good example in establishing standards and judging approximation of them.

12. The Sponsor Should Give Much Time and Thought to the Council's Program.—Sponsoring a student council is a great responsibility because of the group's intimate and complicated relations with all of the activities and organizations of the school, its bothersome financial matters, and the necessity for a wise investment of the enormous amount of time and energy devoted to the many and varied elements of the program. The sponsor who believes that he can successfully discharge his obligations merely by attending council meetings and entering into pertinent discussions will soon discover that he has a mistaken conception of the size of his job. Continuous preparation is necessary because no two council meetings, no two projects, and no two problems are exactly alike. The sponsor can never learn his subject once and for all as he can his classroom material. Each day's work with the council is a new assignment, and as such it requires a new or different application of time and thought.

It is to be regretted that many school administrators have not recognized this fact in a practical way by allowing sufficient time for such required preparation. All too frequently, even in this day of widespread appreciation of the value and place of extracurricular activities, the teacher's assignment to an organization is an addition to an already full teaching load. Under such conditions it is amazing that administrators should expect to have an efficient program, but many of them do; and often they make undeserved and unjustifiable criticisms of the sponsors by presenting an unfair comparison of their work with that of sponsors in more enlightened schools where time provisions are made. This is unjust to the teacher, to the organizations, to the school, and to the students themselves, and asking the impossible is uncomplimentary to the administration.

13. The Sponsor Should Stress and Practice Cooperation.—The council is not a complete and separate unit of the school but an important integrated element, a cooperative organization representing other cooperative organizations. Further, in the interest of a unified participation program, it must cooperate with the various key individuals about the school, the principal, dean, activity director, guidance officer, group sponsors, and others who have related responsibilities which must be recognized. Therefore the council should practice what it preaches and so set a good example. Here again, the sponsor must lead the way. He must recognize that cooperation is two-sided; that he should cooperate with the council, not merely the council with him.

14. The Sponsor Should Not Be Afraid to Experiment.—In many schools the council is a new organization with few established traditions, procedures, and programs and consequently it must feel its way forward in the development of these. As a result of this situation some, perhaps nearly all, of its activities and projects are certain to be largely experimental in type. The inevitable implication is that the sponsor, the leader of the group, must be an educational scientist, an individual who originates, experiments, discards, and improves as careful evaluation of organization, leadership, material, and method establishes proof of relative successes and values. Such scientific investigation will reveal some failures, but each of these, properly capitalized, represents a valuable learning situation. Every elimination of something wrong, bad, or inferior means a closer approach to what is right, good, or superior. Evaluative research always brings some criticism, but the scientist does not allow this to interfere with his program.

15. The Sponsor Should Not Attempt to Prevent All Council Mistakes.—It has been repeatedly emphasized in this book that a failure may represent a most valuable educational opportunity if it is intelligently capitalized. Because of the school's rigid definition of success and failure and its usual lack of a practical policy of recognizing the educational importance of the latter, this idea cannot be overemphasized. Although the mistakes that would be most serious in consequences should be prevented, the adult who steps in and prevents all childish errors is robbing the child of many educational opportunities. The student can often learn far more efficiently and permanently from a choice of his own, a recognition of failure, and a resultant program of improvement headed toward success, than he can from a teacher's admonition to avoid or prevent such failure. Sermonizing the student on what is right and wrong tends to become monotonous and probably will ultimately result in resentment and impair harmony. The group which refuses to listen to the voice of experience must learn in the hard way. An occasional failure will also prevent the council from becoming conceited, arrogant, and self-sufficient.

16. The Sponsor Should Not Become Discouraged.—The road of all pioneering effort is dotted with failures, but no achievement would ever have been accomplished if those responsible had become disheartened and quit. Any accomplishment is an eternal memorial to the courage of those who continued their efforts despite failures and discouragements, which is another way of saying that nothing worth while is ever achieved if failure and discouragement are allowed to dominate the picture.

There have been many failures in student council work, and there will be many more. A proper conception of the relation of failure to success must be recognized and appreciated. The administrator who takes an attitude of "we tried it once and it failed so we dropped it" need never expect to have a successful council, at least until he changes his tune. Educational progress, or any other kind of progress, is made only by those who have "tried it" ten, fifty, or a hundred times, failed, tried it again in some other way, and are still "trying it." Anyone who has any knowledge whatever of council work knows that there is not one "it" but countless "its." A participation plan is not a cloak that can be quickly thrown about a school, but something which must be slowly and laboriously grown into. All learning is a terribly slow and painful process.

The sponsor is a human being and it is but natural that he may often become disheartened about his council work. However, recalling to mind the objectives of the plan and their extreme importance in the lives of his students and his country, and remembering that other schools do have successful councils, should help him to see beyond the discouragement of the moment. Because the students will very easily recognize and reflect it, the sponsor should never show his discouragement. The students should see that when the council fails in some project the sponsor becomes all the more determined to make it a success.

17. The Sponsor Should Study Himself and, If Necessary, Make Personal Readjustments.—It would be illogical to place the blame for all council errors, mistakes, and failures on the student members of the group because undoubtedly some of it should be placed upon the sponsor. He should realize that any failure of the council is a reflection upon himself as well as upon the student members. As has already been pointed out in this chapter, it is not reasonable to expect every teacher to slip easily from one setting in which he dominates into another setting in which he is only an ordinary member. Some difficulty in making this readjustment need not be unexpected. Of course there are other reasons for sponsor inefficiency. The sponsor himself should be the individual most interested in discovering these and, if necessary, remedying them.

If the sponsor notes that the students react somewhat resentfully toward him or ignore him, recognizes that his ideas are criticized too easily and vigorously, sees himself frequently outvoted, or in other ways senses a lack of mutual understanding and harmony, he should not be too ready to place all the blame upon the students; he should begin with a study of himself and his own qualifications—his knowledge, experience, attitudes, personality, ideas, methods of presentation, and personal relationships—in an attempt to discover if part or all of the fault is his own. If the situation is serious enough, he should talk the matter over confidentially with the principal, with his best friend, and even with a few of the most highly respected and competent students. He should be alert to all criticisms and should evaluate them fairly. Naturally, he should undertake this self-study honestly and should, if conditions warrant it, make a sincere attempt to improve the intolerable situation. His investigation should not stop with the acquiring of knowledge; as a result of this acquisition he should do something about it.

18. The Sponsor Should Continue His Training.—The possibilities and implications of the student participation idea are so numerous and broad that no sponsor should ever consider himself completely and finally trained for his job. Because of the rapidity with which the field is developing, even the better experienced sponsors will have to continue their education in order to keep abreast of developments. College courses, books, magazines, conventions, conferences, and visits are the main devices through which this continued education may be secured. An incidental, but important, outcome of such training is increased interest in the plan.

Selected References

ALTSCHULL, H.: Suggestions to the Adviser of an Elementary School Council, *Educational Method*, 22: 281–283, March, 1943.

BOWDEN, A. O., and I. C. CLARKE: "Tomorrow's Americans," Chap. V, G. P. Putnam's Sons, New York, 1930.

The Student-council Sponsor

BROGUE, E. B., and P. B. JACOBSON: "Student-council Handbook," Chap. V, National Association of Secondary School Principals, March, 1940.

DEITTERT, C. C.: Teacher Load and Extra-curricular Activities, *School Activities*, 9: 203, 245, January, 1938.

ELIASSEN, R. H.: The Teacher and Extra-curriculum Activities, *School Review*, 40: 364–371, May, 1932.

ERICKSON, C. E., F. B. DIXON, and L. E. BARTHOLD: "Pupil Participation in School Life," Chap. VIII, Lucas Brothers, Columbia, Mo., 1942.

GOING, C. J.: The Teacher's Place in Student Activities, *Proceedings of the National Education Association*, 65: 622–624, 1927.

KIRKENDALL, L. A.: Duties of a Student Council Faculty Adviser, *Progressive Education*, 3: 208–210, November, 1934.

McKOWN, H. C.: "Activities in the Elementary School," Chap. II, McGraw-Hill Book Company, Inc., New York, 1938.

———: "Home Room Guidance," Chap. XI, McGraw-Hill Book Company, Inc., New York, 1934.

MILLARD, C. V.: "The Organization and Administration of Extra-curricular Activities," Chap. V, A. S. Barnes & Company, New York, 1930.

NEWSOM, N. W., and E. L. BARNDT: Teacher Training for Extra-curricular Sponsorship, *School Activities*, 12: 299–300, April, 1941.

OTTO, J. H., and S. A. HAMRIN: "Co-curricular Activities in Elementary Schools," Chap. XIII, D. Appleton-Century Company, Inc., New York, 1937.

TERRY, P. W.: "Supervising Extra-curricular Activities," Chap. XX, McGraw-Hill Book Company, Inc., New York, 1930.

THOMAS, E. A.: Training for Activities Administration, *School Activities*, 14: 51–52, October, 1942.

WEBB, A. B.: The Selection of Class Sponsors, *School Activities*, 8: 347–348, April, 1937.

Chapter XIII

Evaluating the Student Council

MEASUREMENT in extracurricular activities has been characterized as being "very necessary, quite inadequate, and extremely difficult," and probably no one who is familiar with the field and with the implications of these three points will disagree with this statement. Nor is it likely that anyone would disagree with this statement if it were applied to measurement in the field of student participation in control. A brief explanation of these three points will help to set the stage for a discussion of the specialized techniques of such appraisal.

The organization and operation of a plan of student participation is expensive in time, efforts, and money and, if the plan is to continue to exist, this cost must be satisfactorily justified to those who are asked to meet it. Such satisfactory justification can come only through proof of attainments, and such proof can come only out of evaluation. Further, because the program is somewhat new in most schools—and some of it will be "new" in any school because of the necessity for a continuous adaptation to changed ideals, conditions, and personnel—it is not perfect, hence it can be improved upon. Such improvement cannot be made until the knowledge is obtained as to which parts of the plan are weak and should be strengthened, and which parts are strong and should be maintained. This, also, necessitates appraisal. Obviously, any attempt at evaluation helps to clarify, validate, and establish the objectives of the thing being appraised.

Evaluating the Student Council

Evaluation has always been considered an important part of educational procedure, but, until comparatively recently, most of it was concerned with immediate objectives, such as ability to spell, work problems, write legibly, and recall memorized material; very little was concerned with the ultimate results in the lives and activities of adults. Therefore, because education must be justified on the basis of its ultimate effects, much of our evaluation has been and still is inadequate. This is particularly true in the fields of character education and citizenship training, where end purposes are rather indefinite and general. Too, the recency of the recognition and systematic organization of extracurricular activities have inevitably meant, as in any new field, that appraisal has not kept step with development. Another reason for the present inadequacy of measurement in this field is to be found in the difficulty of making appraisals.

It is comparatively easy to test the student's knowledge of facts and his skill in simple processes because these are limited and immediate goals. Except in extreme cases, it is exceedingly difficult to make corresponding ratings of his attitudes, ideals, and habits in such a general sphere as citizenship, the main objective of the participation plan, because (1) the purposes, materials, methods, and relationships involved are largely intangible; (2) many or nearly all of these ultimate goals are set by the community, not by the school; (3) a considerable period of time usually elapses between training and "real life" utilization; and (4) other agencies than the school make contributions. However, despite these difficulties, attempts at appraisal must be made, and the sooner they are made the sooner will come the development of the devices by means of which the results of participation in school government can be evaluated.[1]

[1] Perhaps the best single pertinent article, one that is original as well as reflective of other articles, is P. R. Grim, Evaluating the School Activities

The Place of Opinion in Evaluation.—Undoubtedly one reason for the neglect of evaluation in the extracurricular field, or at least for neglect of the publication of such appraisals, is an apparent belief that because most of these measurements are based on opinions rather than on "nose-counting" techniques, they will not be comparable in accuracy or in general caliber to those commonly published by the "scientific measurement expert." In other words, the tester by opinions has feared the almost certain derogatory remarks of the tester by objective measures. Hence, a word of encouragement is in order.

The oldest and simplest form of evaluation is the expression of opinion and this measurement, whether it be short, general, and simple or long, detailed, and complex, represents appraisal because it is based upon felt, implied, or definitely stated standards. The coffee taster who rates flavors or the jewel expert who rates colors in a precious stone is using subjective measurement. Naturally, the value of this method will depend upon the competency of the individual using it. A few years ago at the beginning of the so-called "testing movement" this technique of measurement was widely scoffed at as being "subjective—mere opinion." However, today it is being used more and more by professional testers. The reason for this change in attitude is clear—subjective measurement has value, and a very definite place in all programs of educational evaluation.[1]

Program, *School Activities*, 8: 198–200, 208, 213, January, 1937. An excellent general article is R. W. Tyler, The Place of Evaluation in Modern Education, *Elementary School Journal*, 41; 19–27, September, 1940.

[1] Two good recent illustrations of this type of evaluation are the doctoral dissertations of G. Jones, "Extra-curricular Activities in Relation to the Curriculum," Bureau of Publications, Teachers College, New York, 1935; and J. H. Wise, "An Evaluation of Extra-curricular Activities in Large Southern High Schools," George Peabody College for Teachers, Nashville, Tenn., 1935.

How, by Whom, and When Should Evaluation Be Made?—"There is no royal road to learning" is no more true than "There is no royal road to evaluating learning." A complete and accurate measurement of the results of any kind of instruction represents a complicated and arduous task. This is especially true in the case of an activity like participation in which the objectives and elements are so intangible, numerous, varied, and interrelated. Certainly such appraisal is not a one-man, a one-device, or a one-time job. The three most pertinent questions which arise in this connection are (1) How shall evaluation be made? (2) Who shall do the measuring? and (3) When shall this appraisal be made? The purpose of this chapter is to answer these three important questions.

DEVICES FOR EVALUATION

There are a number of devices which may be utilized in appraising the council and its work, and some of these are more suitable for certain types and sizes of schools and plans than for others. However, there is a place for all of them. In fact, a utilization of all forms of measuring devices gives a view from several angles and should thus result in a more complete and accurate picture than if only one of them were used.

In this connection a word of caution is in order. In measuring the participation plan there is a very real danger that this evaluation will overemphasize the elements of the form of the organization and underemphasize the objectives sought. The test of the value of a plan of participation is to be found in what it accomplishes, and although this is dependent to a considerable extent upon the details of organization, yet it does not necessarily follow that a good organization inevitably means good results.

The Questionnaire

The questionnaire is a widely used modern device for discovering attitudes, opinions, reactions, ideas, facts, and materials, and it will be found useful in evaluating the council and its work. A questionnaire may vary in length and complexity from a short and simple form which requests a little definite, easily recalled information to a long and complicated form which requires complete and detailed data and considerable thought. A statement of the purposes of the questionnaire and directions as to how it shall be used are necessary. The questions should be clear and to the point and couched in language easily understood by the questionees. Trying out a questionnaire before finally using it is a good policy. The individual should be encouraged to illustrate his points wherever possible; one good example is often worth a whole page of generalities. Espccially in the case of requests for personal opinions or reactions, no names should be required. A return which is signed will often be valueless because it does not represent the completely frank, honest, and unbiased opinions of the individual signing it. Filling out the questionnaire, even in the case of check lists, should not be hurried because competently thinking about an item and carefully evaluating it require time. The three following sets of questions represent material which may be used in a questionnaire.[1]

The following questions by Lester Kirkendall are "designed to find whether certain features of democracy are present, not whether certain provisions are made for them. A constitution may provide a most democratic framework for council organization, but the operation of the council may be quite

[1] The oral questionnaire or interview is being increasingly used in educational measurement. It has advantages, but also obvious disadvantages: (1) it represents a very slow and tedious process; (2) answers, especially opinions and reactions, are quite likely to be unduly influenced by the setting; and (3) recording is always difficult, sometimes impossible.

undemocratic. If your school can answer fifteen of these questions affirmatively, then your school ranks high as an effective instrument of democracy."[1]

1. Can the president, or the adviser of the council, outline a definite program projecting itself into the future, to which the council is dedicating its efforts?
2. Does the council give consideration to problems which are associated with the determination of school policies?
3. Are election arrangements such as to provide a continuity of officers?
4. Does the principal or superintendent of the school confer often with the council president, or council members?
5. Do faculty members ever attend council meetings, consult with or participate in the deliberations of the council?
6. Is the routine work of the council organization adequately cared for?
7. Does the council keep records of those of its activities which are of vital concern to the school?
8. Is a definite and sufficient time provided for council meetings?
9. Can the council through its president and advisor call special meetings or school forums presided over by the council president for a consideration of important problems?
10. Can the lay members of the student body or faculty members cite any significant contributions made by the council?
11. Are council elections serious referendums in which candidates for office have policies and programs for consideration?

[1] Is Your School an Effective Instrument of Democracy? *The Councilor*, No. 2, pp. 2–3, December, 1942.

12. Does the faculty participate cooperatively in the affairs of the school council by voting or by attending and participating in school forums?
13. Are differences of opinion, even when individuals or groups are involved, considered openly and without rancor?
14. Does the lay pupil know who is the council president, or who are the council officers?
15. Do pupils speak openly when they are opposed in principle to the policies or program of the school?
16. Are home room or school forums provided for group consideration of council problems?
17. Does the council president occupy a prominent place in the life of the school?
18. Does the council employ the talents of students other than council members in its programs?
19. Are meetings conducted according to an orderly parliamentary procedure?
20. Do members of the student body or faculty freely raise issues for the consideration of the council?
21. Do students and faculty members discuss democratic principles involved in matters under consideration?

Another illustrative set of appropriate questions is the following used by Earl C. Kelley in his evaluation of the Milwaukee Vocational School council. Janitors as well as teachers answered these questions.[1]

1. Do you think the advent of student participation in government made the students happier as a whole? Yes______ No______

[1] Kelley, E. C., "An Evaluation of Student Participation in Government in American Secondary Schools" (unpublished doctor's dissertation), Northwestern University, 1940.

2. Did it make the students feel more at home in the school? Yes______ No______
3. Did the legislative functions make the students more aware of the problems of the school? Yes______ No______
4. Did the attempts at cooperation in citizenship carry over into other school work? Yes______ No______
5. Was the general conduct of the students improved? Yes______ No______
6. Was the attitude toward school property improved? Yes______ No______
7. Was regard for the rights of others increased? Yes______ No______
8. Was the students' sense of responsibility increased? Yes______ No______
9. Was student pride in the school increased? Yes______ No______
10. Did student participation in school government enable the students to attach themselves to, or identify themselves with the school more? Yes______ No______
11. Was the student's attitude toward government in general improved? Yes______ No______
12. Did student participation in government release teachers from time-consuming disciplinary efforts to any extent? Yes______ No______
13. Would you recommend student participation in government to other schools as a method of promoting cooperation? Yes______ No______
14. Would you recommend it to other schools as a method of promoting citizenship? Yes______ No______
15. Would you recommend it as a method of improving school conduct? Yes______ No______

If you have any additional comment to make, will you please make it in the space below or use the reverse side of the sheet?

In a slightly different form of appraisal the student is asked to think largely in terms of the influence of the council upon himself and answer such questions as those indicated below.

Directions.—We are attempting to find out just how successful our student-council plan is. You can help us by answering the following questions from your own experience. Give your honest opinions. Do not sign the sheet.

1. Are you glad that your school has a student council? Why, or why not?
2. Are you interested in what the council does? Why, or why not?
3. Do you have a pretty clear idea of the main purpose of our student council plan? What do you think this purpose is?
4. Do you feel that you have any personal responsibility for the success of the plan? Give reasons for your answer.
5. Do you have opportunities to participate in the discussions of school problems?
6. Do you believe that the council is seriously and continuously trying to find opportunities to render service to the school?
7. Do you feel that you yourself are represented in the council?
8. Do you consider the council a serious-minded body?
9. Do you believe that the council has accomplished some really important achievements? If so, will you illustrate?
10. Because of the council's work, do you feel that you understand better the problems of the school? That you take a greater interest in these problems?

11. In general, do you believe that the council is composed of good members? That it has good officers?
12. Has your attitude toward the school changed because of council activities? If so, in what way?
13. Has your attitude toward yourself changed? If so, in what way?
14. Has your attitude toward other students changed? If so, in what way?
15. Because of council activities, do you believe that you have a better understanding of the meaning of democratic government?
16. Do you believe that you are better prepared for adult citizenship?
17. Do you believe that you will take a greater interest in adult citizenship activities?
18. Do you consider yourself a better all-round school citizen because of the council's work? Explain your answer.
19. Does the council make any difference to you in your daily school life? If so, just what?
20. In general, would you say that the council has been (underscore one) Unsuccessful Successful Very successful
21. What are your suggestions for improving the council or its work?

Check List

The check list is another device commonly used in evaluation. In it the various elements, items, activities, procedures, or relationships are listed and the evaluator rates each one in terms of quality, satisfactoriness, or some other measure of worth. The most important advantages of this type of device in council evaluation are that (1) it can cover all specific details, and (2) relatively little time is required for an appraisal. Its main value is in discovering the high and the low spots in organization, activities, procedures, and products. Its most important disadvantages are that (1) it represents largely an appraisal of processes rather than products; (2) it is more or less rigid and hence may not fit all schools and settings equally well; and (3) it does not consider the relative worth of the various items—a dozen "highly satisfactory" items might be outweighed by a single "unsatisfactory" item. In general, the check list is valuable mostly as a tentative or preliminary technique and should be supplemented by other methods The accompanying check list will illustrate this device. The various items are those which have been discussed in this book. Probably the teachers can use this device more successfully than the students. Obviously, some of the items, such as "Bylaws," could not be competently checked by teachers or students not members of the council. If such a list is developed by a school for its own use, extreme care should be taken to ensure that it represents "good," "standard," or "widely recognized and accepted" ideas, items, and procedures, rather than merely those of the local school.

STUDENT-COUNCIL CHECK LIST

Directions.—Read each of the following items, be sure that you understand what it means, and think about its suitability, value, or sufficiency in our own school. Then place a check mark opposite it in the column which represents your best judgment.

	Unsatis-factory	Satis-factory	Highly satis-factory
Objectives			
Success of the council in teaching or developing:			
The theory of democracy			
Sentiments of law, order			
Respect for authority			
Increased self-direction			
Intelligent leadership			
Intelligent followership			
Social cooperation			

	Unsatis- factory	Satis- factory	Highly satis- factory
Personal responsibility			
School morale			
Awareness of objectives			
Type of Organization			
Source of membership			
Powers and authority			
Form of organization			
Relationship of parts			
School knowledge of these			
Principles			
School-felt need for council			
Student body representation			
Faculty representation			
Student-felt representation			
Restrictions on membership			
Council member participation			
Committee participation			
Training of council members			
Size of the council			
Definiteness of duties			
Seriousness of attitude			
Principal's veto power			
Constructiveness of program			
Council's cooperativeness			
Financial policies			
Regularity of meetings			
Time of meetings			
Facilities and equipment			
Continuous adaptation			
Council's study of its record			
Council-groups relationships			
Program of activities			
Program of publicity			
Intercouncil relationships			
Constitution			
Form of publication			
Adaptation to local school			
General form and style			
Source of authority			
Positiveness of emphasis			
Evidence of serious study			

	Unsatis-factory	Satis-factory	Highly satis-factory
Elements of constitution:			
Name of governing body			
Name of student body			
Statement of purpose			
Qualifications of citizens			
Qualifications of councilors			
Statement of powers			
Description of organization			
Description of officers:			
Title or designation			
Term of office			
Reelection			
Eligibility			
Nomination and election			
Vacancies			
Recall procedure			
Duties, responsibilities			
Ratification			
Veto power			
Amendments			
Bylaws			
Quorum			
Meetings:			
Regular			
Special			
Election of officers			
Order of business			
Rules of order			
Voting procedures			
Reports			
Fees, dues, assessments			
Insignia			
Amendments			
Nominations and Elections			
Elections committee			
Method of nominating			
Election campaign:			
General form			
General results			
Election officials:			

	Unsatis-factory	Satis-factory	Highly satis-factory
Number			
Qualifications			
Duties			
Training for jobs			
Materials and equipment:			
Registration lists			
Forms, signs, etc.			
Ballots			
Ballot boxes			
Details of election:			
Time of voting			
Place of voting			
Method of voting			
Instructions to voters			
Internal Organization			
Officers:			
Number			
Designations			
Rating of:			
President			
Vice-president			
Secretary			
Treasurer			
__________			
__________			
__________			
Method of election			
Office-holding restrictions			
Instruction in duties			
Term of office			
Relationships with school			
Committees:			
Number			
Size			
Membership			
Method of appointment			
Instruction in duties			
Number of activities			
Quality of work			
Relationships with school			

	Unsatis-factory	Satis-factory	Highly satis-factory
Activities and Projects			
Number			
Quality or significance			
Interestingness			
Worthiness			
Practicability			
Results in developing:			
Initiative, originality			
Responsibility			
Cooperation			
School citizenship			
Interests and abilities			
General school spirit			
Completeness of program			
General success of program			
Financial Administration			
Sources of funds:			
Number			
General justifiableness			
Adequacy			
General organization:			
Type of plan			
Handling of finances			
Group treasurers			
Central treasurer			
Bonding			
Forms and procedures:			
Activity ticket			
Ticket report			
Central treasurer's receipt			
Pay order			
Requisition			
Treasurer's check			
______________			
______________			
General report			
Bookkeeping:			
General account			
Special accounts			
Account or record books			

	Unsatis-factory	Satis-factory	Highly satis-factory
"Tightness" of plan			
Auditing of accounts			
Budget:			
Basis of apportionment			
Developing, adopting budget			
Publication of budget			
Provisions for adjustments			
Student Court			
General type of court			
Officials:			
Number			
Method of selection			
Power and duties			
Term of office			
Procedures:			
Arrest or citation			
Trial			
Punishments:			
Educational aim			
Appropriateness			
Reasonableness			
Immediacy			
Enforcement			
Penal code			
Jurisdiction of court			
Court room			
Frequency of sessions			
Secret, open trials			
Publicity			
Final authority			
General work of court			
Sponsor			
Number of sponsors			
Method of selection			
Faculty-felt responsibility			
Representation of faculty			
Sponsor's:			
Knowledge of participation			
Sympathy with the idea			
General attitude			
Interest and enthusiasm			

	Unsatis-factory	Satis-factory	Highly satis-factory
Personality			
Sense of humor			
Cooperativeness			
Sense of relative values			
Preparation for meetings			
Loyalty to the council			
Experimental attitude			
Tenacity			
Study of himself			
Continued training			
Student respect, confidence			

STATEMENT OF CRITERIA

This device is somewhat similar to the check list discussed above. However, it is different in that (1) standards are definitely stated, and (2) the assumption is that the evaluator will make the necessary appraisal; no provision is made for recording reactions. Where there are many criteria they are usually grouped under a relatively few main headings. The following standards suggested by the National Association of Student Councils will illustrate. The five criteria include 52 subpoints. Only the first criterion is shown complete with its specifications.

I. A good student council possesses power, authority, and responsibility.
   1. It is the voice of the student body.
   2. It proposes and carries out activities for school improvement.
   3. It coordinates the extracurricular activities of the the school, enlisting the entire personnel.
   4. In doing the above, it:
      a. Promotes and understanding both practice of democratic citizenship.
      b. Trains student leaders.

5. Its source of power lies in the delegation to it by the principal of authority and responsibility for action within specific or general areas; provided, that if in the judgment of the principal, a projected council activity seems detrimental to the best interests of the school, such activity can be vetoed by him.

II. A good student council practices accepted democratic principles in its operations; its constitution and bylaws are carefully planned and democratically conceived.

III. A good student council is supported on the part of the faculty and principal by a true understanding of the council's role; in addition, the attitude of the principal and faculty is sympathetic.

IV. A good student council has a sound functioning organization.

V. An effective student council has prestige, and enlists the ready cooperation of the student body.

Record of Participation

One of the common measures of the effectiveness of a program of extracurricular activities is the number of students who participate directly in it. Such a device is based upon the assumption that if participation is valuable to one student it is valuable to all. Although this represents a measure of quantity and not quality of participation, it does tell something. For instance, if 35 per cent of the students in one school take part in activities, 60 per cent in another, and 85 per cent in another, it is evident that the third school more nearly achieves the ideal of total participation than the other two schools. Consequently, if the extracurricular program is largely under the control and supervision of the council, a comparison of several years' records of the extent of participation should be enlightening. It cannot be assumed that all of any increases or decreases were due to the council, but it can be safely assumed that some of them were.

The nature or quality of the participation should also be appraised because a student may "participate" by being merely a nominal member of an organization and his participation may be worthless as far as practical benefits are concerned. This type of appraisal is exceedingly difficult to make because of the wide variation in forms and relative potentialities of opportunities and students, and also because of the difficulty of evaluating student development in terms of maximal development. But an opinion on the apparent interest, industry, activity, and contributions of the participants does provide some measure of the quality of the participation.

Another type of participation-evaluation is on the basis of the number of noncouncil students who participate directly in council projects and activities. A council which enlists a considerable number of these students in its program certainly should be credited with developing cooperation and followership.

Case Study Technique

In the case study technique an exhaustive analysis is made of some one council project in order to see how this body functions in a special problem or setting. The direct effects on the school, its students, teachers, activities, and organizations are painstakingly investigated, as well as the indirect influences of its many ramifications. Such an appraisal considers the quality as well as the quantity of these results because some of them will be more important than others. It is even possible that some of the effects may be detrimental rather than beneficial. Weaknesses of the project or procedures, as well as strengths, can be noted, and the causes for each studied. In brief, this method is a complete biography of a particular activity. The devices used in it may be any or all of those discussed above.

Descriptive Report of the Council's Work

Often a council will become discouraged when it faces a multitude of tasks ahead of it; and in such an instance it is quite likely to forget the size and importance of the program behind it. One good method of banishing discouragement and restoring confidence is the compilation of a list of the activities which this body has recently carried on. Such a list is easily prepared because the projects are definite and can be readily seen and counted. Almost without exception the resulting picture or record will be an "eye-opener" to all concerned because these activities have a unique way of piling up over the weeks and months to make a very appreciable total.

A further development of this idea represents an excellent appraisal device. Each entry in the list is briefly described and fairly evaluated. It is true that some of the values cannot be readily seen and measured, but it is safe to assume that to some extent many of them can be, and that a serious attempt at evaluation will indicate still others. This record should be written out. Written reports are always more carefully done than oral reports. Regularly publishing these records through the newspaper or the bulletin board is a good policy, good for the council and good for the school. Incidentally, description is becoming more and more accepted as an approved form of educational measurement.

Who Should Evaluate the Participation Plan?

If the council and its work should be evaluated, the question very naturally arises, Who should do this evaluating? The answer to this question is short and inclusive: Everyone who is directly or indirectly affected or influenced by it. A listing of these individuals together with a brief discussion of their potentialities will help to justify this answer.

Students.—The council represents and is designed to influence every student in the school and hence it is clear that the most logical place to begin evaluation is with the student himself. Better than anyone else he is in position to understand in what ways and to what extent he has been influenced by this, his own organization. Because he is closer to the school than any teacher or administrator, he is in better position to observe, firsthand, the results of the council's efforts. It is quite likely that he will underestimate rather than overestimate the value of the council because undoubtedly he will not immediately recognize the sources of some of the influences operative; the results may have been indirectly caused by the council. This means that his evaluation will be more valuable than if he overestimated the council's influence and gave it credit for something for which it was not responsible. The average student is a much better evaluator of general school life and activities than the average teacher or administrator gives him credit for being.[1]

Alumni and Former Students.—These individuals are now older, have been out of school for some time, are less influenced by immediate appeals or contacts, and hence are in a position to make seasoned judgments as to the value of participation in their own lives and activities. Of course it is possible that changed conditions in school and society may have resulted in changed sense of values. However, it is logical to believe that if the plan was designed to make definite contributions to adult citizenship, then the present adult citizen should be able to recognize some of them. Such questions as these might be asked: Did the participation plan help you?

[1] See Voelker, E. W., The Organization and Functioning of Pupil Opinion in High-School Control, *School Review*, 34: 654–667, November, 1926.

How, or in what way? To what extent? Can you illustrate your answers? Where do you believe the plan might have been improved? Why? A world-wide investigation cannot be undertaken, but there are always a number of former students who are available and who undoubtedly would be glad to have some part in such a survey. The group studied should not be top-heavy with former council members and officers because these would be likely to overestimate the value of the organization of which they were a part.[1]

Student Organizations.—Because student groups represent a part of the total sphere of the council, they are in position to appreciate how this central supervisory body has directly or indirectly helped them, or has not helped them. They are in position to suggest ways in which the council can be of greater service to them. Hence, their appraisals can be quite definite and practical. Further, a group discussion of the council and its program will probably result in good ideas due to (1) the number of individuals participating, and (2) the refining influence of such discussion.

The Council.—It goes without saying that the council should continuously evaluate itself and its program, but this idea is worth emphasizing. As a matter of fact the council should be a more severe judge than any organization or individual in the school. The reason is clear. It is hardly complimentary to the council, which has the proper ideals and knowledges and the necessary power and authority, to have some outsider point out errors or weaknesses which it should have seen first. To repeat, the council should be at one and the same time its own most severe and most intelligent critic. Further, it should not limit appraisal to the status quo but extend it to precedents and established customs, some of which may be unjustifiably handicapping its policies. Self-

[1] Pertinent references in the bibliography are those to Cory, and Shannon and Zimmerman.

evaluation may be somewhat biased because of the organization's interest, enthusiasm, and wishful thinking, and traditional organization and well-established attitudes; and the group may be too close to appreciate what is really happening. On the other hand, it is reasonable to believe that a deeply interested and competent group such as this can very constructively and satisfactorily evaluate its own efforts. The sponsor or faculty member himself must set a good example for the student members to follow.

Teachers.—The teacher is in an excellent position to recognize and appreciate changes in school attitudes and activities due to council accomplishments because she has a sort of overview of the setting. Those teachers who have been in school for some time can easily note these changes by making a comparison of the records, attitudes, and achievements, or lack of them, of several years ago with those of today. Not all teachers' evaluations will be equally valid because of differences in interest and competency, but a totaling of these estimates will tend to average or reduce the effect of these errors in judgment.

Faculty Committee.—Often a faculty committee is appointed by the principal to make an appraisal of the council's work. Such a committee represents several heads, several points of view, and several school contacts. The average teacher is thoroughly honest and conscientious and several of these individuals together should do a commendable job of appraisal. The formal appointment of highly respected and competent teachers will dignify the procedure and make for a proper council attitude toward the committee and its activities. The requirement that a written report be turned in also adds to the worth of the evaluation.

The Administrator.—The principal is at the very center of things. He can feel the pulse of the school more accurately than any other individual in it because he is in position to see the entire setting, with all of the various elements in proper perspective. No one is more competent than he to judge school morale. Undoubtedly, his office is a sort of clearing house for the ideas, opinions, and reactions not only of students and teachers but also of parents and patrons. Because in all probability he is not close to specialized organizations, he is unbiased by enthusiasms for particular activities. He, too, can easily make comparisons of the school of today with that of past years. His evaluations may be more general than those of students and teachers, but they will be valuable.

Parents and Patrons.—As in the case of student evaluation of school life and activities, much too little attention is given to the possibilities of parent and patron appraisal. It is true that parental reactions may be a bit incompetent because often they are not based upon firsthand experience but upon somewhat inaccurate, incomplete, and secondhand information, yet they do have a good basis in fact, much greater than the average teacher or administrator realizes. These individuals are adults, experienced in life activities, ideas, and standards, and they should be able to judge the final value of school activities. They are in position to hear reflections of the school from their own children and their children's friends. And these reflections are generally honest because they are uninfluenced by the presence of school teachers or administrators. The parent can also compare the schedule of opportunities which his children have with that which he himself had, or did not have. This parental-evaluation device has considerable merit.[1]

Outside Professional Experts.—The school survey is now an accepted part of educational procedure, not only in curricular, financial, organizational, and building and equipment matters, but also in extracurricular affairs. In every survey of extracurricular activities that has been made, provided a

[1] See Klinedinst's article in the references at the end of the chapter.

council was operative, the participation plan has come in for a good share of attention. The surveyor is a professional, an individual acquainted with the theory of participation and one possessing a wide knowledge of plans existing in other schools and settings. He is in position to make good judgments. It is true that because he does not know the local school background intimately, and because of the brevity of his visit, he cannot learn all about it. He may not be able to understand and fully appreciate all of the reasons behind particular forms of organization, activities, or procedures. At the same time, this lack may mean an appraisal uninfluenced by local traditions, customs, biases, and opinions—a good evaluation. In any case, a competent investigator can do a helpful job of appraisal.

In this connection it is pertinent to emphasize that the surveyor should be competent in this specialized field. In a number of general school surveys the appraisal of extracurricular activities was made by individuals who were not competent to make them, and the resulting published evaluations were, of course, uncomplimentary and worse than useless. A higher degree or a professorship in a school of education qualifies no one for this task. In a less formal type of survey the happy principal or council sponsor will explain his council plan to a visiting guest or speaker, arrange for him to attend a council meeting, and later ask him his opinion of the local organization. Of course, the opinions given are always favorable—and worthless. Such a "survey" in no way represents worth-while evaluation. Really, there are few outsiders who know anything at all about the council idea.

The Time of Evaluation

When should the student council and its program be evaluated? The answer to this question is, Continuously and periodically.

Some of the definite results of certain activities can be appraised immediately. For instance, at the conclusion of a finance campaign it is possible to count and indicate the amount of money raised, and this represents evaluation. However, it represents only partial evaluation of the campaign because the education received, the attitudes formed or changed, and the effects of the use of this money are also results, but these are difficult to measure, and some of them may not be measurable until later. Similarly, the effects of other projects may not be noticeable until weeks, months, or even years have passed. Further, not all projects begin and end at the same time. These facts mean that a continuous watch must be kept for the appearance of results. Making a rather detailed and complete appraisal at the end of the semester or year represents a good council policy, but this procedure is only one phase of evaluation.

The school setting is always changing; old educational aims, emphases, and materials disappear and new aims, emphases, and materials appear; and old administrators, teachers, and students leave, and new administrators, teachers, and students enter. Consequently, as was pointed out earlier in this book, there must be a continuous adaptation to the present setting and, more difficult still, a continuous reselling of the cooperative way of life, and these necessitate continuous evaluation of all phases of the council's organization and interests. In reality, this adaptation represents experimentation because no one knows how a thing will work until it is tried out and the results are measured; therefore the resultant procedure is evaluation, readjustment and evaluation, and readjustment and evaluation until a satisfactory accomplishment has been achieved. But an accomplishment which is satisfactory today may be unsatisfactory tomorrow. Hence, this procedure of evaluation never ends. If it does end, progress ceases.

A possible danger of a continuous evaluation is that it may become cursory and if this happens the appraisal is not worth making. A periodic evaluation, perhaps near the end of each semester and certainly near the end of each year, is as reasonable as a similar periodic evaluation of the student's classwork or the school's safety devices. Rarely, if ever, will such an appraisal become mere routine. In short, continuous and periodic evaluations supplement each other.

The Interpretation and Capitalization of Results

In many a school an administrator, faculty committee, or other individual or group has made an investigation of some phase of educational activity, absence, finance, marks, promotions, or health, given it considerable publicity, and then laid the results away soon to be forgotten. Such a survey is not an evaluation at all because it does not effectively capitalize the results obtained. Similarly, an evaluation of the council and its program is not completed when opinions have been gathered and read, or marks or ratings given. The data must be interpreted and capitalized, else the time and efforts used in gathering them are wasted. The end purpose of all evaluation is improvement.

The interpretation of the results of an investigation comes in answer to the question, What do these data mean? Any good survey of a participation plan will show some low points and some high points in the various phases or elements of its organization, administration, supervision, program, procedures, material, financing, sponsorship, etc., and proper interpretation indicates the reasons for these particular strengths and weaknesses. A knowledge of these reasons and relationships is an essential part of any helpful appraisal plan.

Capitalization, the last step in evaluation, comes in answer to the question, How shall we use these results? Obviously, a mere knowledge of strengths and weaknesses and of the reasons for them is useless until such knowledge results in maintaining the high points and raising the low points of the program. So the information obtained is used as the basis for making what appear to be desirable or necessary readjustments in organization, program, procedures, and the other elements which together constitute the entire plan.

To emphasize again: the real purpose of all evaluation is improvement and an evaluation is not an appraisal worthy of the name until the results of the investigation have been properly and effectively capitalized in the direction of an improved plan of participation.

Selected References[1]

CARVER, W. L.: Student Evaluation of Handbooks, *School Activities*, 6: 7–9, May, 1935.

CORY, F. B. B.: High School Graduates Appraise Extra-curricular Activities, *School Review*, 43: 672–682, November, 1935.

COUNTS, G. S.: Procedures in Evaluating Extracurriculum Activities, *School Review*, 34: 412–421, June, 1926.

COX, P. W. L.: The Evaluation of Student Activities, *Clearing House*, 4: 265–269, January, 1930.

DAVIS, C. O.: The High School as Judged by Its Students, *School and Society*, 20: 121–123, July 6, 1924.

DEBOLT, E. C.: A Home Room Studies Itself, *School Review*, 50: 709–714, December, 1942.

DIXON, F. B.: How Does Your Student Council Rate? *School Activities*, 13: 54, 56, October, 1941.

EELLS, K. W.: A Scale for Evaluation of Pupils' Judgments on Best-liked and Least-liked Aspects of Secondary Schools, *Journal of Educational Research*, 31: 321–334, January, 1938.

———: Evaluating Pupil Activities, *Nation's Schools*, 23: 29–31, January, 1939.

[1] Some of these references reflect activities other than those of the council. However, they describe devices and procedures which can be used in appraising the participation plan.

EELLS, W. C.: Pupil Judgment on Value of Guidance Received, *School Review*, 46: 265–275, April, 1938.

———: What Secondary-School Pupils Think of Pupil Activities, *Clearing House*, 12: 469–475, April, 1938.

ERICKSON, E. E., F. B. DIXON, and L. E. BARTHOLD: "Pupil Participation in School Life," pp. 183–188, Lucas Brothers, Columbia, Mo., 1942.

FULLER, F.: How Good Is Your Pupil Activity Program? *School Activities*, 11: 235–236, February, 1940.

GILCHRIST, R. S.: An Evaluation in Terms of Pupil Participation, *Clearing House*, 7: 358–363, February, 1933.

HARNLY, P. W.: Attitudes of High School Seniors Toward Education, *School Review*, 47: 501–509, September, 1939.

HIATT, L. R.: Junior High School Citizenship, *School Review*, 35: 756–759, December, 1927.

JONES, G.: Survey of Extra-curriculum Activities in the High School, *School Review*, 34: 734–744, December, 1936.

KLINEDINST, P. E.: How Parents Regard Extra-curricular Activities, 6: 10–12, January, 1935.

KOOS, L. V.: Evaluating Extra-curricular Activities, "Twenty-fifth Yearbook," National Society for the Study of Education, Chap. XX, 1926.

MAYBERRY, B. A.: Study of High School Pupils to Determine the Effect of Student Council Participation on the Formation of Certain Habits of Citizenship, *Journal of Educational Research*, 24: 305–307, November, 1931.

MEYER, F.: Judging Student Government, *Clearing House*, 16: 451–453, April, 1942.

MORGART, J. H.: Rating 7B Home Room Groups, *School Activities*, 6: 20–21, March, 1935.

NETTLETON, L.: A Study of Assemblies from the Children's Viewpoint, *Educational Method*, 16: 35–37, October, 1936.

PETTY, H.: Interpreting the Student Council, *School Activities*, 11: 323, 351, April, 1940.

ROEMER, J.: Standards for Judging a Club Sponsor, *Clearing House*, 5: 398–400, March, 1931.

———, C. F. ALLEN, and D. A. YARNELL: "Basic Student Activities," pp. 76–84, Silver Burdett Company, New York, 1935.

SCHNACKE, M. A.: Student Government at Cassville, Missouri, As Seen by the Students, *School and Community*, 19: 18–21, May, 1933.

SHANNON, J. R., and C. ZIMMERMAN: High School Graduates' Estimates of Their High School Annuals, *School Review*, 40: 55–60, January, 1932.

SMITH, E. S.: A Procedure for Appraising Clubs, *School Review*, 48: 108–118, February, 1940.

STRANG, R.: "Group Activities in College and Secondary School," Chap. XII, Harper & Brothers, New York, 1941.

THRASHER, F. M.: The Boys' Club Study, *Journal of Educational Sociology*, 6: 4–16, September, 1932.

TILLINGHAST, C. C.: Can We Measure the Success of Citizenship Training? *Clearing House*, 4: 297–300, January, 1930.

WILLIAMS, C. O.: Student Reactions to Home Rooms, *School Activities*, 6: 3–4, November, 1934.

WRIGHT, C. O.: Student Attitude on School Clubs, *Clearing House*, 9: 48–50, September, 1934.

WRIGHTSTONE, J. W.: Measuring Personal and Social Adjustments, *Teachers College Record*, 36: 224–228, December, 1934.

Index